FAMILY LAW
IN A NUTSHELL®

EIGHTH EDITION

JOHN E.B. MYERS
Visiting Professor of Law
University of California
Hastings College of the Law

444 Cedar Street, Suite 700
St. Paul, MN 55101
1-877-888-1330

Printed in the United States of America

ISBN: 978-1-68561-040-1

For Rowan, Quinn, Oisin,
Zethea, and Zelda

PREFACE

This book is intended for students enrolled in family law. My hope is you find portions of the book useful.

JOHN E.B. MYERS

April, 2022

OUTLINE

Chapter 10. Property Issues in Family Law 237

TABLE OF CASES

References are to Pages

FAMILY LAW
IN A NUTSHELL®

EIGHTH EDITION

CHAPTER 1

INTRODUCTION: SOURCES AND APPLICATIONS OF FAMILY LAW

Family law deals with complex legal and human issues. The practice of family law is challenging, but it can be the most professionally rewarding thing you do.

§ 1-1 FAMILY DEFINED

The meaning of "family" evolves. Fifty years ago, most Americans lived in two-parent married families. Andrew Cherlin writes, "The nuclear family of husband, wife, and children, which was predominant in the first half of the [20th] century, reached its zenith in the 1950s. . . . Since the 1960s . . . the overall percentage of children not living with both parents rose sharply to more than 40%." (Andrew J. Cherlin, Demographic Trends in the United States: A Review of Research in the 2000s, 72 *Journal of Marriage and Family* 403, 410 (2010)). When you think of your own family, you probably think of your parents, brothers and sisters, grandparents, and relatives. Some of us include a stepparent, guardian, adoptive parent, or foster parent. Increasingly, children have "two mommies" or "two daddies." Indeed, as we will see in Chapter 6, states are beginning to recognize the possibility that a child can have more than two parents! With its watershed decision in 2015, the Supreme Court expanded the meaning of family to include same sex marriage. (*Obergefell v. Hodges,* 575 U.S. 994, 135 S Ct. 2071 (2015)).

Martha Minow, writing in the *West Virginia Law Review*, provides insight into the meaning of "family":

> Both the growing diversity in groups across this nation who claim to be families and diversity within the families themselves carry consequences for three basic issues in family law: (1) who is in "the family," (2) what benefits accompany family membership, and (3) what obligations accompany family roles. It may once have seemed that these questions had obvious and uncontroverted answers. It may once have seemed that "family" referred to a natural or obvious social entity created by the biological ties of parent and child and the divine or contractual ties of marriage.

(Martha Minow, All in the Family and In All Families: Membership, *Loving*, and *Owing*, 95 *West Virginia Law Review* 275 (1992/1993)).

Minow points out that the definition of "family" is a social construct that changes over time. The U.S. Supreme Court's decisions striking down bans on interracial marriage (*Loving v. Virginia,* 388 U.S. 1, 87 S. Ct. 1817 (1967)) and same sex marriage (*Obergefell v. Hodges,* 575 U.S. 994, 135 S. Ct. 2071 (2015)) are powerful illustrations of Minow's observation.

Should the law recognize marriage of more than two persons? Polygamy is the practice of having more than one spouse. Although polygamy is illegal in the United States, the practice is legal in some countries. The term polyamory refers to intimate relationships between three or more people. For discussion of "poly" relationships, *see* Casey E. Faucon, Third Parties With Benefits, 17 *Stanford Journal of Civil Rights and Civil Liberties* 185 (2021).

The meaning of family will change during your legal career. As Jaqueline Gaines writes, "Over the last fifty years, the function and definition of 'family' has undergone major cultural shifts caused by no-fault divorce, high divorce rates, increased frequency of childbirth outside of marriage, cohabitation, reproductive technology, genetic testing, delayed marriage, and the Supreme Court's recognition of rights and obligations of unmarried fathers . . . ." Jacqueline V. Gains, The Legal Quicksand 2+ Parents: The Need for a National Definition of a Legal Parent, 46 *University of Dayton Law Review* 105 (2021).

§ 1–2 FAMILY LAW DEFINED

Family law, also known as domestic relations law, is the law governing family relations. Family law covers marriage and divorce, the parent-child relation, child custody, child support, spousal support, property division on divorce, domestic violence, assisted reproduction, adoption, premarital agreements, cohabitation agreements, the constitution and the family, and ethical issues arising in family law practice. This book addresses these subjects and adds analysis of the juvenile court.

§ 1-3 SOURCES OF FAMILY LAW

Family law springs from five sources. First, there is the states' comprehensive common law, statutory, and constitutional law ordering of family relationships. It should be emphasized that there is no family law in a national, unified sense. Instead, every state has its own law on the subject. Second, there are the United States Constitution and state constitutions by which courts have shaped family law. Chapter 2 describes the impact of U.S. Supreme Court decisions on family relations. Third, there is a vast complex of *state* social welfare and tax legislation, including laws providing benefits on the basis of marital status or dependency, tax laws, and laws regulating entitlements. Fourth, an increasing volume of *federal* law and policy, ranging from child support enforcement (Chapter 8) to interstate custody disputes (Chapter 7), has injected federal authority into family law. Fifth, regulation occurs on the local level, including zoning ordinances that impact families.

CHAPTER 2

THE CONSTITUTION AND THE FAMILY

The day-to-day work of family law attorneys seldom takes them into the realm of constitutional law. Yet, there is no gainsaying the impact of the United States and state constitutions on families and on the relationship between government, families, and individuals. This chapter summarizes the principal intersections of constitutional and family law. The chapter focuses on decisions of the United States Supreme Court.

§ 2–1 MARRIAGE IS A FUNDAMENTAL RIGHT

The Supreme Court has long lauded the right to marry and raise a family. In *Skinner v. Oklahoma*, 316 U.S. 535, 62 S. Ct. 1110, 1113 (1942), the Court wrote, "Marriage is one of the basic civil rights of man, fundamental to our very existence and survival." In *Griswold v. Connecticut*, 381 U.S. 479, 486, 85 S. Ct. 1678 (1965), the Court spoke glowingly of marriage, "We deal with a right of privacy older than the Bill of Rights—older than our political parties, older than our school system. Marriage is a coming together for better or for worse, hopefully enduring, and intimate to the degree of being sacred. It is an association that promotes a way of life, not causes; a harmony of living, not political faiths; a bilateral loyalty, not commercial or social projects. Yet it is an association for as noble a purpose as any involved in our prior decisions." In *Loving v. Virginia*,

388 U.S. 1, 87 S. Ct. 1817 (1967), the Court struck down laws against interracial marriage as violations of the Equal Protection Clause of the Fourteenth Amendment. In *Zablocki v. Redhail*, 434 U.S. 374, 379, 98 S. Ct. 673 (1978), the Court ruled unconstitutional a Wisconsin law that forbade certain adults who owed child support from marrying unless the person got a judge's permission. The Court wrote, "Our past decisions make clear that the right to marry is of fundamental importance. . . ." In *Obergefell v. Hodges*, 575 U.S. 994, 135 S. Ct. 2584 (2015), the Court ruled that same sex couples have the right to marry. In *Obergefell,* the Court reiterated the principle expressed long ago in *Skinner,* "The right to marry is fundamental under the Due Process Clause." (135 S. Ct. at 2598).

§ 2-2 STATE INTEREST IN MARRIAGE AND FAMILY

Individuals have a fundamental personal right to marry. At the same time, the state has strong interests in marriage, and the state may regulate many aspects of marriage. (*Maynard v. Hill*, 125 U.S. 190, 204, 8 S. Ct. 723 (1888)). In *Loving v. Virginia*, 388 U.S. 1, 87 S. Ct. 1817, 1821 (1967), the Court observed that "marriage is a social relation subject to the State's police power." Thus, the state may set a minimum age to marry, require a license to marry, establish a system of marital property, prohibit certain forms of marriage, such as polygamy and incestuous marriage, and define the requirements to end marriage.

§ 2-3 PARENTAL RIGHTS

The right of parents to the care, custody, and control of their children has a long constitutional pedigree in the Supreme Court. Parents have broad "authority over minor children." (*Parham v. J.R.*, 442 U.S. 584, 602, 99 S. Ct. 2493 (1979)). In *Meyer v. Nebraska*, 262 U.S. 390, 43 S. Ct. 625 (1923), the state of Nebraska made it illegal in private elementary schools to teach in a language other than English. In striking down the Nebraska law as a violation of substantive due process, the Supreme Court observed that the "liberty" guaranteed by the Fourteenth Amendment includes the right "to marry, establish a home and bring up children" free from unwarranted government intervention. In *Pierce v. Society of the Sisters of the Holy Names of Jesus and Mary*, 268 U.S. 510, 535, 45 S. Ct. 571 (1925), the Court relied on substantive due process to strike down an Oregon law that required all children to attend public school. The Court wrote that the law "unreasonably interferes with the liberty of parents and guardians to direct the upbringing and education of children under their control." In *Wisconsin v. Yoder*, 406 U.S. 205, 92 S. Ct. 1526 (1972), the Court ruled unconstitutional a Wisconsin compulsory attendance law that required Amish parents to send their children to school after eighth grade. The Court acknowledged the authority of the state to require school attendance, but ruled the state's authority has limits, and the authority of the state can be balanced against the parents' First Amendment right to free exercise of religion and the parents' right to direct the religious and educational upbringing of their children.

The most frequently cited parental rights case is *Prince v. Massachusetts*, 321 U.S. 158, 64 S. Ct. 645 (1944), although the adult involved, Sarah Prince, was nine-year-old Betty's guardian rather than her mother. Sarah and Betty were Jehovah's Witnesses. One evening, Betty persuaded Sarah to allow her to go with Sarah onto the streets to distribute religious pamphlets. Sarah was convicted of violating Massachusetts' child labor laws. The Supreme Court began by emphasizing the importance of parental rights, "It is cardinal with us that the custody, care and nurture of the child reside first with the parents, whose primary function and freedom include preparation for obligations the state can neither supply nor hinder. And it is in recognition of this that [there is a] private realm of family life which the state cannot enter." (321 U.S. at 166). Yet, parental rights are not absolute. Parental rights can be balanced against the state's interest in children. The Court described "the interests of society to protect the welfare of children, and the state's assertion of authority to that end [as] no mere corporate concern of official authority. It is the interest of youth itself, and of the whole community, that children be both safeguarded from abuses and given opportunities for growth into free and independent well-developed citizens." (*Id.* at 165). Even when parents combine a claim of parental rights with an assertion of religious liberty, the state is not powerless. In famous language, the Supreme Court wrote, "Parents may be free to become martyrs themselves. But it does not follow they are free, in identical circumstances, to make martyrs of their children before they have reached the age of full and legal discretion when they can make that choice for themselves." (*Id.* at 170).

§ 2-4 RIGHTS OF UNWED FATHERS

The subject of paternity is discussed in Chapter 6. In a series of decisions beginning in 1972 with *Stanley v. Illinois*, 405 U.S. 645, 92 S. Ct. 1208 (1972), the U.S. Supreme Court addressed the rights of unwed fathers regarding their children. In *Stanley*, the Court dealt with an Illinois law that provided that when an unwed mother died, her children automatically became wards of the state. Unwed fathers were presumed to be unfit for custody. Mr. Stanley never married the mother of his children, but he lived with the mother and their children intermittently for 18 years, until the mother died. The children were then made wards of the juvenile court and placed in foster care because Illinois law did not recognize Stanley as a "parent." In striking down the law as a violation of the Equal Protection Clause, the Court ruled that, at a minimum, an unwed father has the right to a hearing to determine whether he is a fit parent. The parental rights of a fit parent cannot be terminated without due process and a hearing.

In *Stanley v. Illinois*, the unwed father's rights deserved constitutional protection because he acted responsibly—he was a father to his children. A similar scenario arose in *Caban v. Mohammed*, 441 U.S. 380, 99 S. Ct. 1760 (1979). Mother and father did not marry, but they lived together for a time, and father helped support the two children. After the parents separated, father had an ongoing relationship with the children. Each parent married, and mother and her husband sought to adopt the children (stepparent adoption, *see* Chapter 14). In the adoption context, New York law afforded unwed mothers more rights than unwed fathers. Basically, an unwed mother could block an adoption but an unwed father could not. The Supreme Court ruled this difference offended the Equal Protection Clause "in cases such as this, where the father has established a substantial relationship with the child and has admitted his paternity. . . ." (441 U.S. at 393).

In *Quilloin v. Walcott*, 434 U.S. 246, 98 S. Ct. 549 (1978), the Court considered an unwed father who had not acted responsibly. Mother and father never married or lived together. When the child was four, mother married another man. When the child was eleven, the stepfather sought to adopt the child he helped raise. The genetic father had a less than sterling record of paying child support, although he often visited the child. The child expressed a desire to be adopted. The genetic father refused to consent to the adoption, which would end his parent-child relationship with the child. After a trial, the judge found adoption to be in the child's best interest. The judge did *not* find that the genetic father was unfit. On appeal, the genetic father argued that because he was not unfit, he had the same right to veto adoption as that possessed by a mother or a formerly married parent. When the case reached the U.S. Supreme

Court, the justices ruled against the genetic father. The Court wrote, "We have recognized on numerous occasions that the relationship between parent and child is constitutionally protected. . . . We have little doubt that the Due Process Clause would be offended if a State were to attempt to force the breakup of a natural family, over the objections of the parents and their children, without some showing of unfitness and for the sole reason that to do so was thought to be in the children's best interest. But this is not a case in which the unwed father at any time had, or sought, actual or legal custody of his child. Nor is this a case in which the proposed adoption would place the child with a new set of parents with whom the child had never before lived. Rather, the result of the adoption in this case is to give full recognition to a family unit already in existence, a result desired by all concerned except appellant. Whatever might be required in other situations, we cannot say that the State was required in this situation to find anything more than that the adoption . . . [was] in the best interests of the child." (434 U.S. at 255).

The Court's decision in *Quilloin v. Walcott* made clear that if an unwed father wants his rights respected, he needs to assume the responsibilities that come with being a parent. This idea was further developed in the Court's 1983 decision in *Lehr v. Robertson,* 463 U.S. 248, 103 S. Ct. 2985 (1983), which originated in New York. The New York Legislature adopted a "putative father" registry where unwed fathers could register their interest in their child. In *Quilloin v. Walcott,* the unwed father did not register. Nor did he live with the mother or provide child support. The mother married another man, and when the child was two, the stepfather sought to adopt. As in *Quilloin v. Walcott,* the unwed father sought to block the adoption, and as in *Quilloin v. Walcott,* he failed. The U.S. Supreme Court wrote:

> The difference between the developed parent-child relationship that was implicated in *Stanley* and *Caban*, and the potential relationship involved in *Quilloin* and this case, is both clear and significant. When an unwed father demonstrates a full commitment to the responsibilities of parenthood by coming forward to participate in the rearing of his child, his interest in personal contact with his child acquires substantial protection under the due process clause. At that point it may be said that he acts as a father toward his children. But the mere existence of a biological link does not merit equivalent constitutional protection. The actions of judges neither create nor sever genetic bonds. The importance of the familial relationship, to the individuals involved and to the society, stems from the emotional attachments that derive from the intimacy of daily association, and from the role it plays in prompting a way of life through the instruction of children as well as from the fact of blood relationship.
>
> The significance of a biological connection is that it offers the natural father an opportunity that no other male possessed to develop a relationship with his offspring. If he grasps that

> opportunity and accepts some measure of responsibility for the child's future, he may enjoy the blessings of the parent-child relationship and make uniquely valuable contributions to the child's development. If he fails to do so, the Federal Constitution will not automatically compel a state to listen to his opinions of where the child's best interests lie. (463 U.S. at 261–262).

In *Lehr v. Robertson,* the unwed father had no significant relationship with the child and had not even bothered to take the simple step of registering with the putative father's registry. His "rights" did not deserve protection by the Constitution.

§ 2-5 TERMINATION OF PARENTAL RIGHTS

Before a state may permanently sever the parent-child relationship due to abuse, neglect, or abandonment, the state must prove parental fault by clear and convincing evidence. In *Santosky v. Kramer*, 455 U.S. 745, 102 S. Ct. 1388 (1982), the Court observed, "The fundamental liberty interest of natural parents in the care, custody, and management of their child does not evaporate simply because they have not been model parents or have lost temporary custody of their child to the state." For Native American children who are protected by the Indian Child Welfare Act, termination of parental rights requires proof beyond a reasonable doubt.

§ 2-6 PRIVACY AND PROCREATION

The Constitution protects privacy and procreative freedom. (*Roe v. Wade*, 410 U.S. 113, 93 S. Ct. 705 (1973)). In *Lawrence v. Texas*, 539 U.S. 558, 123 S. Ct. 2472 (2003), the Supreme Court struck down Texas' sodomy law. The Court noted that people enjoy a constitutional right to make certain decisions regarding intimate sexual conduct, whether gay or straight. The Due Process Clause affords "constitutional protection to personal decisions relating to marriage, procreation, contraception, family relationships, child rearing, and education." (539 U.S. at 574). In *United States v. Windsor*, 570 U.S. 744, 133 S. Ct. 2675, 2682 (2013), the Court ruled unconstitutional the federal Defense of Marriage Act, "which exclude[d] a same-sex partner from the definition of 'spouse' as that term is used in federal statutes." In *H.L. v. Matheson*, 450 U.S. 398, 101 S. Ct. 1164 (1981), the Court ruled that a state cannot prohibit minors from obtaining an abortion, but can impose limitations on minors that would be illegal if applied to adults.

§ 2-7 CHILDREN HAVE CONSTITUTIONAL RIGHTS

Children have constitutional rights. In *Planned Parenthood of Central Missouri v. Danforth,* 428 U.S. 52, 74, 96 S. Ct. 2831 (1976), the Supreme Court wrote, "Constitutional rights do not mature and come into being magically only when one attains the state-defined age of majority. Minors, as well as adults, are protected by the Constitution and possess constitutional rights." The Court explained in *In re Gault,* 387 U.S. 1, 13, 87 S. Ct. 1428 (1967), "Neither the Fourteenth Amendment, or the Bill of Rights, is for adults alone."

Although children enjoy constitutional rights, their rights are not the same as adult rights. They are, after all, children. In *Parham v. J.R.*, 442 U.S. 584, 99 S. Ct. 2493 (1979), the Supreme Court established the constitutional parameters governing psychiatric hospitalization of children. The Court acknowledged "that a child, in common with adults, has a substantial liberty interest in not being confined unnecessarily for medical treatment. . . ." (442 U.S. at 600). The Court held that although parents do not have unbridled authority to psychiatrically hospitalize children, parents play the key role in this decision, along with medical professionals. The Court understood, "Most children, even in adolescence, simply are not able to make sound judgments concerning many decisions, including their need for medical care or treatment. Parents can and must make those judgments." (*Id.* at 603).

CHAPTER 3

PREMARITAL AGREEMENTS

This chapter analyzes premarital agreements, or as they are called in some states, antenuptial or prenuptial agreements. Most couples who enter a premarital agreement do so to opt out of the marital property system. (*Marriage of I.C. and Q.C.*, 551 S.W.3d 119 (Tex. 2018)). Premarital agreements traditionally have been used by wealthy individuals seeking to protect wealth from claims by new partners, and by older individuals with children from a previous marriage who desire to pass their property to their children. (*Sanderson v. Sanderson*, 245 So. 3d 421 (Miss. 2018); Linda J. Ravdin, Gray Divorce, 48 *Estate Planning* 4 (2021)). Premarital agreements are available to young people getting married but most young couples see no need for a prenup.

§ 3–1 PREMARITAL AGREEMENT DEFINED

The National Conference of Commissioners on Uniform State Laws (NCCUSL), also known as the Uniform Law Commission, was created in 1892 to promote uniformity in state laws. In 1983, NCCUSL promulgated the Uniform Premarital Agreement Act (UPAA). More than half the states adopted the 1983 Act, often with modifications. In 2012, NCCUSL updated the UPAA and expanded it to cover agreements during as well as in contemplation of marriage. The 2012 Act defines premarital agreement as "An agreement between individuals who intend to marry which affirms, modifies, or waives a marital right or obligation during the marriage or at separation, marital dissolution, death of one of the spouses, or the occurrence or nonoccurrence of any other event." (§ 2(5)).

The American Law Institute (ALI), like NCCUSL, is devoted to improving the law. Indeed, ALI and NCCUSL sometimes collaborate on projects. The ALI produces Restatements of law, including the *Restatement of Torts* and the *Restatement of Contracts.* In 2002, the ALI published *Principles of the Law of Family Dissolution: Analysis and Recommendations,* which defines premarital agreement as "an agreement between parties contemplating marriage that alters or confirms the legal rights and obligations that would otherwise arise under" applicable law. (§ 7.01(a)).

A premarital agreement is a contract and is governed by principles of contract law. (*Marriage of Bliss and Evans*, 382 Mont. 370, 367 P.3d 395 (2016); *Marriage of I.C. and Q.C.*, 551 S.W.3d 119 (Tex. 2018)). Courts scrutinize premarital agreements more closely than ordinary commercial contracts because of the intimate relationship between the parties. (*Andrew B. v. Abbie B.*, 494 P.3d 522, 539 (Alaska 2021) ("more protection is required to ensure that a prenuptial agreement is truly voluntary."); (*Matter of Nizhnikov*, 132 A.3d 412 (N.H. 2016)).

Under the 1983 UPAA, a premarital agreement must be in writing and signed by the parties. (UPAA § 2) (2012 Act § 6). The agreement is enforceable without consideration (UPAA § 2) (2012 Act § 6), and becomes effective upon marriage. (UPAA § 4) (2012 Act § 7). The 1983 UPAA defines property as "an interest, present or future, legal or equitable, vested or contingent, in real or personal property, including income and earnings." (UPAA § 1(2)) (2012 Act § 2(6)). The 1983 UPAA gives couples broad latitude to contract regarding property in the event of separation, divorce, or death. (UPAA § 3).

Premarital agreements generally contain a choice of law clause specifying what state's law governs interpretation of the agreement. Choice of law clauses are generally enforceable. (*Gal v. Gal*, 243 So.3d 466 (Fla. Ct. App. 2018)).

For in depth discussion of "nonmarital contracts" *see* Albertina Antognini, Nonmarital Contracts, 73 *Stanford Law Review* 67 (2021).

§ 3-2 PUBLIC POLICY REGARDING PREMARITAL AGREEMENTS THAT CONTEMPLATE DIVORCE

When people marry they hope their marriage will last " 'til death do us part." They are sure their love will endure. In addition to the strong individual desire for "a marriage that lasts," the state has an interest in supporting marriage. In the past, the state interest in stable marriage led courts to conclude that premarital contracts that contemplate divorce are against public policy. (*Silverman v. Silverman*, 206 A.3d 825 (Del. 2019)). The California Supreme Court wrote in *Marriage of Bonds*, 24 Cal. 4th 1, 5 P.3d 815, 99 Cal. Rptr. 2d 252 (2000), "At one time, a premarital agreement that was not made in contemplation that the parties would remain married until death was considered to be against public policy in California and other jurisdictions." Premarital agreements that focused only on distribution of property at death were acceptable because they did not encourage divorce.

Courts have changed their views regarding premarital agreements that contemplate divorce. (*Marriage of Dawley*, 17 Cal. 3d 342, 551 P.2d 323, 131 Cal. Rptr. 3 (1976); *Penrod v. Penrod*, 624 S.W.3d 905, 910 (Mo. Ct. App. 2021)). Today, premarital agreements that deal overtly with the possibility of divorce are enforceable. Indeed, public policy favors premarital agreements. (*See Marriage of Sauls and Worley*, 2021 WL 5364775 (Tex. Ct. App. 2021)). The New York Court of Appeals wrote in *Van Kipnis v. Van Kipnis*, 11 N.Y.3d 573, 900 N.E.2d 977, 980, 872 N.Y.S.2d 426 (2008), "It is well settled that duly executed prenuptial agreements are generally valid and enforceable given the strong public policy favoring individuals ordering and deciding their own interests through contractual arrangements." The West Virginia Supreme Court of Appeals noted in *Ware v. Ware*, 224 W. Va. 555, 687 S.E.2d 382, 387 (2009), "This Court has held that prenuptial agreements are presumptively valid."

§ 3–3 PROPERTY ASPECTS OF PRENUPTIAL AGREEMENTS

Couples signing premarital agreements have broad latitude regarding property. If they like, a couple can contract entirely out of the marital property system. (*See Marriage of Bonds*, 24 Cal. 4th 1, 13, 5 P.3d 815, 99 Cal. Rptr. 2d 252 (2000);

Poythress v. Poythress, 865 S.E.2d 892 (N.C. Ct. App. 2021)). The New York Court of Appeals observed in *Van Kipnis v. Van Kipnis*, 11 N.Y.3d 573, 900 N.E.2d 977, 981, 872 N.Y.S.2d 426 (2008), that a premarital agreement "may specifically designate as separate property assets that would ordinarily be defined as marital property subject to equitable distribution. . . . Such property would then remain separate property upon dissolution of the marriage." Indeed, the desire to avoid creation of marital or community property is the most common reason for premarital agreements.

§ 3-4 WAIVER OF SPOUSAL SUPPORT

May parties to a premarital agreement waive or limit spousal support in the event the marriage ends in divorce? Older decisions said no, reasoning that prospective waiver of spousal support was against public policy. The law is changing. (*Posner v. Posner*, 233 So. 2d 381 (Fla. 1970)). The 1983 UPAA authorizes premarital agreements that modify or eliminate spousal support. (UPAA § 3(4)). However, Section 6(b) of the 1983 Act places the following limit on waivers of spousal support: "If a provision of a premarital agreement modifies or eliminates spousal support and that modification or elimination causes one party to the agreement to be eligible for support under a program of public assistance at the time of separation or marital dissolution, a court, notwithstanding the terms of the agreement, may require the other party to provide support to the extent necessary to avoid that eligibility." (*Accord* 2012 Act § 9(e)). In *O'Daniel v. O'Daniel*, 419 S.W.3d

280 (Tenn. Ct. App. 2013), a premarital agreement waived spousal support. Enforcement of the agreement would likely render the wife eligible for welfare. The Tennessee Court of Appeals ruled the waiver of spousal support was not enforceable.

Premarital agreements that waive spousal support are increasingly viewed as enforceable. The California Supreme Court wrote in *Marriage of Pendleton and Fireman,* 24 Cal. 4th 39, 53, 5 P.3d 839, 99 Cal. Rptr. 2d 278 (2000), "When entered into voluntarily by parties who are aware of the effect of the agreement, a premarital waiver of spousal support does not offend contemporary public policy." (*See also, Anonymous v. Anonymous*, 27 N.Y.S.3d 583, 137 A.D.3d 583 (2016)). Turner and Morgan write, "Forty-three jurisdictions have abandoned the common law restrictions of premarital waivers of spousal support. In 22 jurisdictions, premarital waivers of spousal support are authorized by statutes. . . ." (Brett R. Turner & Laura W. Morgan, *Attacking and Defending Marital Agreements* p. 381 (2d ed. 2001)).

States have varying rules regarding waiver of spousal support. California, for example, provides that a premarital agreement waiving spousal support is enforceable at divorce only if the party seeking support was represented by an attorney when the agreement was signed. (Cal. Family Code § 1612(c)). Even if the party seeking support was represented by counsel, a waiver of support is *un*enforceable if the waiver is "unconscionable at the time of enforcement."

§ 3–5 CHILD SUPPORT

A premarital agreement cannot affect a parent's duty to support children. (*Marriage of Erpelding*, 917 N.W.2d 235 (Iowa 2018)). The 1983 UPAA provides, "The right of a child to support may not be adversely affected by a premarital agreement." (UPAA § 3(b) (2012 Act § 10(b)(1))).

Although a premarital agreement cannot diminish a parent's duty to support children, a premarital agreement *can* impose child support duties that the law normally does not require, and courts enforce such agreements. Thus, an agreement to support stepchildren if a marriage ends is enforceable. So too is an agreement to pay for private school, college, or to support children past the age of majority.

In *Marriage of Erpelding*, 917 N.W.2d 235 (Iowa 2018), the Iowa Supreme Court ruled that a prenuptial agreement cannot waive the right to seek attorney fees regarding child custody, child support, or spousal support.

§ 3–6 DEFENSES TO ENFORCEMENT OF PREMARITAL AGREEMENT

When a marriage ends in divorce, one party may seek to enforce a premarital agreement against the other party, who may acquiesce in the agreement or attack it. There are two basic defenses to enforcement of a premarital agreement: (1) The party against whom enforcement is sought did not execute the agreement voluntarily (1983 UPAA § 6(a)(1)), and (2) The agreement is unconscionable (1983 UPAA § 6(a)(2)).

§ 3–6[A] VOLUNTARINESS

Under the 1983 UPAA, a premarital agreement is enforceable only if it was signed voluntarily. (§ 6(a) (2012 Act § 9). A signature under duress is not voluntary. The New Hampshire Supreme Court wrote, "To establish duress, a party must ordinarily show that it involuntarily accepted the other party's terms, that the coercive circumstances were the result of the other party's acts, that the other party exerted pressure wrongfully, and that under the circumstances the party had no alternative but to accept the terms set out by the other party." (*Matter of Nizhnikov*, 132 A.3d 412 (N.H. 2016)). Courts agree that it is not duress for one party to say, "I won't marry you without a prenuptial agreement." (*In re Matter of Yannalfo and Yannalfo,* 794 A.2d 795 (N.H. 2002)).

A court evaluating voluntariness examines the totality of the circumstances. (*Penrod v. Penrod,* 624 S.W.3d 905 (Mo. Co. App. 2021); *Hutchins v. Hutchins*, 393 Mont. 283, 430 P.3d 502 (2018)). How much time did the party resisting enforcement of the agreement have to consider the agreement? For example, was the agreement presented for the first time a few days before the wedding or, in an extreme case, on the wedding day? In *Andrew B. v. Abbie B.,* 494 P.3d 522 (Alaska 2021), wife was presented with a premarital agreement the night before the wedding, while she was intoxicated. In *Penrod v.*

Penrod, 624 S.W.3d 905 (Mo. Ct. App. 2021), the Missouri Court of Appeals upheld a premarital agreement presented to wife the day before the wedding. The couple had discussed the agreement four days earlier, and wife had the advice of an attorney. In *Estate of Hollett,* 150 N.H. 39, 834 A.2d 348 (2003), the New Hampshire Supreme Court wrote, "To avoid invalidation on grounds of involuntariness, it has been recommended that the contract should be presented well in advance of the ceremony, usually thirty days." California law dictates that the party against whom enforcement is sought must have at least seven days to consider the agreement (Cal. Family Code § 1615(c)(2); *Marriage of Clarke and Akel,* 19 Cal. App. 5th 914, 228 Cal. Rptr. 3d 483 (2018)). How sophisticated and well educated is the party? Did the parties have equal bargaining power? (*Matter of Nizhnikov,* 168 N.H. 525, 132 A.3d 412 (2016)). Did the party against whom enforcement is sought have an attorney? If not, was the party advised to seek legal advice? Was the party fully informed of the wealth of the other party?

Is a prenuptial agreement voluntary if wedding plans are far advanced? Consider Tom and Wendy who will soon marry. Invitations have been mailed. The wedding site is reserved. The caterer is employed. The cake is ordered. The wedding dress is at the seamstress following the final fitting. Dresses for the bridesmaids are hanging in closets. Relatives and friends from far and wide have made airline and hotel reservations. In the midst of these happy but hectic preparations, Tom tells Wendy, "I think it would be a good idea for us to have a prenup. I asked my lawyer to draft one for us. Here it is. What do you think?" Should the advanced state of wedding preparations be a factor in deciding whether Wendy's signature on the prenup is voluntary? Proximity to the wedding day can be a factor. (*See Edwards v. Edwards*, 16 Neb. App. 297, 744 N.W.2d 243 (2008) (the fact that wife had made wedding plans did not mean she was coerced into signing prenuptial agreement)); *Porter v. Porter*, 281 Or. App. 169, 381 P.3d 873 (2016) (prenup was not signed voluntarily). A prenuptial agreement signed under duress is not enforceable. (*Kremer v. Kremer*, 912 N.W.2d 617 (Minn. 2018)).

§ 3–6[B] UNCONSCIONABILITY

In *Grabe v. Hokin,* 341 Conn. 360, 267 A.3d 145 (2021), the Connecticut Supreme Court defined unconscionability: "Unconscionable is a word that defies lawyer-like definition. The classic definition of an unconscionable contract is one which no individual in his senses, not under delusion, would make, on the one hand, and which no fair and honest individual would accept, on the other." The Connecticut Court continued, "Unfairness or inequality alone does not render a prenuptial agreement unconscionable; spouses may agree on an unequal distribution of assets at dissolution. The mere fact that hindsight may indicate the provisions of the agreement were improvident does not render the agreement unconscionable."

The 1983 UPAA invalidates a premarital agreement that was unconscionable when it was signed unless, prior to signing, the party against whom enforcement is sought was provided with fair and reasonable disclosure of other party's property. (§ 6(2) (2012 Act § 9(f)). The UPAA allows a party to waive, in writing, the right to disclosure of the other party's property (UPAA § 6(2)(ii) (2012 Act § 9)). (*See Blanchard v. Blanchard*, 148 A.3d 277 (Me. 2016) (premarital agreement was not unconscionable; wife had adequate notice, understood the agreement, and insisted on certain changes before signing); *Sanderson v. Sanderson*, 245 So. 3d 421 (Miss. 2018) (17-year marriage, at end of which husband had more than $3 million in separate property, while wife left the marriage with $425,000; the prenuptial agreement was not unconscionable when it was signed).

In *Marriage of Woodrum*, 426 Ill. Dec. 99, 115 N.E.3d 1021 (Ct. App. 2018), the Illinois Appellate Court ruled that language in a premarital agreement stating that "full and complete disclosure" of property had been made did not control, and what was important was whether the *actual* disclosure was full, fair, and reasonable. Disclosure can be reasonable without being complete in every detail.

Note that under the UPAA an unconscionable premarital agreement regarding property *can be* valid and enforceable so long as the party against whom enforcement is sought was fully informed or gave up the right to be informed. (*Silverman v. Silverman*, 206 A.3d 825 (Del. 2019)). In *Gottlieb v. Gottlieb*, 138 A.D.3d 30, 25 N.Y.S.3d 90 (2016), the Appellate Division of the New York Supreme Court wrote, "Despite the presumption of validity, an agreement between prospective spouses can be set aside where it is shown to be the product of fraud, duress, overreaching resulting in manifest unfairness, or other inequitable conduct. In the absence of such inequitable conduct, however, courts should not redesign the bargain reached by the parties merely because in retrospect the provisions might be viewed as improvident or one-sided."

Iowa law allows a judge to refuse to enforce an unconscionable premarital agreement. The Iowa Supreme Court wrote in *Marriage of Shanks,* 758 N.W.2d 506, 514 (Iowa 2008), "In contrast to the UPAA approach, unconscionability alone is sufficient to render a premarital agreement unenforceable under the [Iowa] IUPAA, notwithstanding fair and reasonable financial disclosure.... Under the IUPAA, courts may address unconscionability claims whether or not appropriate financial disclosures are made."

Connecticut law provides that a premarital agreement is not enforceable if the party against whom enforcement is sought proves the agreement was unconscionable when it was executed or when enforcement is sought (Conn. Stats. § 46b–36g(a)).

The American Law Institute's *Principles of the Law of Family Dissolution* grapple with the enforceability of premarital agreements that turn out to be unfair when they are enforced in divorce proceedings years after they are signed. The ALI *Principles* state that a premarital agreement should not be enforced if enforcement would "work a substantial injustice." (American Law Institute, *Principles of the Law of Family Dissolution: Analysis and Recommendations* § 7.05, p. 982 (2002)). The *Principles* state, "When many years have passed since the agreement was executed, when the parties first have children in common after execution, or when the circumstances of the parties have unforeseeably changed, courts must examine the agreement before enforcing it to ensure . . . that such enforcement will not work a 'substantial injustice.' " (§ 7.02, p. 955).

§ 3–6[C] BURDEN OF PROOF

Who should have the burden of proof regarding enforceability of a premarital agreement? The party seeking to enforce the agreement? Or the party seeking to invalidate the agreement? The 1983 UPAA places the burden of proof on the party challenging a premarital agreement. (§ 6(a) (2012 Act § 9(a)). In *Marriage of Woodrum,* 426 Ill. Dec. 99, 115 N.E.3d 1021 (Ct. App. 2018), the Illinois Appellate Court ruled that the party seeking to avoid enforcement of a premarital agreement has the burden of proving the disclosure of property was not fair and reasonable. The American Law Institute places the burden of proof on the party seeking to enforce a premarital agreement. (American Law Institute, *Principles of the Law of Family Dissolution: Analysis and Recommendations* § 7.04, p. 960 (2002)).

§ 3–7 ARE PARTIES TO A PRENUPTIAL AGREEMENT IN A CONFIDENTIAL RELATIONSHIP?

Married couples are in a confidential relationship and owe each other duties of honesty and candor. Should a couple planning to marry, and thinking about a premarital agreement, be considered in a confidential relationship? In *Marriage of Rudder*, 230 Or. App. 437, 217 P.3d 183, 193 (2009), the Oregon Court of Appeals wrote, "The relationship between the parties to a premarital agreement is 'fiduciary in character' if entered into in contemplation of marriage." The Connecticut Supreme Court discussed the issue in *Friezo v. Friezo,* 281 Conn. 166, 914 A.2d 533, 549 (2007), "Our review of [the] case law indicates that when a party's independent knowledge is insufficient and the other party must disclose financial information in a prenuptial agreement, the extent of the required disclosure depends on how the court views the relationship. Courts in the majority of jurisdictions regard the parties as involved in a confidential relationship of mutual trust that demands the exercise of the highest degree of good faith, candor and sincerity in all matters bearing on the proposed agreement. . . . Jurisdictions that treat the parties as involved in an arm's-length relationship on the theory that parties who are not yet married are not presumed to share a confidential relationship, impose a duty on each spouse to inquire and investigate the financial condition of the other, and consequentially, the disclosure requirement is less demanding. Connecticut regards the parties to a premarital agreement as involved in a confidential relationship." (*See Andrew B. v. Abbie B.*, 494 P.3d 522 (Alaska 2021); *Kremer v. Kremer*, 912 N.W.2d 617, 627 (Minn. 2018) ("antenuptual agreements typically involve parties in a confidential relationship.")). In *Marriage of Hill and Dittmer*, 202 Cal. App. 4th 1046, 136 Cal. Rptr. 3d 700 (2011), the California Court of Appeal ruled that a couple entering a premarital agreement do not owe each other fiduciary duties.

§ 3-8 RELIGIOUS PRENUPTIAL AGREEMENTS

In Muslim weddings the parties may execute a document called a nikah or wedding agreement. The nikah may contain a mahr which is an agreement by which a wife is guaranteed a dowry. (*Oleiwi v. Shlahi*, 73 Misc.3d 913, 156 N.Y.S.3d 825 (Sup. Ct. N.Y. 2021)). The mahr provides an amount of money to be paid at the time of marriage and an amount to be paid in the event of divorce. In *Ahmed v. Ahmed*, 261 S.W.3d 190 (Tex. Ct. App. 2008), the Texas Court of Appeal ruled that a mahr was not enforceable. In *Marriage of Obaidi and Qayoum*, 154 Wash. App. 609, 226 P.3d 787 (2010), the Washington Court of Appeals applied neutral principles of contract law to conclude that a mahr was not valid. In *Nouri v. Dadgar*, 245 Md. App. 324, 226 A.3d 797 (2018), the Maryland Court of Special Appeals ruled that trial courts could apply neutral principles of contract law to enforce a mahr. In *Oleiwi v. Shlahi*, 73 Misc.3d 913, 156 N.Y.S.3d 825 (Sup. Ct. N.Y. 2021), a New York trial court concluded that a mahr that was executed in Iraq would be enforced in New York. The judge wrote, "New York has long held that comity should be extended to uphold the validity of foreign nuptial matters unless recognition of the judgment would do violence to a strong public policy of New York. . . . Therefore, a duly executed prenuptial agreement executed in a foreign nation in accordance with that nation's laws will be found to be valid and enforceable in New York."

In the Jewish tradition, a ketuba is a document signed prior to a wedding. In the document, the couple agree to abide by Jewish law governing marriage. A "get" is a document that releases a woman from the obligations of the ketuba, and allows her to remarry in the faith. In a number of secular divorce cases, women sought court orders forcing unwilling husbands to grant a get so the woman could remarry. (*See* Lara Traum (Note) Involved, Empowered and Inspired: How Mediating Halakhic Prenuptual Agreements Honors Jewish and American Law and Builds Happy Families, 17 *Cardozo Journal of Conflict Resolution* 179 (2015)). In *Marriage of Goldman*, 554 N.E.2d 1016, 196 Ill.App.3d 785 (1990), the Illinois Appellate Court ruled that the wording of a ketuba allowed specific performance of a husband's promise to procure a get. In *Avitzur v. Avitzur,* 58 N.Y. 2d 108, 446 N.E.2d 136, 459 N.Y.S.2d 572 (1983), the New York Court of Appeals found nothing in law or policy that precludes courts from enforcing the secular provisions of a ketuba. Wife brought an action to enforce a provision of her ketuba in which the parties agreed to appear before a religious tribunal called the Beth Din. The Court of Appeals wrote: "The present case can be decided solely upon the application of neutral principles of contract law, without reference to any religious principle." *See also*, *Victor v. Victor*, 177 Ariz. 231, 866 P.2d 899 (Ct. App. 1994) (financial obligations of ketuba were not enforceable).

§ 3-9 PROFESSIONAL RESPONSIBILITY ISSUES REGARDING PREMARITAL AGREEMENTS

Can the same attorney represent both parties to a premarital agreement? (*See Furman v. Furman*, 233 So. 3d 1280 (Fla. Ct. App. 2018)). The West Virginia Supreme Court of Appeals addressed this question in *Ware v. Ware*, 224 W. Va. 599, 687 S.E.2d 382, 390 (2009), where the court wrote:

> This Court has previously recognized that, in certain instances, dual representation is never appropriate, even if both parties are willing to consent. It is improper for a lawyer to represent both the husband and the wife at any stage of the separation and divorce proceeding, even with full disclosure and informed consent. The likelihood of prejudice is so great with dual representation so as to make adequate representation of both spouses impossible, even where the separation is "friendly" and the divorce uncontested.
>
> Like divorce actions, the nature of prenuptial agreements is such that the parties interests are fundamentally antagonistic to one another. Indeed, the purpose of a prenuptial agreement is to preserve the property of one spouse, thereby

preventing the other from obtaining that to which he or she might otherwise be legally entitled. . . . Accordingly, the Court holds that one attorney may not represent, nor purport to counsel, both parties to a prenuptial agreement.

CHAPTER 4
COHABITATION

Half a century ago, living together in an intimate relationship outside marriage was considered "living in sin." Today, it is common for lovers to live together. Indeed, in the twenty-first century, cohabitation is normal. (Margaret Ryznar & Anna Sporek, Cohabitation Worldwide Today, 35 *Georgia State University Law Review* 299 (2019)).

Unmarried couples often accumulate property during the relationship. The system of marital/community property applies to married couples and registered domestic partners, not to cohabitants. Thus, cohabitants do not acquire marital or community property. Courts may apply principles of non-marital property law to partition interests in property. (*Brooks v. Allen,* 168 N.H. 707, 137 A.3d 404 (2016); *Wynkoop v. Stratthaus,* 201 Vt. 158, 136 A.3d 1180 (2016)). The Oregon Supreme Court rejected the argument that regular rules of cotenancy govern division of property between unmarried cohabitants. *Beal v. Beal,* 282 Or. 115, 577 P.2d 507 (1978). In *Manley v. McKinney,* 313 Or. App. 544, 496 P.3d 663, 665 (2021), the Oregon Court of Appeals explained: "[W]hen dealing with property disputes between two people who have been living together in a nonmarital domestic relationship, courts should distribute the property based upon the express or implied intent of the parties. . . . [O]nce cohabitation ends, the regular rules of cotenancy apply."

When cohabitants have children, the rules for child custody and child support are the same as for married parents.

§ 4-1 CONTRACTS BETWEEN UNMARRIED COHABITANTS

At an earlier time, courts believed it was against public policy to enforce contracts between intimate partners living together. In 1979, for example, the Illinois Supreme Court ruled in *Hewitt v. Hewitt*, 77 Ill. 2d 49, 394 N.E.2d 1204, 31 Ill. Dec. 827 (1979) that such contracts are unlawful. The Illinois Supreme Court reaffirmed this stance in 2016 in *Blumenthal v. Brewer*, 410 Ill. Dec. 289, 69 N.E.3d 834 (2016). Today, in most states, unmarried cohabitants can contract with each other regarding property, support, children, and other matters. (*Tomal v. Anderson,* 426 P.3d 915 (Alaska 2018)). The leading case is *Marvin v. Marvin*, 18 Cal. 3d 660, 557 P.2d 106, 134 Cal. Rptr. 815 (1976), decided by the California Supreme Court in 1976. Lee Marvin was a famous movie star. Lee and Michelle lived together for seven years, but did not marry. All property acquired during the relationship was in Lee's name. When the relationship ended, Michelle claimed an oral contract existed in which Lee promised that all property acquired during the relationship belonged to both of them, and that Lee would support her for the rest of her life. Lee denied a contract existed. The California Supreme Court held that "courts should enforce express contracts between nonmarital partners except to the extent that the contract is explicitly founded on the consideration of meretricious sexual services. In the absence of an express contract, the courts should inquire into the conduct of the parties to determine whether that conduct demonstrates an implied contract, agreement of partnership or joint venture, or some other tacit understanding between the parties. The courts may also employ the doctrine of *quantum meruit*, or equitable remedies such as constructive or resulting trusts, when warranted by the facts of the case." (557 P.2d at 110).

Alexander Lindey and Louis Parley wrote a detailed guide to drafting *Marvin* agreements. (Alexander Lindey & Louis I. Parley, *Lindey and Parley on Separation Agreements and Antenuptual Contracts* (2d ed. 2000)).

New Jersey law provides that an agreement "by one party to a non-marital personal relationship to provide support or other consideration for the other party, either during the course of such relationship or after its termination" must be in writing. (N.J. Rev. Stat. § 25:1–5(h)).

§ 4–2 PALIMONY

Alimony is reserved for married couples. The term "palimony" was coined to refer to support paid to a former non-marital partner. As stated earlier, absent an agreement, there generally is no legal obligation to support a former non-marital partner. In cases where there is an express or implied agreement to provide support, the support is often called palimony.

CHAPTER 5

MARRIAGE AND DIVORCE

This chapter focuses on marriage and divorce, with most of the attention on divorce. Subsequent chapters address critical aspects of divorce.

§ 5-1 MARRIAGE

Individuals have a constitutional right to marry. (*See* Chapter 2). At the same time, the state has authority to regulate marriage. (*Id.*). States set the minimum age to marry and require couples to get a marriage license. (*MacDougall v. Levick*, 66 Va. App. 50, 782 S.E.2d 182 (2016)). States have detailed laws governing marital property, liability for debts, and the duty of spouses to deal honestly with each other in matters of money and property. When a spouse dies, state law governs the characterization and distribution of property.

Apart from guaranteeing the constitutional right to marry, federal law has little direct impact on marriage. However, federal law has an enormous impact on the economic aspects of marriage, ranging from Social Security to taxes. In *United States v. Windsor*, 570 U.S. 744, 133 S. Ct. 2675, 2683 (2013), the Supreme Court noted that there are more than a thousand federal laws mentioning "marital or spousal status."

§ 5–2 COMMON LAW (INFORMAL) MARRIAGE

A common law or informal marriage occurs when a couple agrees to be married, considers themselves married, and holds themselves out to the world as married, but the couple does not meet the legal requirements of a marriage license and a ceremony. Texas is one of the few states that still allow common law marriage. Texas Family Code § 2.401(a)(2) provides that informal marriage may be established with evidence that a couple "agreed to be married and after the agreement they lived together in this state as husband and wife and there represented to others that they were married." Colorado allows common law marriage. In *People v. Lucero*, 747 P.2d 660, 663 (Colo. 1987), the Colorado Supreme Court wrote, "A common law marriage is established by the mutual consent and open assumption of a marital relationship." In *LaFleur v. Pyfer,* 479 P.3d 869 (Colo. 2021), the Supreme Court ruled same-sex couples can enter common law marriages in Colorado. (*See also, Estate of Yudkin*, 478 P.3d 732 (Colo. 2021); *Hogsett v. Neale*, 478 P.3d 713 (Colo. 2021) (same-sex couple did not have common law marriage).

The Texas Court of Appeals, in *Assoun v. Gustafson,* 493 S.W.3d 156 (Tex. Ct. App. 2016), made the following useful observations about common law marriage:

> An agreement to be informally married, like any ultimate fact, may be established by direct or circumstantial evidence. Evidence of cohabitation and "holding out" in some cases

may constitute some evidence of an agreement to be married. However, it is difficult to infer an agreement to be married from cohabitation in modern society. Thus, evidence of holding out must be particularly convincing to be probative of an agreement to be married. Occasional informal references to another as their spouse will not prove an agreement to be married. Circumstantial evidence can entirely fail to overcome direct evidence from both members of the alleged marriage that there is no agreement to be married.

States that do not allow common law marriage recognize as valid a common law marriage from a state that allows such marriages.

§ 5–3 DIVORCE

Much day-to-day work of family law attorneys concerns divorce. The details of the job are endless, and include meeting with clients and prospective clients; helping clients understand the divorce process; gathering financial information; drafting and filing pleadings; conducting discovery; filing motions; conducting research; negotiating settlements; consulting with and employing experts (*e.g.*, forensic accountants, psychologists); and preparing for and appearing in court.

In addition to purely legal work, family law attorneys need to decide how much "hand holding" to do. Some clients are in crisis. They are going through the worst experience of their life. Many clients are angry, scared, depressed, anxious, and uncertain about the future. When children are involved, emotions run even higher. Attorneys have an important counseling role, but lawyers are not mental health professionals. Sometimes, it is appropriate to refer a client to a mental health professional who can help the client with the emotional aspects of divorce. Even when counselors are involved, there is no escaping the emotional side of family law. If you are uncomfortable dealing with strong emotions, and with people who are hurting or angry, family law may not be for you. You can do a great deal of good as a family law attorney, but it is not for everyone.

The divorce rate fluctuates over time. Cherlin writes, "The aggregate risk of a marriage ending in divorce appears to have declined from the peak that occurred around 1980. Perhaps half of marriages that were begun around that time will end in divorce, but the lifetime level of divorce may not be as high for marriages begun recently. . . . Divorce rates are diverging by education. During the 1960s and 1970s, the probability that a marriage would end in divorce rose sharply for all groups. Since then, however, the probability of divorce has declined among married couples in which the spouses have college degrees, whereas divorce probabilities have stayed roughly the same or even increased for the less educated." (Andrew J. Cherlin, Demographic Trends in the United States: A Review of Research in the 2000s, 72 *Journal of Marriage and Family* 403–419, 405 (2010)). In 2020, the divorce rate hit an historic low.

§ 5-4 BRIEF HISTORY OF DIVORCE

Divorce existed in antiquity. In ancient Greece, an Athenian could petition a magistrate for a divorce. Divorce was available in Rome. As the Catholic Church gained power in Europe, the law of domestic relations came under ecclesiastical control. The church considered marriage a sacrament instituted by God, and by the tenth century, the church put a stop to divorce.

Although complete divorce—*a vinculo matrimonii*—was not available under church law, the church did allow "legal separation"—divorce *a mensa et thoro,* or divorce from bed and board. A divorce *a mensa et thoro* authorized a married couple to live apart. Importantly, however, the couple remained married. Today, legal separation is available although it is seldom used because absolute divorce is readily available and most couples who break up choose divorce. Why would a couple today prefer legal separation to divorce? In some families, one spouse has a chronic medical condition. If the ill spouse is on the medical insurance of the other spouse and they divorce, the insurance will eventually end. If they remain married but obtain a legal separation, they may be able to continue the medical coverage because they are "still married." Some separating couples prefer legal separation because they don't want to take that last step of divorce.

In addition to permitting divorce *a mensa et thoro,* the church authorized annulment of marriage. Annulment is discussed in Chapter 11.

Divorce, as we know it today—*a vinculo matrimonii*—did not become available in England until 1857. Prior to that time, a few wealthy individuals obtained divorces by act of Parliament—that is, legislative divorce. When the United States became a nation, legislative divorce was available and was used occasionally. (*Maynard v. Hill*, 125 U.S. 190, 205–206, 8 S. Ct. 723 (1888)). Legislative divorce died out during the nineteenth century as state legislatures authorized courts to grant divorce.

§ 5–4[A] FAULT-BASED DIVORCE

When divorce became more readily available in the nineteenth century, it was based on marital fault. Only a spouse who was innocent of fault could get a divorce. The spouse seeking a divorce commenced a divorce action and had to prove that their spouse was at fault. Grounds for fault-based divorce varied slightly from state to state. Grounds generally included adultery (also known as "criminal conversation"), physical or mental cruelty, desertion, fraud, impotence, conviction of a felony, habitual drunkenness, failure to support, and incurable insanity.

§ 5–4[B] DEFENSES TO DIVORCE DURING THE ERA OF FAULT

During the era of fault based divorce, which lasted into the 1980s, a spouse who was sued for divorce could raise one of three defenses: recrimination, connivance, or condonation. If a defense was established, the divorce case was dismissed and the parties remained married.

With recrimination, the defendant spouse who was charged with marital fault filed a counter suit charging the plaintiff spouse with fault. For example, a defendant who was sued for divorce based on mental cruelty might counter sue based for mental cruelty. Or a spouse charged with adultery might counter sue for cruelty. If both spouses were "guilty" of marital fault, *neither could obtain a divorce!* In the 1894 case of *Brenot v. Brenot*, 102 Cal. 294, 296, 36 P. 672 (1894), for example, husband sued wife for divorce, accusing her of adultery. Wife counter sued, claiming extreme cruelty. The trial court found the allegations of both parties true, denied all relief, and dismissed the case. The California Supreme Court approved, writing, "There is also no question but that a court of equity is authorized to enter a judgment dismissing an action of divorce, where both parties are seeking a decree, and the evidence discloses them to be equally guilty of the misconduct alleged."

To ameliorate the harsh result sometimes brought about by strict application of recrimination, some states adopted the principle of comparative rectitude. Under comparative rectitude, if both spouses were at fault, the spouse whose fault was less serious could get a divorce.

The defense of connivance applied when the spouse seeking divorce connived with others to create grounds for divorce. In *Sargent v. Sargent*, 114 A. 428 (N.J. Chancery 1920), husband sued for divorce, based on wife's adultery with the family chauffeur.

Husband suspected the chauffeur's motives, but did not fire the chauffeur. Rather husband kept the chauffeur in his employ, realizing his wife would often be alone with the chauffeur. Husband hired detectives to spy on them. When adultery occurred, husband sued for divorce. Wife raised the defense of connivance and the court denied husband's suit for divorce.

Condonation as a defense arose when one spouse committed marital fault but the innocent spouse forgave the trespass. So long as the forgiveness—condonation—was voluntary, it foreclosed a later suit for divorce. In *Murphy v. Murphy*, 204 Pa. Super. 576, 205 A.2d 647 (1964), husband committed burglary and armed robbery. Shortly after the crimes were committed, wife allowed husband to hide in their home. She also spent some of the ill-gotten gain. Husband was captured and sent to prison. Wife filed for divorce, but the court denied divorce because wife condoned her husband's crimes. She was not an "innocent and injured spouse."

§ 5–4[C] "GOING TO RENO"

During the era of fault, many couples who shared a desire to divorce but who lacked grounds to divorce contrived—that is, made up—grounds for divorce. Judges generally turned a blind eye. Another tactic was for one spouse to file a complaint for divorce and for the other spouse to default. A third technique was for one spouse to leave the state, and move temporarily to a state that had liberal grounds for divorce. Such states—notably Nevada—became known as "divorce mills." During the first half of the twentieth century, hundreds of thousands of married Americans got divorced in Nevada. Indeed, the practice was so common that "Going to Reno" was understood to mean going there for a divorce. The practice was known as "the Reno cure."

§ 5-4[D] NO FAULT DIVORCE

The 1960s brought increased calls to do away with fault-based divorce. As a step in that direction, a number of states passed laws allowing divorce when the parties lived apart for a number of years. In 1969, California adopted no fault divorce. Indeed, in California today it is improper even to mention fault in a petition for divorce. (Cal. Family Code § 2335). By 1985, all states had some form of no-fault divorce. Although states allow no fault divorce, a number of states retain fault based grounds for divorce. (*Matter of Blaisdell*, 174 N.H. 187, 261 A.3d 306 (2021); *Matter of Henry*, 163 N.H. 175, 37 A.3d 320 (2012).

With no fault divorce, a married person files a petition asserting the marriage is "irretrievably broken" or that "irreconcilable differences" have caused the irremediable breakdown of the marriage. Basically, "irreconcilable differences" is whatever one spouse thinks is a good reason to end the marriage. Judges seldom second guess claims of irreconcilable differences.

No fault divorce can be unilateral. That is, one spouse can get a divorce even if the other spouse wants to stay married. In the era of no fault, the defenses of condonation, connivance, and recrimination are largely irrelevant. A few states retain watered down versions of the traditional defenses. (*Denham v. Denham*, 2022 WL 290890 (Miss. Ct. App. 2022); *Anderson v. Anderson*, 266 So.3d 1058 (Miss. Ct. App. 2019); *Ware v. Ware*, 7 So. 3d 271 (Miss. Ct. App. 2008); *Chastain v. Chastain*, 381 S.C. 295, 672 S.E.2d 108 (Ct. App. 2008)).

§ 5–5 COVENANT MARRIAGE

Concerned about high divorce rates, Arizona, Arkansas, and Louisiana created so-called covenant marriage. The Arizona covenant marriage statute contains a pledge to be taken by couples entering covenant marriage. The couple pledges to stay married for life. (Ariz. Stat. § 25–901(B)). The pledge is not binding, however, and couples can divorce. Interestingly, to make divorce more difficult, Arizona reintroduced the traditional fault grounds for divorce including adultery, commission of a felony, abandonment, physical abuse of the spouse, habitual abuse of alcohol or drugs, and living separate and apart. (§ 25–903). Most of the "teeth" of the Arizona statute are removed by a clause that allows a covenant married couple to divorce if they agree to end the marriage. Louisiana's grounds for dissolution of covenant marriage are similar to Arizona's, except that Louisiana does not provide for dissolution when "the husband and wife both agree to a dissolution of marriage."

§ 5-6 JURISDICTION IN DIVORCE LITIGATION

A divorce action is a lawsuit, and as with all lawsuits, the court must have jurisdiction. In analyzing jurisdiction, it is helpful to break the divorce into four parts: (1) the divorce itself, (2) parentage, (3) child custody, and (4) the financial aspects of divorce—child support, spousal support, property division, and attorneys fees.

In most litigation the court must have subject matter jurisdiction *and* personal jurisdiction. In divorce litigation, subject matter jurisdiction is always necessary. Personal jurisdiction, however, is not always necessary.

§ 5-6[A] JURISDICTION TO GRANT DIVORCE

A court has subject matter jurisdiction to grant divorce if at least one spouse is domiciled in the state. (*Williams v. North Carolina,* 325 U.S. 226 (1945); *Mbatha v. Cutting,* 356 Ga. App. 743, 746, 848 S.E.2d 920 (2020) ("a Georgia court has jurisdiction to terminate a marriage when one spouse is domiciled in Georgia"); *Evans v. Evans,* 300 Va. 134, 860 S.E.2d 381 (2021)).

All states have a residency requirement for divorce. (*Hayduk v. Hayduk,* 2022 WL 108011 (S.C. Ct. App. 2022) (husband did not meet residency requirement for divorce)). California, for example, requires residence in the state for six months and the county where the divorce is filed for three months. (Cal. Family Code § 2320). Georgia law requires six months' residence in the state (Ga. Code § 19–5–2). Other states are similar.

If a couple gets married in Texas and has always lived in Texas, no jurisdictional issues are likely to arise. The court clearly has subject matter jurisdiction *and* personal jurisdiction over the parties. Similarly, if a couple married in Indiana but moved to Texas years ago, jurisdictional issues regarding divorce are unlikely to arise. But what of the following situation? A married couple lives in Virginia. One of them moves to Texas and meets the Texas residency requirement. The other spouse has never set foot in Texas. Can the spouse living in Texas get divorced in Texas? Texas has no personal jurisdiction over the spouse remaining in Virginia. The U.S. Supreme Court's decision *Williams v. North Carolina*, 317 U.S. 287, 63 S. Ct. 207 (1942) supplies the answer. Subject matter jurisdiction to grant a divorce is based on domicile. If at least one spouse is domiciled in the state, the courts of the state may grant a divorce. The divorce is entitled to full faith and credit in other states. The divorcing state does *not* have to have personal jurisdiction over the absent spouse, although due process requires notice to the absent spouse. (*Evans v. Evans,* 300 Va. 134, 860 S.E.2d 381, 386 (2021)). In sum, jurisdiction to grant a divorce requires domicile of at least one of the parties. Personal jurisdiction over the absent party is not required.

§ 5–6[B] JURISDICTION TO ESTABLISH THE PARENT-CHILD RELATIONSHIP

State law establishes subject matter jurisdiction over parentage. (*See* Chapter 6). In addition to subject matter jurisdiction, the court must have personal jurisdiction over both parties. (*David L. v. Superior Court*, 29 Cal. App. 5th 359, 240 Cal. Rptr. 3d 462 (2018)).

§ 5–6[C] JURISDICTION OVER THE FINANCIAL ASPECTS OF DIVORCE

A court must have subject matter jurisdiction *and* personal jurisdiction over both parties to adjudicate the financial aspects of divorce, including property division, support, and attorney's fees. (*Kulko v. Superior Court*, 436 U.S. 84, 98 S. Ct. 1690 (1978). *See also, Walden v. Fiore*, 571 U.S. 277, 134 S. Ct. 1115 (2014); *Evans v. Evans*, 300 Va. 134, 860 S.E.2d 381, 386 (2021)). A state may employ its long-arm statute to acquire personal jurisdiction over a spouse. (*Evans v. Evans*, 300 Va. 134, 860 S.E.2d 381, 386 (2021)).

§ 5–6[D] JURISDICTION OVER CHILD CUSTODY

Personal jurisdiction over both parents is *not* required to adjudicate child custody. Jurisdiction over child custody is governed by two statutes, the federal Parental Kidnapping Prevention Act and the state Uniform Child Custody Jurisdiction and Enforcement Act. Both acts are analyzed in Chapter 7.

§ 5-7 DOMESTIC RELATIONS EXCEPTION TO FEDERAL JURISDICTION

Actions for divorce, support, and child custody are not litigated in federal court. In *Ankenbrandt v. Richards*, 504 U.S. 689, 112 S. Ct. 2206 (1992), the Supreme Court ruled that the domestic relations exception to federal jurisdiction "divests the federal courts of power to issue divorce, alimony, and child custody decrees." (*See Bailey v. MacFarland,* 5 F.4th 1092 (9th Cir. 2021); Bradley G. Silverman (Note) Federal Questions and the Domestic-Relations Exception, 125 *Yale Law Journal* 1364 (2016)).

The United States is a party to the Hague Convention on the Civil Aspects of International Child Abduction, a treaty that facilitates return of children wrongfully removed by a parent from the child's home country. Civil actions under the Hague Convention *may* be brought in federal or state court. The Convention is discussed in Chapter 7.

§ 5-8 DIVORCE ACTION ABATES ON DEATH

A pending divorce action abates if one party dies. (*Stuhr v. Oliver*, 363 S.W.3d 316 (Ark. 2010); *Bomer v. Dean*, 195 A.D.3d 1518 (2021); *Maier v. Maier*, 266 A.3d 778 (Vt. 2021)). Death divests the family court of jurisdiction over a divorce action.

§ 5-9 ALTERNATIVES TO LITIGATION—MEDIATION; COLLABORATIVE LAW

Litigating family law issues takes a toll on couples' pocketbooks and egos. The breakdown of a marriage is often accompanied by hurt feelings and anger. Pitting one spouse against the other in court magnifies the pain and anger. Much of the work of the family law attorney involves helping clients *avoid* litigation. The vast majority of family law cases settle out of court.

During the past several decades, progress has been made integrating alternatives to litigation into family law practice. (*See* Nancy Ver Steegh, Family Court Reform and ADR: Shifting Values and Expectations Transform the Divorce Process, 42 *Family Law Quarterly* 659 (2008)).

§ 5-9[A] MEDIATION

Mediation is a popular way to avoid acrimonious and costly litigation. The mediator is a neutral third party. Some attorneys train as mediators. Indeed, some family law attorneys mediate full time. All states encourage mediation of child custody disputes, and quite a few states require parents to attempt mediation before bringing child custody matters to court.

§ 5-9[B] COLLABORATIVE FAMILY LAW

Some divorcing couples choose "collaborative family law" in which they agree to avoid litigation. Collaborative law is described by the National

Conference of Commissioners on Uniform State Laws: "The distinctive feature of collaborative law . . . is that parties are represented by lawyers ('collaborative lawyers') during negotiations. Collaborative lawyers do not represent the party in court, but only for the purpose of negotiating agreements. The parties agree in advance that their lawyers are disqualified from further representing parties" if either party decides to litigate in court. (*Uniform Collaborative Law Act* (2009)).

Tindall and Smith describe collaborative law in the *Family Law Reporter*, "The superiority of collaborative law is multidimensional. One such dimension greatly valued by clients is the economy of the process with regard to time. While cases in traditional litigation may drag on for months with time consuming court appearances, the average length of time between the start of the process with signing of the participation agreement and court approval of resolution within the [authors' law firm] has been approximately six months. . . . In contrast to litigation, collaborative law pushes parties to recognize and acknowledge the other party's goals and interests, even if not shared. Collaborative law is further unlike litigation as the process is intended to result in a mutually beneficial outcome rather than one party prevailing over the other." (Harry L. Tindall & Jennie R. Smith, Collaborative Law: An Innovation Here to Stay, 38 *Family Law Reporter* 1132–1138, at 1137 (2012)).

§ 5-10 DISCOVERY IN DIVORCE LITIGATION

The family law attorney needs a large amount of information about both spouses. When divorcing couples are on good terms and when they are honest, most or all of the information can be obtained informally without the need for formal discovery. When litigation is required, however, the full panoply of discovery tools is available to the family law practitioner. Thus, it is sometimes necessary to depose the parties and their experts. Interrogatories, requests for production of documents, and subpoenas are available. Failing to conduct necessary discovery can constitute legal malpractice. (*See* Andrew S. Grossman, Avoiding Legal Malpractice in Family Law Cases: The Dangers of Not Engaging in Financial Discovery, 33 *Family Law Quarterly* 361 (1999)).

§ 5-11 ATTORNEY FEES IN FAMILY LAW MATTERS

The matter of attorney fees arises in two settings. First, unless an attorney is representing a client *pro bono*, the client and the attorney enter a contract regarding attorney's fees. Second, in some cases, one spouse files a motion asking the court to order the other spouse to pay some or all of the moving spouse's attorney fees.

§ 5–11[A] AGREEMENT REGARDING ATTORNEY FEES

A written agreement is executed regarding fees. In many cases, the attorney requires a retainer, that is, an advance payment of fees. The advance is placed in the client's trust account and may not be commingled with the attorney's own funds. Contingent fee agreements are not typical in family law proceedings.

§ 5–11[B] COURT-ORDERED ATTORNEY FEES

The court has authority to order one spouse to pay some or all of the other spouse's attorney fees. Such orders allow the spouses to be on an equal footing in court. As the Colorado Supreme put it in *Marriage of Ikeler*, 161 P.3d 663, 668–669 (Colo. 2007), "Attorney's fees are intended to equalize the parties and ensure neither party suffers undue economic hardship because of the dissolution of marriage." An award of attorney fees is based on the parties' needs as well as the parties' ability to pay.

§ 5–12 RESTORATION OF PRE-MARRIAGE LAST NAME

Earlier in our history it was common for women to take the husband's last name upon marriage. Many couples continue this custom, although nowadays the man occasionally changes his name or the couple selects a hyphenated last name or each party keeps her/his own last name. Upon divorce, a spouse may ask the court to reinstate the pre-marriage name.

§ 5-13 SERVICEMEMBERS CIVIL RELIEF ACT

In 1940, when America was on the cusp of entering Word War II, Congress enacted the Soldiers and Sailors Relief Act (SSRA). SSRA put civil litigation on temporary hold while service members were deployed. The purpose of SSRA was to allow service members to devote their full attention to military duties without worrying about lawsuits back home.

Congress updated the law in 2003 and renamed it the Servicemembers Civil Relief Act (SCRA) (50 U.S.C. App. §§ 501 et seq.). A service member can apply to a court for a 90 day stay of proceedings in litigation concerning divorce, custody, or paternity. (*Real v. Real,* 3 A.3d 1196 (Me. 2010)). The service member must support the application for a stay with a "letter or other communication from the servicemember's commanding officer stating that the servicemember's current military duty prevents appearance and that military leave is not authorized for the servicemember at the time of the letter." (50 U.S.C. App. § 522(b)(2)(B)).

The non-servicemember party can argue that a stay is unnecessary. Mark Sullivan, in his book *The Military Divorce Handbook* (3d ed. 2019), notes that the attorney for the nonmilitary party can ask the judge to determine whether the servicemember acted in good faith in requesting a stay of proceedings. If a stay is granted, it can be extended. The SCRA limits the ability to obtain a default judgment against a service member.

§ 5–14 FROM PETITION TO JUDGMENT

A divorce is started with a pleading called a petition or a complaint. The petition for divorce, along with a summons, is served on the respondent, who has a limited time (typically 30 days) to file a response or answer. If the respondent fails to file a timely response, a default judgment may be entered. (*Moore v. Moore*, 568 S.W.3d 725 (Tex. Ct. App. 2019) (the characterization of property in a default judgment is *res judicata*, even if incorrect)). If a response is filed, the parties or their attorneys endeavor to resolve the case without further litigation.

The document that dissolves a marriage and returns the parties to the status of unmarried persons is a divorce decree or judgment signed by a judge. Like other judgments, a judgment of divorce is *res judicata*—a thing decided. States have detailed laws governing judgments and procedures to modify, reopen, or set aside judgments.

A divorce judgment is final regarding the marriage itself. As well, the property aspects of a divorce judgment are *res judicata*. (*Quijada v. Quijada*, 437 P.3d 876 (Ariz. Ct. App. 2019) (a party is generally "stuck" with the property division in a divorce judgment even if it later turns out that some aspect of the division was incorrect—again, *res judicata*); *Hilton v. Hilton,* 496 P.3d 839 (Idaho 2021)).

As explained in § 7–12, the child custody provisions of a judgment are *res judicata* regarding the facts before the court when the judgment was entered. However, the court retains continuing jurisdiction to modify child custody if the facts change.

The court has continuing jurisdiction to modify child support.

The court has continuing jurisdiction to modify spousal support although the law in many states permits parties to agree at the time of the divorce that spousal support cannot be modified in the future.

CHAPTER 6

PARENT-CHILD RELATIONSHIP ESTABLISHING PARENTAGE

Every state has elaborate laws to establish the parent-child relationship. Giving birth generally, although not invariably, establishes a mother-child relationship. (*See* Chapter 15). If the woman who gives birth is married, the law creates a presumption that her spouse is a parent. In *LC v. MG*, 143 Hawai'i 302, 430 P.3d 400 (2018), the Hawai'i Supreme Court ruled the marital presumption applies to same sex couples. Not every child born during marriage is the genetic offspring of the couple, and the law grapples with this reality.

Issues of parentage arise most often when the woman who gave birth is not married. To use the antiquated phrase, the child was born "out of wedlock." If the biological father steps forward and assumes his parental responsibilities, issues of parentage seldom arise. Sometimes, however, the likely father is less than enthusiastic about assuming the responsibilities of parenthood, including paying child support. In some cases, more than one man may be the father. When an unwed mother receives public benefits to support her child, child support officials are keen to establish parentage and enforce father's duty to support his children.

A child can have two mommies or two daddies. Is it possible for a child to have more than two parents? As explained below, increasingly, the answer is yes.

§ 6-1 "ILLEGITIMATE" CHILDREN

At common law, a child born out of wedlock was "illegitimate"—a "bastard." Early law treated "illegitimate" children harshly. William Blackstone (1723–1780), in his *Commentaries on the Laws of England,* had the following to say about "illegitimate" children:

> I proceed next to the rights and incapacities which appertain to a bastard. The rights are very few, being only such as he can *acquire;* for he can *inherit* nothing, being looked upon as the son of nobody, and sometimes called *filius nullius*, sometimes *filius populi*. Yet he may gain a surname by reputation, though he has none by inheritance. All other children have their primary settlement in their father's parish; but a bastard in the parish where born, for he hath no father. The incapacity of a bastard consists principally in this, that he cannot be heir to any one, neither can he have heirs but of his own body; for, being *nullius filius*, he is therefore of kin to nobody, and has no ancestor from whom any inheritable blood can be derived.

Legal discrimination against "illegitimate children" continued into the twentieth century. A 1962 Note in the *Harvard Law Review* described the unfinished business of advancing the interests of these children: "Though [the child's] outlook would be less dismal today [than at common law], he would by no means have attained equality. . . . Today he could almost everywhere be made legitimate by the subsequent marriage of his parents. Even as an illegitimate he usually would be entitled to inherit from his mother, but his right to inherit from her or her kindred would be much more limited. Only a minority of states would permit him to inherit from or through his father." (Note, The Rights of Illegitimates Under Federal Statutes, 76 *Harvard Law Review* 337, 337 (1962)).

In 1966, Harry Krause observed, "The traditional status of the illegitimate child does not rest on a fair and impartial adjustment of the conflicting interests involved, but springs from ancient prejudice based on religious and moral taboos. . . ." (Harry D. Krause, Bringing the Bastard Into the Great Society—A Proposed Uniform Act on Legitimacy, 44 *Texas Law Review* 829, 830 (1966). *See also*, Harry D. Krause, Equal Protection for the Illegitimate, 65 *Michigan Law Review* 477 (1967)).

A series of United States Supreme Court decisions in the 1970s struck down many restrictions on the rights of children born out of wedlock. In *Weber v. Aeta Casualty & Surety Co.,* 406 U.S. 164, 92 S. Ct. 1400 (1972), the Court ruled unconstitutional a Louisiana worker's compensation law that granted benefits to "legitimate" children of injured workers but denied benefits to "illegitimate" children of workers. The Court wrote, "The status of illegitimacy has expressed through the ages society's condemnation of irresponsible liaisons beyond the bonds of marriage. But visiting this condemnation on the head of an infant is illogical and unjust. Moreover, imposing disabilities on the illegitimate child is contrary to the basic concept of our system that legal burdens should bear some relationship to individual responsibility or wrongdoing. Obviously, no child is responsible for his birth and penalizing the illegitimate child is an ineffectual—as well as an unjust—way of deterring the parent. Courts are powerless to prevent the social opprobrium suffered by these helpless children, but the Equal Protection Clause does enable us to strike down discriminatory laws relating to status or birth where—as in this case—the classification is justified by no legitimate state interest, compelling or otherwise." (92 S. Ct. at 1406–1407). The Supreme Court revisited the issue in *Trimble v. Gordon*, 430 U.S. 762, 97 S. Ct. 1459 (1977), where the Court struck down an Illinois law that allowed "legitimate" children to inherit by intestate succession from both parents, but allowed "illegitimate" children to inherit only from the mother.

Today, the term "illegitimate child" is an anachronism. The 2017 Uniform Parentage Act (UPA) abolishes the concept of illegitimacy with the following language: "A parent-child relationship extends equally to every child and parent, regardless of the marital status of the parent." (§ 202).

§ 6–2 UNIFORM PARENTAGE ACT

States have complex statutes governing parentage. The most influential law is the Uniform Parentage Act (UPA), first published in 1973. The UPA was revised in 2000 and again in 2017. Key components of the 2017 UPA are discussed in this section.

Parentage laws vary from state to state, and the reader is referred to local law for details.

§ 6–2[A] PARENT DEFINED

The 2017 UPA defines five categories of "parent." (1) An "acknowledged parent" has an established parent-child relationship. (UPA § 102(1)). (2) An "adjudicated parent" has been adjudged by a court to be a child's parent. (§ 102(2)). (3) An "alleged genetic parent" is a person who claims to be a child's genetic parent (§ 102(3)). (4) An "intended parent" is a person who intends to be a parent by means of assisted reproduction. (§ 102(13)). (5) A "presumed parent" is a person who is presumed by the UPA to be a child's parent. (§ 201(17)).

§ 6–2[B] ESTABLISHING PARENT-CHILD RELATIONSHIP

The identity of a child's mother is usually clear. The woman who gives birth to a child is typically a parent. (UPA § 201(1)). The UPA provides that a woman who fulfills the role of a surrogate is not a "parent." (§ 201(1)). Surrogacy is discussed in Chapter 13.

Issues of parentage arise most often regarding the father-child relationship. Section 201 of the UPA provides that the parent-child relationship can be established when a man: (1) Is a presumed parent, (2) Is an adjudicated parent, (3) Adopts a child, (4) Signs an acknowledgement of parentage, (5) Becomes a parent through assisted reproductive technology, or (6) Becomes a parent through surrogacy.

§ 6–2[C] PARENTS OF SAME GENDER

A child can have two mothers or two fathers. (*See D.M.T. v. T.M.H.*, 129 So. 3d 320 (Fla. 2013); *Matter of W.L. and G.L.*, 312 Kan. 367, 475 P.3d 338 (2020); *Schaberg v. Schaberg*, 637 S.W.3d 512 (Mo. Ct. App. 2021); *Brooke S.B. v. Elizabeth A.C.C.*, 28 N.Y.3d 1, 61 N.E.3d 488, 39 N.Y.S.3d 89 (2016)). For discussion, *see* § 7–11. The language of many state parentage laws speaks of women and men, but courts interpret the statutes in gender-neutral fashion.

§ 6–2[D] PRESUMPTION OF PARENTAGE

Under the 2017 UPA and corresponding state laws, a person—woman or man—is a presumed parent under the circumstances outlined below. These presumptions are rebuttable.

A person is a presumed parent when the person is married to the woman who gave birth to the child. (UPA § 204(a)(1)(A)). In 2018, the Hawai'i Supreme Court held that the marital presumption applies to same sex married couples. (*LC v. MG,* 143 Hawai'i 302, 430 P.3d 400 (2018)).

A person is a presumed parent if the person lived in the same household as the child for the first two years of the child's life and openly held the child out to the world as the person's child. (§ 204(a)(2)). Quite a few states have variations of this presumption. In California, for example, a person is a presumed parent when the person "receives the child into his or her home and openly holds out the child as his or her natural child." (Cal. Family Code § 7611(d)).

In some cases, two or more persons are presumed parents. With competing presumptions, who wins? The 1973 UPA provided that when two presumed parents were in competition to establish a parent-child relationship, the court determined which presumption was founded on the weightier considerations of policy and ruled accordingly. The 2002 UPA eliminated this balancing approach to competing presumptions. The official Comment to the 2002 Act states: "Nowadays the existence of [genetic] testing obviates this old approach to the problem of conflicting presumptions when a court is to determine paternity." The 2017 UPA, like the 2002 Act, abandons a balancing test for resolving conflicting presumptions. Under the 2017 UPA, the court considers the best interests of the child, including the child's age, the child's relationship with each presumed parent, and the harm to the child likely to be caused by ending the relationship with a presumed parent. (2017 UPA § 613). Some states continue to balance competing presumptions of parentage.

§ 6–2[E] ACKNOWLEDGMENT OF PARENTAGE

States have a procedure to establish parentage by signing a voluntary acknowledgement/declaration of parentage. (2017 UPA § 301). An acknowledgement of parentage that is filed with the appropriate agency is equivalent to a court judgment of parentage and confers all the rights and duties of a parent. (UPA § 305(a)). A person who signs an acknowledgement of parentage has 60 days to change her or his mind and rescind the acknowledgment. (UPA § 308). After the

60 days expires, a person may challenge an acknowledgement of parentage if the person acts within two years and a court finds fraud, duress, or material mistake of fact. (UPA § 309).

§ 6–2[F] REGISTRY OF PARENTAGE

More than half the states have a state-wide registry of parentage. The 2017 UPA specifies such a registry (UPA Article 4). Section 402 of the UPA provides that if an unmarried man wants to be notified of a pending adoption, the man must register within 30 days of the child's birth. In *Lehr v. Robertson*, 463 U.S. 248, 103 S. Ct. 2985 (1983) (*See* Chapter 2), the Supreme Court upheld the constitutionality of a parentage registry.

§ 6–2[G] GENETIC TESTING

Courts routinely order genetic testing to determine parentage. (2017 UPA § 503).

§ 6–2[H] PROCEEDING TO ESTABLISH PARENTAGE

Court proceedings to establish parentage occur in several settings. (2017 UPA §§ 601 et seq.). First, to collect child support, a parentage action may be commenced in family court. A support-motivated proceeding may be commenced by a parent or by a child support enforcement agency. Second, a person who claims to be a child's parent may commence a family court action to establish the parental relationship. Third, in juvenile court proceedings to protect children from abuse or neglect, the juvenile court establishes parentage. Personal jurisdiction is required to establish parentage. (2017 UPA § 604).

§ 6-3 MORE THAN TWO PARENTS?

Children have two parents, right? A mother and a father or two parents of the same gender. But can a child have more than two parents? In most states, the answer is no. (Myrisha S. Lewis, Biology, Genetics, Nurture, and the Law: The Expansion of the Legal Definition of Family to Include Three or More Parents, 16 *Nevada Law Review* 743, 745 (2016)). In 2014, the California Legislature made it possible for a child to have more than two parents. California Family Code § 7612(c) provides, "In an appropriate action, a court may find that more than two persons with a claim to parentage . . . are parents if the court finds that recognizing only two parents would be detrimental to the child."

In *In re Donovan L., Jr.*, 244 Cal. App. 4th 1075, 198 Cal. Rptr. 3d 550 (2016), Shannon and Donovan were married when the child was conceived. Shannon had an affair with David and became pregnant by him. David took little interest in the baby for the first year of the child's life. Shannon and the child stayed at David's apartment for two weeks when she and Donovan had marital problems. In juvenile court proceedings the trial judge ruled Donovan was a presumed father because of the marriage, and that David was a presumed father because the child lived in his home for two weeks and David acknowledged he was the child's genetic father (Cal. Family Code § 7611(d)). The judge ruled the child had three parents despite the fact that the court concluded David did not have a meaningful relationship with the child. The Court of Appeal disagreed, finding that this was "not 'an appropriate action' to recognize three parents . . . because the juvenile court determined [the child] did not have an existing relationship with David."

Another case interpreting California's "three parent" law is *Matinez v. Vaziri,* 246 Cal. App. 4th 373, 200 Cal. Rptr. 3d 884 (2016). Mother was in a long term non-marital relationship with Anthony. Mother became pregnant by the genetic father—not Anthony—who abandoned mother during pregnancy. Mother had sole legal and physical custody, with no visitation for the genetic father who was by then in prison. Although Anthony knew he was not the genetic father, he fully participated in caring for the child, living with the child and mother for the first six months of the baby's life and continuing his involvement after moving to his own apartment. When the child was one year old, Anthony spanked the child and left bruises. Child protective services became involved. Anthony brought an action to establish paternity. No one disputed that Anthony was a presumed parent under California law (§ 7611(d)). Yet, the trial judge declined to rule in Anthony's favor. The judge refused to apply the "three parent" law. The Court of Appeal ruled that the trial judge misconstrued the statute and remanded for further proceedings.

In *C.A. v. C.P.,* 29 Cal. App. 5th 27, 30, 240 Cal. Rptr. 3d 38 (2018), the California Court of Appeal considered a case involving "a little girl bonded to and loved by each of her three parents." The trial court decided this was one of the rare cases where a child has three parents, and the appellate court affirmed.

In *M.M v. D.V.*, 66 Cal. App. 5th 733, 281 Cal. Rptr. 3d 361 (2021), the biological father of a child sought a court order naming him the child's third parent. The biological father had no existing relationship with the two-year-old child. In denying third parent status, the California Court of Appeal wrote that Family Code § 7612(c) "allows a court to recognize three parents only in rare cases where a child truly has more than two parents. Specifically, an appropriate action for application of section 7612, subdivision (c) requires a court to find an *existing*, rather than *potential*, relationship between a putative third parent and the child, such that recognizing only two parents would be detrimental to the child. . . . [O]nly a person with a claim to parentage is eligible to be a third parent. Thus, not only must a person seeking to become a third parent show that it would be detrimental to the child to have only two parents, the putative third parent must meet the *preliminary* hurdle of establishing that he or she qualifies as a presumed parent." (emphasis in original).

§ 6–4 PARENTAGE BY ESTOPPEL

A person who holds herself or himself out to the world as a child's parent may be estopped from denying parentage. In *A.S. v. I.S.*, 130 A.3d 763, 769 (Pa. 2015), the Pennsylvania Supreme Court wrote,

"The doctrine of paternity by estoppel provides that where a party assertively holds himself out as a child's father, that party may be estopped from subsequently denying this status."

§ 6-5 DE FACTO PARENTAGE

An emerging area of law grants parental rights or parent-like rights to persons who are not presumed or biological parents. The 2017 UPA defines such individuals as de facto parents (*Young v. King*, 208 A.3d 762 (Maine 2019); *E.N. v. T.R.*, 474 Md. 346, 255 A. 3d 1 (2021)).[1] Section 609(d) of the 2017 UPA allows a finding of de facto parent where there is only one other parent, and the de facto parent proves by clear and convincing evidence that: (1) the person lived with the child for a substantial time, (2) the person consistently cared for the child, (3) the person undertook the normal responsibilities of parenthood, without expecting to be paid, (4) the person held the child out to the world as her or his child, (5) the person and the child are constructively bonded to each other, (6) the other parent supported the relationship, and (7) continuing the relationship is in the child's best interest.

---

[1] In California, the term de facto parent is used in juvenile court to describe a non-parent who has an established relationship with a neglected or abused child, and who is permitted to participate in a limited fashion in juvenile court proceedings to protect the child. *See In re B.S.*, 65 Cal. App. 5th 888, 280 Cal. Rptr. 3d 259 (2021) (in juvenile court, de facto parent lacked standing to challenge court's placement decision); *see also, State ex rel. C.H. and S.H. v. Faircloth*, 815 S.E.2d 540 (W. Va. 2018).

The Comment to Section 609 states:

> This section adds a new means by which an individual can establish a parent-child relationship. . . .
>
> In most states, if an individual can establish that he or she has developed a strong parent-child relationship with the consent and encouragement of a legal parent, the individual is entitled to some parental rights and possibly some parental responsibilities. Some states extend rights to such persons under equitable principles. . . .
>
> In addition, by statute and through case law, several states recognize such persons as legal parents. . . .
>
> Under this new section, an individual who has functioned as a child's parent for a significant period such that the individual formed a bond and dependent parent-child relationship may be recognized as a legal parent. (§ 609 Comment).

In 2019, the Washington State Legislature updated Washington Uniform Parentage Act to recognize de facto parents who form strong parent-child bonds with children. Washington Code § 26.26A.440(4) provides that to establish de facto parent status, a person must (1) reside with the child as a regular member of the child's household for a significant period, (2) engage in consistent caretaking of the child, (3) undertake full parental responsibilities without expectation of payment, (4) hold the child out as her or his own child, (5) have a bonded and dependent relationship with the child that is parental in nature, (6) another parent supported the relationship, and (7) continuing the relationship is in the child's best interest. (*See Matter of Custody of SA-M*, 17 Wash. App. 2d 939, 489 P.3d 259 (2021); *Matter of L.J.M.,* 15 Wash. App. 2d 588, 476 P.3d 636 (2020)).

CHAPTER 7

CHILD CUSTODY

This chapter addresses the most emotionally charged aspect of family law, child custody. Fortunately, most divorcing parents agree on the custodial arrangement that is best for their family and custody litigation is avoided. When parents agree on custody, the judge seldom second guesses the parents. This is not to say that parental decisions regarding custody are binding on the court. In the final analysis, judges decide custody, although, again, judges usually defer to custody agreements reached by parents.

When parents cannot agree on custody, litigation is necessary and full blown custody litigation breeds tremendous ill-will, stress, and heartache. Custody fights are hard on clients and on kids. Even lawyers, who ostensibly are detached professionals, lose sleep over these cases. Indeed, there are family law attorneys who will not do custody. They will do everything else, but not custody.

Most custody litigation is between biological parents in the context of divorce or the breakup of non-marital relationships. Occasionally, child custody issues arise between adults who are not genetically related to a child. Chapter 6 discusses who is considered a child's parent. When a same-sex couple—married or unmarried—has a baby through intrauterine insemination or surrogacy and the adults break up, both may seek custody. (*See* Chapter 13). Courts are increasingly receptive to claims of custody brought by step-parents who have a strong bond with step-children. (*See* 750 Illinois Statutes 5/601.2(b)(4); *Sharpe v. Westmoreland,* 2020 IL 124863 (Ill. 2020); Barbara A. Atwood, Marriage as Gatekeeper: The Misguided Reliance on Marital Status Criteria to Determine Third-Party Standing, 58 *Family Court Review* 971 (2020)).

§ 7-1 IMPACT OF DIVORCE ON CHILDREN

Psychologists have studied the impact of divorce on children. Most research suggests divorce is a risk factor for adjustment problems. (*See* Hyun Sik Kim, Consequences of Parental Divorce for Child Development, 76 *American Sociological Review* 487–511 (2011); Daniel Potter, Psychosocial Well-Being and the Relationship Between Divorce and Children's Academic Achievement, 72 *Journal of Marriage and Family* 933–946 (2010)). Amato reviewed the literature available in 2010 and wrote, "Research during the last decade continued to show that children with divorced parents, compared with children with continuously married parents, score lower on a variety of emotional, behavioral, social, health, and academic outcomes, on average." (Paul R. Amato, Research on Divorce: Continuing Trends and New Developments, 72 *Journal of Marriage and Family* 650–666, 653 (2010)). Melton and his colleagues note that divorce is nearly always stressful for children. The effects of divorce vary among children and are influenced by many factors. "Negative effects are not inevitable or necessarily long term." Gary B. Melton, John Petrila, Norman G.

Poythress, Christopher Slobogin, Randy K. Otto, Douglas Mossman & Lois O. Condie, *Psychological Evaluations for the Courts: A Handbook for Mental Health Professionals and Lawyers* p. 543 (4th ed. 2018).

Although divorce is difficult for children, many children of divorce do well. Divorce is a risk factor not a fait accompli. Indeed, a divorce that ends a bad, abusive marriage can be good for children. (Hyun Sik Kim, Consequences of Parental Divorce for Child Development, 76 *American Sociological Review* 487–511 (2011)). Melton and his colleagues write, "[T]he divorce 'crisis' is exacerbated if there is very high conflict between the parents; in such cases, children are worse off when the parents stay in contact." (Gary B. Melton, John Petrila, Norman G. Poythress, Christopher Slobogin, Randy K. Otto, Douglas Mossman & Lois O. Condie, *Psychological Evaluations for the Courts: A Handbook for Mental Health Professionals and Lawyers* p. 542 (4th ed. 2018)).

§ 7-2 HIGH-CONFLICT DIVORCE

Most divorcing couples recover from the hurt and anger involved in divorce. The couple—and the children—move on. Divorced parents have disagreements as children grow up, but so do parents in intact marriages. Fortunately, most divorced parents find ways to support each other in the difficult job of raising kids. Sadly, however, up to twenty percent of divorcing parents get locked in seemingly endless acrimony. They return again and again to family court, seeking changes to custody, visitation, and child support. Family law attorneys sometimes cynically refer to these parents as "frequent fliers." Haddad, Phillips, and Bone describe high-conflict couples:

> A high-conflict divorce is defined as a divorce process that lasts longer than two years, which is characterized by a high degree of anger, hostility, and distrust, intensive custody litigation, ongoing difficulty in communicating about the care of their children, and higher than usual rates of nonpayment of child support. . . .
>
> A high-conflict divorce can destroy people. Long-term effects on children, parents, and extended family and friends can be devastating for years. . . .
>
> The literature is clear in identifying that parents need to stop the high-conflict process. What is not clear is how to stop the process, and why some cases are high-conflict and some are not.

(Lisa Haddad, Kenneth D. Phillips & J. Michael Bone, High-Conflict Divorce: A Review of the Literature, 29 *American Journal of Family Law* 243, 243–244 (2016)).

§ 7–3 ATTACHMENT THEORY; BONDING BETWEEN PARENT AND CHILD

John Bowlby (1907–1990) was an English psychoanalyst. Bowlby was the "father" of attachment theory. As a young psychiatrist, Bowlby focused his work on the quality of the relationship between infants and parents, especially mothers. Bowlby believed the quality of this relationship has a profound impact on the developing child. In 1951, Bowlby published a report for the World Health Organization describing the importance of the bond between children and parents. Bowlby wrote: "The services which mothers and fathers habitually render their children are so taken for granted that their magnitude is forgotten. In no other relationship do human beings place themselves so unreservedly and so continuously at the disposal of others. This holds true even of bad parents. . . . It must never be forgotten that even the bad parent who neglects her child is none the less providing much for him. Except in the worst cases, she is giving him food and shelter, comforting him in distress, teaching him simple skills, and above all is providing him with that continuity of human care on which his sense of security rests. . . . Unless his parents have wholly rejected him, he is secure in the knowledge that there is *someone* to whom he is of value and who will strive, even though inadequately, to provide for him until such time as he can fend for himself." (John Bowlby, *Maternal Care and Mental Health* pp. 67–68 (1951) (World Health Organization)).

Bowlby and other child development experts emphasize the trauma that can come from disrupting the parent-child bond. Dozier and Rutter write, "During the second half of the first year of life, children typically develop attachment relationships to specific caregivers. . . . Thus experiences of separation, maltreatment, and privation, even early in the first year of life, may have long-term developmental consequences." (Mary Dozier & Michael Rutter, Challenges to the Development of Attachment Relationships Faced by Young Children in Foster and Adoptive Care. In Jude Cassidy & Philip R. Shaver (Eds.), *Handbook of Attachment: Theory, Research, and Clinical Applications* 698–717, at 699 (2nd ed. 2008)). Kobak and Madsen write, "Unchallenged maintenance of an attachment bond contributes to a feeling of security. . . . When an individual perceives a threat to a caregiver's availability, he or she will feel anxious and angry. . . . A persistent disruption of an attachment bond will result in feelings of sadness and despair." (Roger Kobak & Stephanie Madsen, Disruptions in Attachment Bonds: Implications for Theory, Research, and Clinical Intervention. In Jude Cassidy & Philip R. Shaver (Eds.), *Handbook of Attachment: Theory, Research, and Clinical Applications* 23–47, at 24 (2nd ed. 2008)).

Bowlby's most famous student was Mary Ainsworth (1913–1999), an American psychologist who conducted groundbreaking research on attachment. Ainsworth described three types of attachment—secure, insecure-avoidant, and insecure-ambivalent/resistant. Secure attachment is most likely to occur when parents are loving, warm, consistent, and sensitive to their baby's needs. In the United States, approximately 70% of babies become securely attached. The securely attached baby views the parent as a "secure base." The baby feels comfortable exploring the environment, confident that the secure base is there. The typical securely attached baby is relatively easy to sooth when upset. During the preschool years, the securely attached child is likely to develop good self-esteem and be flexible and able to problem solve. These positive attributes continue as the child matures. Berlin, Cassidy, and Appleyard write, "Individuals with secure attachments to their mothers during infancy also have more harmonious and mutually supportive relationships with siblings, friends, peers, and romantic partners, even 20 years later." (Lisa J. Berlin, Jude Cassidy, & Karen Appleyard, The Influence of Early Attachments on Other Relationships. In Jude Cassidy & Philip R. Shaver (Eds.), *Handbook of Attachment: Theory, Research, and Clinical Applications* 333–347, at 343 (2nd ed. 2008)). Parents who are themselves in a supportive, loving relationship are in the best position to provide the nurturing that leads to secure attachment. Belsky and Fearon write, "An abundance of evidence indicates that a supportive relationship with a spouse or partner during the infancy and toddler years is correlated with the very kinds of parenting theorized (and found) to predict attachment security." (Jay Belsky & R.M. Pasco Fearon, Precursors of Attachment Security. In Jude Cassidy & Philip R. Shaver (Eds.), *Handbook of Attachment: Theory, Research, and Clinical Applications* 295–316 at 307 (2nd ed. 2008)).

Insecure-Avoidant attachment is more likely to occur when the primary caretaker is often emotionally unavailable or rejecting of the child. The baby cannot count on the parent for consistent nurturance. The baby may become unpredictably angry and unresponsive to the parent.

Insecure-Ambivalent attachment is more likely to develop when the primary caretaker is inconsistent or disorganized. The parent does not seem "in tune" with the baby. The baby cannot predict the behavior of the most important person in the baby's life. This leads to insecurity and, often, anger.

Some children do not fit neatly into one of Ainsworth's three categories of attachment. Main and Solomon described a fourth type of attachment observed in a small number of children: Disorganized/disoriented. (M. Main & J. Solomon, Discovery of a New, Insecure Disorganized/ Disoriented Attachment Pattern. In T.B. Brazelton & M. Yogman (Eds.), *Affective Development in Infancy* pp. 95–124 (1986)). Kobak and Madsen describe this fourth type of attachment: "A traditional focus on the availability of an attachment figure assumes that the attachment relationship will serve as a source of safety; however, children exposed to abuse or extreme forms of punishment must manage a profound dilemma, as their attachment figures are potential sources of danger. . . . Infants who have been unpredictably frightened by their attachment figures are caught in a conflict when placed in a situation that normally elicits attachment behavior. Although these infants may display the typical secure and insecure attachment strategies, many show temporary lapses in their strategies; such lapses are marked by fear, freezing, and disorientation. . . . The infant and adult disorganized classifications have been consistently linked to a variety of adjustment difficulties and to psychopathology." (Roger Kobak & Stephanie Madsen, Disruptions in Attachment Bonds: Implications for Theory, Research, and Clinical Intervention. In Jude Cassidy & Philip R. Shaver (Eds.), *Handbook of Attachment: Theory, Research, and Clinical Applications* 23–47, at 35–36 (2nd ed. 2008)).

Insecure attachment is a risk factor for problems down the road. Deklyen and Greenberg write, "Most of the research linking attachment with psychopathology has considered attachment as a potential risk or protective factor. . . . Attachment exerts its influence *in the context of other risk factors* within the child and the family ecology." (Michelle Deklyen & Mark T. Greenberg, Attachment and Psychopathology in Childhood. In Jude Cassidy & Philip R. Shaver (Eds.), *Handbook of Attachment: Theory, Research, and Clinical Applications* 637–665, at 638 (2nd ed. 2008) (emphasis in original)). Not all insecurely attached babies and toddlers have adjustment problems as they mature. Insecure attachment is a risk factor, not a death sentence. Moreover, insecure attachment is *not* itself a disorder or mental illness. Deklyen and Greenberg write, "It is clear that insecure attachment is not itself a form of psychopathology but may set a trajectory that, along with other risk factors, can increase the risk for either externalizing or internalizing psychopathology." (p. 657).

Attachment—secure or insecure—typically occurs between ages six months to a year. Babies become attached to abusive and neglectful parents. The quality of attachment may suffer, but attachment occurs. Babies can become attached to more than one person. Cassidy writes, "The majority of children become attached to more than one familiar person during their first year." (Jude Cassidy, The Nature of the Child's Ties. In Jude Cassidy & Philip R. Shaver (Eds.), *Handbook of Attachment: Theory, Research, and Clinical Applications* 3–22, at 14 (2nd ed. 2008)).

It is common for expert witnesses in child custody litigation, in protective proceedings in juvenile court, and in termination of parental rights cases to use the terms "attachment" and "bonding." For example, *J.W. v. C.M.*, 627 N.W.2d 687, 693 (Minn. Ct. App. 2001) was a custody case. The child had been cared for since birth by foster parents. The trial court "found a strong attachment existed between [the child and the foster parents] but none existed between [the child and the genetic father] because of his canceled and failed visitations." In *In re K.C.F.*, 928 A.2d 1046 (Pa. Super. 2007), an expert witness in a termination of parental rights case used attachment terminology. In *In re C.L.*, 178 Vt. 558, 878 A.2d 207 (2005), an expert's report stated that a child was attached to foster parents and that it would be risky to remove the child from the foster parents and return the child to the genetic father. (*See also, In re Gustavus E.*, 182 A.3d 153, 158 (Me. 2018)).

In addition to case law, one finds the terminology of attachment in legislation. For example, when

California's juvenile court law addresses family reunification for children in foster care, the statute asks whether "the child is closely and positively attached to that parent." (Welfare and Institutions Code § 361.5(c)). At another point, the statute refers to "the degree of parent-child bonding."

Judges, legislators, and expert witnesses often use the terminology of attachment rather loosely and in ways that have little connection to the "attachment theory" developed by Bowlby, Ainsworth, and others. Most of the time, what the speaker is referring to is the psychological connection between child and caretaker.

An article by psychiatrist David Arredondo and Judge Leonard Edwards offers guidance on the use and misuse of the terms "attachment" and "bonding." (David E. Arredondo & Leonard P. Edwards, Attachment, Bonding, and Reciprocal Connectedness, 2 *Journal of the Center for Families, Children and the Courts* 109–125 (2000)). Arredondo and Edwards conclude, "The term 'attachment' (as usually conceived) is too narrow to be of much use to the court. . . ." (p. 110). Arredondo and Edwards write:

> Forensic testimony based on attachment theory may mislead courts in three ways. First, the concept of attachment draws distinctions in black and white, whereas courts often need to decide questions in the gray areas of human relations. . . . In a forensic setting, attachment theory is critically limited because it describes attachment in terms of categories instead of

> more accurately conceptualizing interrelatedness as a spectrum of continuously distributed variables. . . .
>
> Second, attachment theory may mislead courts because it excludes from its scope the attitudes of adult caregivers. . . .
>
> Third, the concept of attachment is vague. As applied in both research and forensic psychology, the terms "bonding" and "attachment" have multiple meanings that sometimes diverge from their ordinary meanings. (pp. 110–111).

In place of testimony about attachment or bonding, Arredondo and Edwards recommend the concept of "reciprocal connectedness," which they define as follows: "Reciprocal connectedness paints a more comprehensive and subtle picture of relationships than do 'bonding' and 'attachment'. In the context of decision making in the family court setting, we can define it as a mutual interrelatedness that is characterized by two-way interaction between a child and an adult caregiver and by the caregiver's sensitivity to the child's developmental needs." (p. 112).

§ 7–4 HISTORY OF CHILD CUSTODY LAW

For much of the nineteenth century, courts ruled that fathers normally had the right to custody. (*See, e.g., Wand v. Wand,* 14 Cal. 512 (1860)). Joel Bishop was a leading nineteenth century commentator on family law, and in 1891, Bishop wrote, "The father is at the common law the guardian of his minor children." (Joel P. Bishop, *New Commentaries on Marriage, Divorce, and Separation* vol. 2, § 1152, p. 449 (1891)).

Gradually, the presumption in favor of fathers was replaced with the "tender years" presumption which held that children of tender years should normally be with mother. In the 1960s, the argument was made that the tender years presumption constituted gender-based discrimination, and the tender years presumption was replaced with a gender-neutral preference for the "primary caretaker," that is, the parent who provides most of the day-to-day parenting. In *Williams v. Williams,* 368 P.3d 539 (Wyo. 2016), the Wyoming Supreme Court discussed the centrality of the primary caretaker, "A parent's role as the primary caregiver is a weighty factor that the court must consider when fashioning a custody arrangement that is in the best interests of the child. While primary caregiver status is not determinative, it is a crucial factor in many custody disputes." The overarching priority is to make a custody decision that serves the best interests of the child.

§ 7-5 CUSTODY TERMINOLOGY

States vary slightly in the terms used to describe custody. For example, Texas uses the term "managing conservator." In all states, a distinction exists between legal and physical custody. Legal custody is the right to make decisions for a child about medical care, where the child goes to school, and innumerable day-to-day issues. Physical custody is the right to have the child live with the custodial parent all or part of the time.

Sole physical custody means the child lives full time with the custodial parent. Joint physical custody means the child lives part of the time with each parent. Parents can have joint legal and physical custody, or one parent can have sole physical custody while the parents share legal custody.

The preference in custody matters is to maximize involvement of both parents in the child's life. In Michigan, for example, "If the parents agree on joint custody, the court shall award joint custody unless the court determines on the record based upon clear and convincing evidence that joint custody is not in the best interests of the child." (Mich. Comp. Laws Ann. § 722.26a(2)).

§ 7–6 BEST INTERESTS OF THE CHILD

To decide custody, judges employ the best interests of the child standard. For a classic analysis of the best interest standard, *see* Robert H. Mnookin, Child-Custody Adjudication: Judicial Functions in the Face of Indeterminancy, 39 *Law and Contemporary Problems* 226–293 (1975). The Vermont Supreme Court discussed best interest analysis in *Miller-Jenkins v. Miller-Jenkins,* 189 Vt. 518, 12 A.3d 768 (2010), "The family court's sole focus in a custody dispute must be the best interests of the child. Although the parents are the ones who appear before the court in a custody dispute, and it is therefore easy to become caught up in their rights and interests rather than the child's welfare, the family court must not take into consideration the competing, often antagonistic, desires of the parents without upsetting the delicate nature of custody proceedings and trivializing the welfare of the child." The question is always, what custody arrangement will be best for this child?

In conducting a best interest analysis, the judge considers all evidence shedding light on a child's short- and long-term interests—the totality of the circumstances. (*Hinds v. Hinds-Holm*, 2022 WL 244537 (Utah Ct. App. 2022)). As the South Carolina Supreme Court put it is *Parris v. Parris*, 319 S.C. 308, 460 S.E.2d 571, 572 (1995), "The totality of the circumstances peculiar to each case constitutes the only scale upon which the ultimate decision can be weighed." The judge has broad discretion in evaluating the evidence and reaching a decision.

Every state has a statute describing factors to consider in the best interest analysis. The Illinois and Michigan statutes are typical. The Illinois statute provides: "(c) In determining the child's best interests for purposes of allocating significant decision-making responsibilities, the court shall consider all relevant factors, including, without limitation, the following: (1) the wishes of the child, taking into account the child's maturity and ability to express reasoned and independent preferences as to decision-making; (2) the child's adjustment to his or her home, school, and community; (3) the mental and physical health of all individuals involved; (4) the ability of the parents to cooperate to make decisions, or the level of conflict between the parties that may affect their ability to share decision-making; (5) the level of each parent's participation in past significant decision-making with respect to the child; (6) any prior agreement or course of conduct between the parents relating to decision-making with respect to the child; (7) the wishes of the parents; (8) the child's needs; (9) the distance between the parents' residences, the cost and difficulty of transporting the child, each parent's and the child's daily schedules, and the ability of the parents to cooperate in the arrangement; (10) whether a restriction on decision-making is appropriate under Section 603.10 [Section 603.10 deals with a parent who abused or neglected the child]; (11) the willingness and ability of each parent to facilitate and encourage a close and continuing relationship between the other parent and the child; (12) the physical violence or threat of physical violence by the child's parent directed against the child; (13) the occurrence of abuse against the child or other member of the child's household; (14) whether one of the parents is a sex offender, and if so, the exact nature of the offense and what, if any, treatment in which the parent has successfully participated; and (15) any other factor that the court expressly finds to be relevant. (750 Illinois Stats. § 5/602.5(c)).

Michigan uses different words to attain the same goal: "As used in this act, best interests of the child means the sum total of the following factors to be considered, evaluated, and determined by the court: (a) The love, affection, and other emotional ties existing between the parties involved and the child. (b) The capacity and disposition of the parties involved to give the child love, affection, and guidance and to continue the education and raising of the child in his or her religion or creed, if any. (c) The capacity and disposition of the parties involved to provide the child with food, clothing, medical care or other remedial care recognized and permitted under the laws of this state in place of medical care, and other material needs. (d) The length of time the child has lived in a stable, satisfactory environment, and the desirability of maintaining continuity. (e) The permanence, as a family unit, of the existing or proposed custodial home or homes. (f) The moral fitness of the parties involved. (g) The mental and physical health of the parties involved. (h) The home, school, and community record of the child. (i) The reasonable preference of the child, if the court considered the child to be of sufficient age to express preference. (j) The willingness and ability of each of the parties to facilitate and encourage a close and continuing parent-child relationship between the child and the other parent or the child and the parents. (k) Domestic violence, regardless of whether the violence was directed against or witnessed by the child. (*l*) Any other factor considered by the court to be relevant to a particular child custody dispute." (Mich. Compiled Laws § 722.23).

The best interest standard has always had critics. (*See* Steven N. Peskind, Determining the Undeterminable: The Best Interest of the Child Standard as an Imperfect But Necessary Guidepost to Determine Child Custody, 25 *Northern Illinois University Law Review* 449 (2005)). The strength *and* weakness of the standard is that it is standardless.

On the negative side, decision making tools that lack relatively clear guidelines for application result in unpredictable outcomes, especially in close cases. Every judge conducting a best interest analysis has a personal history. Most judges are parents, and judges are almost certainly influenced by their experience with their own kids. Not only is every judge different, every judge was once a lawyer, not a psychologist or social worker trained in child development, but a lawyer trained in contracts, torts, and crimes. What makes us think judges have any particular skill in deciding what is best for children? On the other hand, judges have a solemn responsibility to do justice—a responsibility the vast majority of judges take very seriously, and this judicial responsibility is at the core of the principle strength of the best interest standard: Individualized decisions for each child, made by a judge whose only interest is the child's welfare. Judges understand that few decisions they make are more important than decisions about children. As well, judges are skilled at sorting through conflicting evidence to find kernels of truth. Thus, we can be fairly confident that the gravity of the office, combined with experience and an appreciation of the importance of "getting it right," equips judges to reach correct decisions most of the time.

§ 7–6[A] ABUSE OF ALCOHOL OR DRUGS

Parental consumption of alcohol in moderation generally is not relevant to a child's best interests. When alcohol consumption impairs a parent's ability to care for children, however, especially drinking and driving or alcoholism, judges take note. (*Jessica HH v. Sean HH*, 196 A.D.3d 750, 151 N.Y.S.3d 449 (2021) ("The mother has exhibited signs of excessive alcohol use on numerous occasions and has failed to submit urine screens as required by the terms of her probation.").

Parental use of illegal drugs hardly sets a wholesome model for children. It should surprise no one that judges view parental drug abuse as a serious matter. (*Whittington v. Stracener*, 964 So. 2d 407 (La. Ct. App. 2007); *Klein v. Larson*, 724 N.W.2d 565 (N.D. 2006)). Of course, recovery and sobriety are possible, and a parent who proves she is clean and sober may convince the court accordingly. (*Bauer v. Bauer*, 97 S.W.3d 515 (Mo. Ct. App. 2002) (mother had been sober quite some time); *Long v. Ledug*, 237 Or. App. 652, 241 P.3d 340 (2010) (parent's drug problems were in the past)). In *Marriage of Brinkly*, 223 Or. App. 113, 195 P.3d 405, 408 (2008), a mother's long term recovery from methamphetamine use constituted a substantial change in circumstances warranting a fresh look at best interests.

§ 7–6[B] CRIMINAL CONDUCT AND INCARCERATION

Not every violation of the law paints one a bad parent. Judges consider the type of offense, whether it was a one-of-a-kind mistake or the latest episode in a life of crime. (*Jessica HH v. Sean HH*, 196 A.D.3d 750, 151 N.Y.S.3d 449 (2021); *Klein v. Larson*, 724 N.W.2d 565 (N.D. 2006)) (mother had numerous convictions during time child was in her care). A parent who is incarcerated for years is not in a position to parent or support children. Yet, most incarcerated parents love their kids, and their kids love them. An incarcerated parent cannot exercise physical custody, but incarceration should not, in the run of cases, blot the parent out of the child's life. The Appellate Division of the New York Supreme Court observed in *Coley v. Mattice*, 25 N.Y.S.3d 452, 136 A.D.3d 1231 (2016), that while visitation with an incarcerated parent is often in a child's best interest, the presumption in favor of visitation may be rebutted.

§ 7–6[C] STABILITY AND EMPLOYMENT

A pattern of instability in housing or employment sometimes indicates lack of responsibility and maturity. The North Dakota Supreme Court noted in *Klein v. Larson*, 724 N.W.2d 565, 569 (N.D. 2006), "A parent's frequent moving and inability to maintain steady employment are significant indicators of the parent's inability to provide a stable environment for the child."

§ 7–6[D] SEXUAL BEHAVIOR; SEXUAL ORIENTATION

In the not too distant past, gay and lesbian parents faced a steep uphill battle for custody of their children. In *Bachman v. Bradley*, 171 Pa. Super. 587, 91 A.2d 379 (1952), father acknowledged bisexuality. The trial judge denied him custody and the Pennsylvania appellate court affirmed, writing, "We think the cumulative weight of the evidence is to the effect that the children in the custody of [father] may be exposed to improper conditions and undesirable influences." In 1967, a California trial judge ruled that "the homosexuality of [mother] as a matter of law constitutes her not a fit or proper person to have the care custody and control of the minor child of the parties." The judge refused even to consider the facts of the case, ruling, essentially, that no gay or lesbian parent is fit for custody. The Court of Appeal ruled the judge should have evaluated the evidence. (*Nadler v. Superior Court*, 255 Cal. App. 2d 523, 63 Cal. Rptr. 352 (1967)). In *Roe v. Roe*, 228 Va. 722, 324 S.E.2d 691 (1985), father lived with his same-sex partner. They slept in the same bed and were affectionate in front of father's child, but did not "flaunt" their homosexuality. The Virginia Supreme Court wrote, "The father's continuous exposure of the child to his immoral and illicit relationship renders him an unfit and improper custodian as a matter of law."

Today, courts hold that sexual orientation itself has no bearing on custody. In *Miller-Jenkins v. Miller-Jenkins*, 189 Vt. 518, 12 A.3d 768, 777 (2010), the Vermont Supreme Court wrote, "The State of Vermont has determined that same-sex couples have the same rights and responsibilities as opposite-sex couples—thus, the sexual orientation of the parents is irrelevant in a custody determination." In *Weisberger v. Weisberger*, 154 A.D.3d 41, 60 N.Y.S.3d 265, 273 (2017), the Appellate Division wrote, "[T]o the extent the mother's sexual orientation was raised at the hearing, we note that courts must remain neutral toward such matters, such that the focus remains on the continued best interests and welfare of the children." The Washington Supreme Court wrote in *Marriage of Black,* 188 Wash. 2d 114, 392 P.3d 1041, 1048 (2017), "[A] trial court may not consider a parent's sexual orientation as a factor for custody decisions absent an express showing of harm to the children."

What *can* be relevant to best interests is sexual behavior, not sexual orientation. Exposing a child to inappropriate sexual behavior—gay or straight—between the parent and their unmarried partner or spouse is relevant to custody. (*DiStefano v. DiStefano*, 60 A.D.2d 976, 401 N.Y.S.2d 636 (1978)). The South Carolina Court of Appeals explained in *Reed v. Pieper,* 393 S.C. 424, 713 S.E.2d 309 (Ct. App. 2011), "A parent's morality, while a proper consideration in custody disputes, is limited in its force to what relevancy it has, either directly or indirectly, to the welfare of the child."

§ 7–6[E] RACE, ETHNICITY, AND CHILD CUSTODY

Race or ethnicity is generally not a relevant factor in custody decision making. The United States Supreme Court's decision in *Palmore v. Sidoti,* 466 U.S. 429, 104 S. Ct. 1879 (1984), addresses the constitutional dimensions of race and child custody. When Linda and Anthony Sidoti divorced in 1980, Linda received custody of their three-year-old child, Melanie. The following year, Anthony returned to family court seeking custody because Linda was living with a person of a different race. The trial judge found both parents competent and devoted to the child. Nevertheless, the judge changed custody to Anthony because Linda "has chosen for herself and for her child, a life-style unacceptable to the father and to society. The child is, or at school age will be, subject to environmental pressures not of choice. [Anthony's] evident resentment of the mother's choice of a black partner is not sufficient to wrest custody from the mother. . . . This Court feels that despite the strides that have been made in bettering relations between the races in this country, it is inevitable that Melanie will, if allowed to remain in her present situation and attains school age and thus more vulnerable to peer pressures, suffer from the social stigmatization that is sure to come." The case found its way to the U.S. Supreme Court, which reversed. The Court wrote:

> It would ignore reality to suggest that racial and ethnic prejudices do not exist or that all manifestations of those prejudices have been eliminated. There is a risk that a child living with a stepparent of a different race may be subject to a variety of pressures and stresses not present if the child were living with parents of the same racial or ethnic origin.
>
> The question, however, is whether the reality of private biases and the possible injury they might inflict are permissible considerations for removal of an infant child from the custody of its natural mother. We have little difficulty concluding that they are not. The Constitution cannot control such prejudices but neither can it

> tolerate them. Private biases may be outside the reach of the law, but the law cannot, directly or indirectly, give them effect. Public officials sworn to uphold the Constitution may not avoid a constitutional duty by bowing to the hypothetical effects of private racial prejudice that they assume to be both widely and deeply held. . . . The effects of racial prejudice, however real, cannot justify a racial classification removing an infant child from the custody of its natural mother found to be an appropriate person to have such custody.

§ 7–6[F] PARENT WITH DISABILITY

The fact that a parent is disabled is no reason to deny or change custody. The California Supreme Court wrote in *Marriage of Carney,* 24 Cal. 3d 725, 598 P.2d 36, 157 Cal. Rptr. 383 (1979), "We do not mean, of course, that the health or physical condition of the parents may not be taken into account in determining whose custody would best serve the child's interests. In relation to the issues at stake, however, this factor is ordinarily of minor importance. . . . In particular, if a person has a physical handicap it is impermissible for the court simply to rely on that condition as prima facie evidence of the person's unfitness as a parent or of probable detriment to the child; rather, in all cases the court must view the handicapped person as an individual and the family as a whole."

For an argument that disability can unfairly disadvantage a parent *see* Nicole Buonocore Porter,

Mothers with Disabilities, 33 *Berkeley Journal of Gender, Law, and Justice* (2018).

§ 7–6[G] DOMESTIC VIOLENCE

States have a presumption against custody for perpetrators of domestic violence. (Cal. Family Code § 3044; *Noble v. Superior Court*, 71 Cal. App. 5th 567, 286 Cal. Rptr. 3d 522 (2021); *S.Y. v. Superior Court,* 29 Cal. App. 5th 324, 240 Cal. Rptr. 3d 137 (2018); *Caroline J. v. Theodore J.*, 354 P.3d 1085 (Alaska 2015) (because father had a history of domestic violence "there was a rebuttable presumption that he could not be awarded joint physical or legal custody of the children."); *Stacey-Ann v. Ian J.*, 190 A.D.3d 456, 139 N.Y.S.3d 63 (2021); *Fountain v. Fountain*, 12 N.Y.S.3d 641, 130 A.D.3d 1107 (2015) (domestic violence is a factor in best interest analysis); *Schurmann v. Schurmann*, 877 N.W.2d 20 (N.D. 2016) (domestic violence can be relevant to changed circumstances); *D.B. v. J.R.*, 235 W.Va. 409, 774 S.E.2d 75 (2015)). The offender must demonstrate rehabilitation to earn the way back into contention for custody.

§ 7–6[H] CHILD ABUSE

Parental abuse of a child is serious misconduct. Yet, in many cases it is difficult to prove abuse, especially sexual abuse of a young child. Fabricating allegations of abuse against an innocent spouse is itself abuse. (*Kortright v. Bhoorasingh*, 137 A.D. 3d 1037, 27 N.Y.S.3d 235 (2016)).

§ 7–6[I] RELIGIOUS BELIEFS AND PRACTICES

When parents' religious beliefs differ, compromise can be difficult. A particularly thoughtful decision on this issue was handed down by the Appellate Division of the New York Supreme Court in *Weisberger v. Weisberger,* 154 A.D.3d 41, 60 N.Y.S.3d 265 (2017).

§ 7–6[J] TRANSGENDER AND GENDER-NONCONFORMING CHILDREN

An emerging issue in family law relates to custody disputes regarding transgender and gender-nonconforming children. A law review article by Katherine Kuvalanka and colleagues provides an excellent introduction to the issue. Katherine A. Kuvalanka, Camellia Bellis, Abbie E. Goldberg & Jenifer K. McGuire, An Exploratory Study of Custody Challenges Experienced by Affirming Mothers of Transgender and Gender Non-Conforming Children, 57 *Family Court Review* 54 (2019). *See also,* Marie-Amelie George, Exploring Identity, 55 *Family Law Quarterly* 1 (2021).

In *Sacklow v. Betts*, 450 N.J. Super. 425, 163 A.3d 367 (2017), the New Jersey appellate court ruled that the best interests of a transgender child were supported by changing the child's name. (*See also, Matter of H.C.W.,* 123 N.E.3d 1048 (Ohio Ct. App. 2019)).

§ 7–6[K] WHEN A PARENT DIES

When one parent dies, the other parent automatically assumes full custody. (*Alukonis v. Smith*, 431 S.C. 41, 846 S.E.2d 600 (2021)).

§ 7–6[L] "FRIENDLY PARENT" PROVISIONS

Numerous states provide that a factor in the best interest analysis is the willingness of a parent to facilitate and support the child's relationship with the other parent. Illinois law considers a parent's "willingness and ability . . . to facilitate and encourage a close and continuing relationship between the other parent and the child." In normal circumstances, so-called friendly parent provisions make sense. Sometimes, however, particularly in cases involving domestic violence, a violent parent uses the friendly parent rule to his advantage by denying any abuse and claiming the victim parent is unfit because the victim does not encourage contact between the child and the abuser. *See* Emmaline Campbell, How Domestic Violence Batters Use Custody Proceedings in Family Courts to Abuse Victims, and How Courts Can Put a Stop to It, 24 *UCLA Women's Law Journal* 41 (2017), where Campbell writes, "Batterers often portray themselves as the reasonable and flexible parent. In contrast, victims may appear rigid and uncooperative for being unwilling to maintain a co-parenting relationship with the batterer. The National Council of Juvenile and Family Court Judges notes that 'it is often legitimate for the partner of an abusive parent to try to protect the children from exposure to abuse, or to try to secure his or her own safety from the abusive partner by limiting the partner's contact with the children." (*See Hinds v. Hinds-Holm*, 2022 WL 244537 (Utah Ct. App. 2022) (mother consistently refused to support young child's relationship with father)).

§ 7–7 SHOULD CHILDREN TESTIFY IN CUSTODY CASES?

In custody litigation, should children testify? Can you think of anything *less* appropriate than putting a child on the witness stand in open court, in front of her parents, and asking the child to "pick a parent"? For in-depth discussion of this issue, *see* Barbara A. Atwood, The Child's Voice in Custody Litigation: An Empirical Survey and Suggestions for Reform, 45 *Arizona Law Review* 629 (2003); Jacqueline Clarke, Do I Have A Voice? An Empirical Analysis of Children's Voices in Michigan Custody Litigation, 47 *Family Law Quarterly* 457 (2013); Laureen A. D'Ambra, The Importance of Conducting In-Camera Testimony of Child Witnesses in Court Proceedings: A Comparative Legal Analysis of Relevant Domestic Relations, Juvenile Justice, and Criminal Cases, 19 *Roger Williams University Law Review* 323 (2014).

With older children, judges sometimes talk to the children in chambers, without the parents. (*Ynclan v. Woodward*, 237 P.3d 145 (Okla. 2010)). By statute or case law, judges have authority to take children's testimony in chambers. The testimony should be "on the record," that is, recorded by a court reporter or mechanically. (*Spruell v. Spruell*, 356 Ga. App. 722,

848 S.E.2d 896 (2020); *Sorrells v. Sorrells*, 178 So.3d 288 (La. Ct. App. 2015); *Hutchinson v. Cobb*, 90 A.3d 438 (Me. 2014) (in chambers testimony from children must be on the record). Parents cannot force a judge to hear from the children. (*Addison v. Addison*, 463 S.W.3d 755 (Ky. 2015)).

Although it is appropriate for the court to hear from older children, children do not decide custody. (*Neumann v. Smith*, 2016 Ark. App. 14, 480 S.W.3d 197 (2016)).

§ 7-8 PSYCHOLOGICAL EVALUATION/ TESTING IN CUSTODY CASES

In contested custody cases, judges sometimes order custody evaluations performed by mental health professionals. The Association of Family and Conciliation Courts approved *Model Standards of Practice for Child Custody Evaluation* (2006) (AFCC *Model Standards*). The AFCC *Model Standards* define custody evaluation: "The child custody evaluation process involves the compilation of information and the formulation of opinions pertaining to the custody or parenting of a child and the dissemination of that information and those opinions to the court, to the litigants, and to the litigants' attorneys."

In normal litigation, each side hires one or more experts to support its position. Child custody litigation is different. The custody evaluator should be neutral. The AFCC *Model Standards* state, "Evaluators shall always function as impartial examiners." (¶ 2). Many custody evaluators will only take cases when they are appointed by the court and when they are guaranteed access to both parties and the child.

There is no psychological test or battery of tests that determines best interests. Garber and Simon write, "Assessing people in the midst of crisis tends not to capture their typical functioning. The intense social, emotional, and financial pressures associated with contested custody litigation can induce or exacerbate, acute and reactive anxiety, anger, and regression among otherwise healthy high functioning adults." (Benjamin D. Garber & Robert A. Simon, Individual Adult Psychometric Testing in Child Custody Evaluations: If the Shoe Doesn't Fit, Don't Wear It, 30 *Journal of the American Academy of Matrimonial Lawyers* 325–341, 330 (2018)). Although Garber and Simon recognize that most psychologists utilize psychological tests as part of custody evaluations, Garber and Simon argue, "Child custody evaluations that rely upon test data risk misleading the court, breaching relevant ethical rules, creating unnecessary, time-consuming and expensive legal straw-men, and doing harm to families and to the vulnerable children whose best interests the court must serve." (Id. at 327). Other experts agree. McCurley, Murphy and Gould write, "It is important to note that no personality tests measure parenting competency, nor has any constellation of personality tests been linked to skill as a caregiver. It is impossible to determine from test results alone if a parent's measured response patterns are related, either directly or indirectly, to parenting competencies." (Mary Johanna McCurley,

Kathryn J. Murphy & Jonathan W. Gould, Protecting Children from Incompetent Forensic Evaluations and Expert Testimony, 19 *Journal of the American Academy of Matrimonial Lawyers* 277 (2005)). Virginia Luftman writes, "Traditional psychological tests do not address parenting ability, the nature of the parent-child relationship, and the parent's abilities to communicate or foster the child's relationship with the other parent." (Virginia H. Luftman, Practice Guidelines in Child Custody Evaluations for Licensed Clinical Social Workers, 33 *Clinical Social Work Journal* 327 (2005). Melton and colleagues write: "It is our contention that psychological tests assessing clinical constructs (e.g., intelligence, depression, personality, academic achievement) are frequently unnecessary and often used inappropriately. Tests of intellectual capacity, achievement, personality style, and psychopathology assess constructs that are linked only indirectly, at best, to the key issues concerning custody and visitation." (Gary B. Melton, John Petrila, Norman G. Poythress, Christopher Slobogin, Phillip M. Lyons, Jr. & Randy K. Otto, *Psychological Evaluations for the Courts: A Handbook for Mental Health Professionals and Lawyers* 559 (3d ed. 2007)). The American Academy of Child and Adolescent Psychiatry published *Practice Parameters for Child Custody Evaluation.* The Parameters provide: "In most cases, psychological testing of the parents is not required. Psychological tests, such as the Minnesota Multiphasic Personality Inventory, the Thematic Apperception Test, or the Rorschach, were not designed for use in parenting evaluations. The introduction into a legal process leads to professionals battling over the meaning of raw data and attorneys making the most findings of 'psychopathology' but may have little use in assessing parenting." (American Academy of Child and Adolescent Psychiatry, Practice Parameters for Child Custody Evaluations, 36 *Journal of the American Academy of Child and Adolescent Psychiatry* 57S–68S, at 54S (1997)).

A custody evaluation cannot answer the ultimate question of a child's best interest. Custody evaluators do not have a magic bullet that makes the custody decision easy. A good custody evaluation gives the judge insight into parenting style and psychological functioning. The evaluator provides information about the child's psychological needs. The evaluator offers suggestions regarding the "fit" between parenting attributes and the child's psychological needs. The American Psychological Association's *Guidelines for Child Custody Evaluations* (2010) (APA 2010 *Guidelines*) remark, "The most useful and influential evaluations focus upon skills, deficits, values, and tendencies relevant to parenting attributes and a child's psychological needs. Comparatively little weight is afforded to evaluations that offer a general personality assessment without attempting to place results in the appropriate context." (American Psychological Association, Guidelines for Child Custody Evaluations in Family Law Proceedings, 65 *American Psychologist* 863–867, at 864 (2010)). Thus, an evaluation that says, "Mother is depressed" does little to help the judge. Plenty of depressed parents are wonderful with their children. The judge needs concrete information about the impact of parental strengths and weaknesses on day-to-day parenting. The court is not required to accept the recommendations of a custody evaluator (*T.W. v. S.A.*, 504 P.3d 163 (Utah Ct. App. 2021)).

In 2022, as this book went to press, the APA was about to release updated child custody guidelines. The updated guidelines continue the principles from the 2010 guidelines.

As mentioned above, custody evaluators prefer to interview both parents. A mental health professional who has not personally evaluated a parent should not opine on the parent's psychological functioning. The APA 2010 *Guidelines* provide: "Psychologists provide an opinion of an individual's psychological characteristics only after they have conducted an examination of the individual adequate to support their statements and conclusions. The only exception to this occurs in those particular instances of record review, consultation, or supervision (as opposed, in each case, to evaluations) in which an individual examination is not warranted or necessary for the psychologist's opinion. The court typically expects the psychologist to examine both parents as well as the child." (p. 866).

Custody evaluations provide valuable information. But should custody evaluators take the final step and offer specific recommendations regarding custody? The APA 2010 *Guidelines* state, "The profession has not reached consensus about whether psychologists should make recommendations to the court about the final child custody determination (*i.e.*, 'ultimate opinion' testimony)." (p. 866). The 2022 version of the *Guidelines* continue the theme that the profession has not reached a consensus about whether psychologists should make specific custody recommendations. Many custody evaluators are comfortable recommending specific custody arrangements. Melton and his colleagues argue mental health professionals have little to offer regarding who should have custody. Melton writes, "[T]he state of the literature does not promote confidence about the validity of ultimate opinions concerning dispositions judges might consider in custody cases." (Gary B. Melton, John Petrila, Norman G. Poythress, Christopher Slobogin, Randy K. Otto, Douglas Mossman & Lois O. Condie, *Psychological Evaluations for the Courts: A Handbook for Mental Health Professionals and Lawyers* p. 531 (4th ed. 2018)).

§ 7-9 ROLES OF MENTAL HEALTH PROFESSIONALS

Mental health professionals (MHP) play key roles in family law. (Robert A. Simon & Daniel H. Willick, Therapeutic Privilege and Custody Evaluations: Discovery of Treatment Records, 54 *Family Court Review* 51 (2016)). As mentioned above, MHPs conduct custody evaluations. As well, MHPs provide psychotherapy for parties and children. MHPs consult with attorneys. MHPs testify as fact witnesses and as expert witnesses. Each role raises complex issues regarding privileged communications and confidentiality. (*See* John E.B. Myers, *Legal*

Issues in Treating Victims of Violence: A Clinician's Guide (2017)).

To help parents reach agreement regarding custody, and to avoid costly and emotionally draining litigation, states encourage or require parents to participate in mediation performed by MHPs. (Cal. Family Code § 3170). The Illinois statute states, "The court shall order mediation to assist the parents in formulating or modifying a parenting plan or in implementing a parenting plan unless the court determines that impediments to mediation exist." (750 ILCS 5/602.10(c)).

Mental health professionals should avoid mixing clinical and forensic roles. Thus, a MHP who provides therapy should not also perform a custody evaluation in the same case. A custody evaluation is forensic mental health practice. The American Psychological Association defines forensic practice: "Forensic psychology refers to professional practice by a psychologist working within any subdiscipline of psychology (*e.g.*, clinical, developmental, social, cognitive) when applying the scientific, technical, or specialized knowledge of psychology to the law to assist in addressing legal, contractual, and administrative matters." (American Psychological Association, *Specialty Guidelines for Forensic Psychology* (2013)). Knapp and VandeCreek observe that clinical practice and forensic practice are generally incompatible. They write, "Psychologists should avoid mixing treatment and forensic relationships" (Samuel J. Knapp & Leon D. VandeCreek, *Practical Ethics for Psychologists: A*

Positive Approach p. 166 (2002)). The American Psychological Association's *Guidelines, supra,* state, "Providing forensic and therapeutic psychological services to the same individual or closely related individuals involves multiple relationships that may impair objectivity and/or cause exploitation or other harm." (Guideline 4.02.01). Knapp and VandeCreek conclude, "Any time psychologists write letters recommending custody or visitation arrangements, they are making a custody recommendation." (p. 167).

What is *not* forensic practice? The fact that a MHP is aware of the forensic implications of therapy does not transform the clinician into a forensic practitioner. Nor does testifying, unless the testimony focuses squarely on psycholegal issues. Reporting suspected child abuse is not forensic practice. The fact that a client has been ordered into therapy by a judge does not render therapy forensic.

§ 7–10 INDIAN CHILD WELFARE ACT

The Federal Indian Child Welfare Act (ICWA) governs "child custody proceedings" concerning Indian children. (25 U.S.C. § 1903). ICWA defines "child custody proceeding" to include foster care, termination of parental rights, preadoptive placement, and adoption. ICWA does not apply to child custody litigation between parents. ICWA is discussed in Chapter 15.

§ 7-11 CUSTODY TO NON-GENETIC PARENT

Most custody litigation is between biological parents. Increasingly, custody litigation is waged between a biological parent and an adult who is not the child's biological parent. For example, Jane and Anne are in a committed non-marital relationship. They decide to have a baby. Anne becomes pregnant through intrauterine insemination. Both women parent the child. When the child is seven, Jane and Anne break up. Anne refuses to allow Jane any contact with "her" child. Does Jane have a right to custody or visitation? Although Jane is not genetically related to the child, Jane may be able to establish that she is entitled to rights as a parent. (*See* Chapter 6 on parentage. *See also, Matter of W.L. and G.L.*, 312 Kan. 367, 475 P.3d 338 (2020)).

Consider the dilemma faced by Jorge. When Jorge and Sara married, Sara had two young children from a previous marriage. Jorge developed a great relationship with his step-kids. The biological father, Juan, lived in another state and saw the children only once or twice a year. After five years of happy marriage, Sara died in a car crash. Juan insists the children live with him. Jorge wonders, "I've been the children's father-figure for five years. Do I have any rights?" Increasingly, the answer is yes. In some states, Jorge may achieve the status of de facto parent. (*See* § 6–5. *See also,* 750 Illinois Stats. 5/701.2(b)(4)).

Statutory and case law is evolving regarding the custody/visitation rights of non-biological parents.

(*See Bethany v. Jones,* 378 S.W.3d 731 (Ark. 2011); *Boseman v. Jarrell,* 364 N.C. 537, 704 S.E.2d 494 (2010)). Indiana allows persons other than parents to bring "an independent custody action." (Ind. Code § 31–17–2–3(2); *Custody of M.B.,* 51 N.E.3d 230 (Ind. 2016)), as does Texas. (*In re H.S.*, 550 S.W.3d 151 (Tex. 2018). In *C.G. v. J.H.,* 193 A.3d 891 (Pa. 2018), the Pennsylvania Supreme Court grappled with a case involving a same sex non-married couple. The Court ruled that the woman who was not genetically related to the child lacked standing to seek custody. In *Watkins v. Nelson,* 163 N.J. 235, 748 A.2d 558 (2000), the New Jersey Supreme Court struggled with "the appropriate standard for deciding a custody dispute between a biological parent and a third party following the death of the custodial parent. We hold that a presumption exists in favor of the surviving biological parent. That presumption can be rebutted by proof of gross misconduct, abandonment, unfitness, or the existence of exceptional circumstances, but never by a simple application of the best interests." The Mississippi Supreme Court weighed in in *Wilson v. Davis*, 181 So. 3d 991, 995 (Miss. 2016), where the court wrote, "This Court has consistently held that it is presumed that the best interests of a child are served by being in the custody of his or her natural parent as opposed to a third party." The Mississippi Supreme court ruled that the presumption in favor of parents can be rebutted by clear and convincing evidence of parental fault. If the presumption is rebutted, the judge examines the child's best interests. In *In re C.J.C.,* 603 S.W.3d 804, 807 (Tex. 2020), the Texas Supreme Court wrote:

"The question presented in this case is whether the presumption that fit parents act according to the best interest of their children applies when modifying an existing order that names a parent as the child's managing conservator. Because a fit parent presumptively acts in the best interest of his or child and has a 'fundamental right to make decisions concerning the care, custody, and control; of that child, we hold that it does."

In some states, adults who fulfill a parenting role but who are not genetically related to a child may claim the status of de facto parent. (*See Young v. King*, 208 A.3d 762 (Maine 2019); *E.N. v. T.R.*, 474 Md. 346, 255 A.3d 1 (2021); *Carroll v. Gould*, 308 Neb. 12, 952 N.W.2d 1 (2020); *C.G. v. J.H.*, 193 A.3d 891 (Pa. 2018)). The 2017 Uniform Parentage Act recognizes de facto parents (§ 609).

In *McAllister v. McAllister,* 779 N.W.2d 652 (N.D. 2010), the North Dakota Supreme Court recognized the concept of a psychological parent. The court wrote that although custody is normally given to biological parents, in "exceptional circumstances" custody may be awarded to a psychological parent. (*See also, Stoddard v. Singer,* 954 N.W.2d 696 (N.D. 2021); *Alukonis v. Smith,* 431 S.C. 41, 846 S.E.2d 600 (2021) (grandfather was child's psychological parent)).

Courts occasionally employ the ancient doctrine of *in loco parentis* to allow a non-parent to seek custody. (*Peister v. Eurek,* 30 Neb. App. 366, 969 N.W.2d 134 (2021); *Tina K. v. Adam B.,* 307 Neb. 1, 948 N.W.2d 182 (2020)). In *C.G. v. J.H.,* 648 Pa. 418, 193 A.3d 891 (2018), the Pennsylvania Supreme Court wrote:

> The phrase '*in loco parentis*' refers to a person who puts oneself in the situation of a lawful parent by assuming the obligations incident to the parental relationship without going through the formality of a legal adoption. The status of *in loco parentis* embodies two ideas; first, the assumption of a parental status, and second, the discharge of parental duties. The rights and liabilities arising out of an *in loco parentis* relationship are, as the words imply, exactly the same as between parent and child. The third party in this type of relationship, however, can not place himself *in loco parentis* in defiance of the parents' wishes and the parent/child relationship. (193 A.3d 907).

In *C.G. v. J.H.,* the Pennsylvania Court ruled *in loco parentis* did not apply.

The Illinois Legislature conducted a major overhaul of Illinois custody law and added provisions allowing certain step-parents and grandparents to petition for custody. (*See* Illinois Stats. § 5/601.2; *Sharpe v. Westmoreland,* 2020 IL 124863 (Ill. 2020)).

§ 7–12 MODIFICATION OF CHILD CUSTODY

A final custody decision is *res judicata.* A parent who is dissatisfied with a final custody decision can appeal, but cannot re-litigate the same facts. However, courts retain continuing jurisdiction over custody until children reach adulthood. Following a final custody decision, a parent may return to court and ask the court to modify custody. Before a court will revisit a final custody determination, the parent seeking modification must prove a substantial change in circumstances that warrants a fresh look at custody. (*Roberts v. Roberts,* 595 S.W.3d 15 (Ark. Ct. App. 2020) (high parental conflict following divorce can constitute substantial change in circumstances); *Mintner v. Mintner*, 29 So. 3d 840 (Miss. Ct. App. 2010)). The California Supreme Court described the changed circumstances rule in *Marriage of Brown and Yana,* 37 Cal. 4th 947, 956, 127 P.3d 28, 38 Cal. Rptr. 3d 610 (2006), "Once the trial court has entered a final or permanent custody order reflecting that a particular custodial arrangement is in the best interest of the child, the paramount need for continuity and stability in custody arrangements—and the harm that may result from disruption of established patterns of care and emotional bonds with the primary caretaker—weigh heavily in favor of maintaining that custody arrangement. In recognition of this policy concern, we have articulated a variation on the best interest standard, known as the changed circumstance rule. . . . Under the changed circumstance rule, custody modification is appropriate only if the parent seeking modification demonstrates a significant change of circumstances indicating that a different custody arrangement would be in the child's best interest." In a similar vein, the Arkansas Supreme Court wrote in *Alphin v. Alphin*, 364 Ark. 332, 219 S.W.3d 160, 165 (2005), "A judicial award of custody should not be modified unless it is shown that there are changed conditions that demonstrate that a modification of the decree is in the best interest of the child. . . . Courts impose more stringent standards for modifications of custody than they do for initial determinations of custody. The reasons for requiring these more stringent standards for modifications . . . are to promote stability and continuity in the life of the child, and to discourage the repeated litigation of the same issues." In Missouri, a parent seeking to change custody from joint to sole custody must establish a substantial change of circumstances. (*Hark v. Hark*, 567 S.W.3d 671 (Mo. Ct. App. 2019)).

At the outset of a divorce case, one parent may seek an order for temporary custody. A temporary order remains in place until the trial court decides custody on the merits. The court may alter temporary custody without evidence of changed circumstances. Nor does the changed circumstances rule apply when parents reach an informal custody agreement without involving a court. Of course, if an informal arrangement persists a long time, the court will take this into account in deciding custody.

What constitutes substantially changed circumstances? The facts of each case are considered. Remarriage of either parent can be but is seldom a change of circumstances warranting changed custody. As mentioned earlier, if the custodial parent dies, the non-custodial parent normally has the right to custody and does not have to get a court order.

In a recurring scenario, a parent with custody frustrates the non-custodial parent's ability to visit the child. Does such obstructionist behavior amount to substantial changed circumstances? Judges seldom change custody on this basis, although a protracted course of deliberate interference with visitation might persuade a judge to revisit custody.

§ 7-13 MOVE AWAY CASES

Consider a recurring scenario: Beth and John fell in love and married in law school. They had a baby girl, Joy, during their third year. Upon graduation, John got a job with the state. Beth went to work for a large corporate law firm and worked crazy hours. They bought a home and settled in. Unfortunately, the marriage deteriorated and they divorced. They agreed on joint legal custody. They also agreed that John would have primary physical custody. Joy lives with John because his work schedule for the state is more flexible than Beth's long hours at the law firm. Beth has visitation three days a week, mostly on weekends. Several years pass with Beth and John working cooperatively to co-parent. Then John gets an offer to join the faculty at a law school across the country. John proposes to take Joy with him. Beth says, "No way. If you move and take her with you how am I supposed to be a mother?" This scenario plays out daily in our mobile society and there are no easy answers.

A large body of case law addresses move aways. (*See, e.g., Saffir v. Wheeler,* 436 P.3d 1009 (Alaska 2019); *Rego v. Rego,* 259 P.3d 447 (Alaska 2011); *Marriage of Brown and Yana,* 37 Cal. 4th 947, 127 P.3d 28, 38 Cal. Rptr. 3d 610 (2006); *Marriage of Levites,* 2021 IL App. (2d) 200552 (2021) (one factor is the extent to which the non-moving parent exercised visitation); *Welch v. Peery,* 26 Neb. App.

966, 925 N.W.2d 375 (2019); *Jennings v. Yillah-Chow*, 84 A.D.3d 1376, 924 N.Y.S.2d 519 (2011); *Pember v. Shapiro*, 794 N.W.2d 435 (N.D. 2011); *Ainsworth v. Ainsworth*, 186 A.3d 1074 (R.I. 2018) (Mother wanted to move with the children to Australia; move was denied). Trial judges consider all circumstances related to a proposed move, and decide what is best for the children. In *Korth v. Korth*, 309 Neb. 115, 958 N.W.2d 683, 695 (2021), the Nebraska Supreme Court wrote: "To determine whether removal to another jurisdiction is in the child's best interests, a trial court should consider (1) each parent's motive for seeking or opposing the move, (2) the potential that the move holds for enhancing the quality of life for the child and the custodial parent, and (3) the impact such a move will have on contact between the child and noncustodial parent when viewed in light of reasonable visitation."

When the parent proposing to move has sole custody and has a good reason to move, the move is likely to be approved. (*Yannas v. Frondistou-Yannas*, 395 Mass. 704, 711, 481 N.E.2d 1153 (1985)). The Nebraska Court of Appeals observed, "To prevail on a motion to remove a minor child, the custodial parent must first satisfy the court that he or she has a legitimate reason for leaving the state." (*Hiller v. Hiller*, 23 Neb. App. 768, 876 N.W.2d 685 (2016)). It should be added that a custodial parent does not have an unconditional right to move with children. (*Marriage of Burgess*, 13 Cal. 4th 25, 913 P.2d 473, 51 Cal. Rptr. 2d 444 (1996)). A judge will not approve a move that, on balance, will be detrimental to children.

When parents share custody and are both actively involved in the children's lives, a judge is less likely to approve a move, especially a move that significantly interferes with the non-moving parent's relationship with the children. The Massachusetts Supreme Judicial Court observed in *Mason v. Coleman*, 447 Mass. 177, 850 N.E.2d 513 (2006), "Where physical custody is shared, the 'best interest' calculus pertaining to removal is appreciably different from those situations that involve sole physical custody. Where physical custody is shared, a judge's willingness to elevate one parent's interest in relocating freely with the children is often diminished. No longer is the fortune of simply one custodial parent so tightly interwoven with that of the child; both parents have equal rights and responsibilities with respect to the children. The importance to the children of one parent's advantage in relocating outside the Commonwealth is greatly reduced. Where physical custody is shared and neither parent has a clear majority of custodial responsibility, the child's interests will typically favor protection of the child's relationships with both parents because both are, in a real sense, primary to the child's development. Distant relocation often impedes frequent and continued contact with the remaining joint custodian."

The New York Court of Appeals captured the complexity of move aways in *Tropea v. Kenward*, 87 N.Y.2d 727, 665 N.E.2d 145, 642 N.Y.S.2d 575 (1996), where the court wrote:

Relocation cases ... present some of the knottiest and most disturbing problems that our courts are called upon to resolve. In these cases, the interests of a custodial parent who wishes to move away are pitted against those of a noncustodial parent who has a powerful desire to maintain frequent and regular contact with the child. Moreover, the court must weigh the paramount interests of the child, which may or may not be in irreconcilable conflict with those of one or both of the parents. . . .

In reality, cases in which a custodial parent's desire to relocate conflicts with the desire of a noncustodial parent to maximize visitation opportunity are simply too complex to be satisfactorily handled within any mechanical . . . analysis that prevents or interferes with a simultaneous weighing and comparative analysis of all of the relevant facts and circumstances. Although we have recognized and continue to appreciate both the need of the child and the right of the noncustodial parent to have regular and meaningful contact, we also believe that no single factor should be treated as dispositive or given such disproportionate weight as to predetermine the outcome. There are undoubtedly circumstances in which the loss of midweek or every weekend visits necessitated by a distant move may be devastating to the relationship between the noncustodial parent and the child. However, there are undoubtedly also many cases where less frequent but more extended visits over summer and school vacations would be equally conducive, or perhaps even more conducive, to the maintenance of a close parent-child relationship, since such extended visits give the parties the opportunity to interact in a normalized domestic setting. In any event, given the variety of possible permutations, it is counterproductive to rely on presumptions whose only real value is to simplify what are necessarily extremely complicated inquires. . . .

We hold that each relocation request must be considered on its own merits with due consideration of all the relevant facts and circumstances and with predominant emphasis being placed on what outcome is most likely to serve the best interests of the child. While the respective rights of the custodial and noncustodial parents are unquestionably significant factors that must be considered, it is the rights and needs of the children that must be accorded the greatest weight, since they are innocent victims of their parents' decision to divorce and are the least equipped to handle the stresses of the changing family situation.

In addition to the custodial parent's stated reasons for wanting to move and the noncustodial parent's loss of access, another factor that may well become important in a particular case is the noncustodial parent's interest in securing custody, as well as the feasibility and desirability of a change in custody. Obviously, where a child's ties to the noncustodial parent and to the community are so strong as to make a long-distance move undesirable, the availability of a transfer of custody as a realistic alternative to forcing the custodial parent to remain may have a significant impact on the outcome. By the same token, where the custodial parent's reasons for moving are deemed valid and sound, the court in a proper case might consider the possibility and feasibility of a parallel move by an involved and committed noncustodial parent as an alternative to restricting a custodial parent's mobility.

Other considerations that may have a bearing in particular cases are the good faith of the parents in requesting or opposing the move, the child's respective attachments to the custodial and noncustodial parent, the possibility of devising a visitation schedule that will enable the noncustodial parent to maintain a meaningful parent-child relationship, the quality of the life-style that the child would have if the proposed move were permitted or denied, the negative impact, if any, from continued or exacerbated hostility between the custodial and noncustodial parents, and the effect that the move may have on any extended family relationships. Of course, any other facts or circumstances that have a bearing on the parties' situation should be weighed with a view toward minimizing the parents' discomfort and maximizing the child's prospects of a stable, comfortable and happy life. . . .

> We hold that, in all cases, the courts should be free to consider and give appropriate weight to all of the factors that may be relevant to the determination. (665 N.E.2d at 150–151).

When a non-custodial parent proposes to move and take the child along, the moving parent bears a heavy burden to prove that remaining with the custodial parent would cause detriment to the child. *Marriage of C.T. and R.B.,* 33 Cal. App. 5th 87 (Cal. Ct. App. 2019).

A number of states have move away statutes. (*See* 750 ILCS 5/609.2). The Colorado statute, for example, applies when a parent with primary custody plans a move that will substantially change the non-custodial parent's ties to the child. (Colo. Rev. Stat. Ann. § 14–10–129). The statute instructs judges to consider all factors relevant to the child's best interests. Specifically, the judge considers the reasons for the proposed move, objections of the non-moving parent, quality of each parent's relationship with the child, educational opportunities for the child here and there, presence or absence of extended family here and there, advantages of the child remaining with the moving custodial parent, and the likely impact of the move on the child. The Colorado statute directs judges to consider the totality of circumstances.

West Virginia's move away statute instructs judges to consider the following factors: "A parent who has been exercising a significant majority of the custodial responsibility for the child should be allowed to relocate with the child so long as that parent shows that the relocation is in good faith for a legitimate purpose and to a location that is reasonable in light of the purpose. The percentage of custodial responsibility that constitutes a significant majority of custodial responsibility is seventy percent or more. A relocation is for a legitimate purpose if it is to be close to significant family or other support networks, for significant health reasons, to protect the safety of the child or another member of the child's household from significant risk of harm, to pursue a significant employment or educational opportunity or to be with one's spouse who is established, or who is pursuing a significant employment or educational opportunity, in another location. The relocating parent has the burden of proving the legitimacy of any other purpose. A move with a legitimate purpose is reasonable unless its purpose is shown to be substantially achievable without moving or by moving to a location that is substantially less disruptive of the other parent's relationship to the child." (W. Va. Code § 49–8–403(d)(1)).

Parents who desire to move with children sometimes argue that denying the move violates the parent's constitutional right to travel. This argument fails because when a judge denies a move away, the judge's order prevents the children from moving, not the parent. (*Mason v. Coleman*, 447 Mass. 177, 850 N.E.2d 513 (2006)).

§ 7-14 WHEN A PARENT IS IN THE MILITARY

Congress enacted the Soldiers and Sailors Civil Relief Act to protect servicemembers from civil lawsuits while the servicemember is deployed and not in a position to defend the case. The Act requires judges to stay civil actions against servicemembers until the member is available to respond. The court may grant "a stay of proceedings for a minimum period of 90 days." (50 U.S.C. App. § 521(d)). The servicemember may request an additional stay. When a servicemember does not make an appearance, "the court may not enter a judgment until after the court appoints an attorney to represent the defendant." (50 U.S.C. App. § 521(b)(2)).

The Act, which is now called the Servicemembers Civil Relief Act. (50 U.S.C. App. §§ 501 et seq.), applies to divorce actions, including child custody proceedings. Moreover, the Act continues in effect for three months after a servicemember is released from military service.

Servicemembers who are parents endure long separations from their children. In intact marriages, the stay-at-home parent keeps the home fires burning and cares for the kids during deployment. Things are more challenging for single parent servicemembers. Often, the servicemember's relatives step in. Sometimes, a servicemember/parent is divorced and has custody. In this situation, the servicemember may appoint someone else to care for the child.

Often, a former spouse assumes custody during deployment. Problems arise when a parent is deployed and the other parent starts proceedings to obtain custody or to modify an existing custody order. The Servicemembers Civil Relief Act can stay such actions.

In custody cases involving servicemembers, should the judge consider the impact on children of lengthy military deployments? States have statutes on this question. *See, e.g.,* California Family Code § 3047. Jeri Hanes grapples with this issue in an article in *Army Lawyer*. (Jeri Hanes, Fight for Your Country, Then Fight to Keep Your Children: Military Members May Pay the Price . . . Twice, 2011 *Army Lawyer* 27–50 (2011)).

§ 7-15 JURISDICTION REGARDING CHILD CUSTODY

Subject matter jurisdiction regarding child custody is governed by two statutes, the federal Parental Kidnapping Prevention Act (PKPA) (28 U.S.C. § 1738A), which is binding on the states, and the Uniform Child Custody Jurisdiction and Enforcement Act (UCCJEA). Personal jurisdiction over both parents is *not* required for child custody.

When child custody disputes cross international borders, attention focuses on the UCCJEA and the 1996 Hague Convention on Jurisdiction, Applicable Law, Recognition, Enforcement and Cooperation in Respect of Parental Responsibility and Measures for the Protection of Children. In addition, certain cases of international child abduction by parents are governed by The Hague Convention on the Civil Aspects of International Child Abduction (Hague Convention). (*See* § 7–19).

§ 7-16 WHY THE UCCJEA WAS CREATED

The first version of the UCCJEA was the Uniform Child Custody Jurisdiction Act (UCCJA), promulgated in 1968. The UCCJA was intended to remedy uncertainty about interstate child custody determinations. Prior to the UCCJA, courts ruled that subject matter jurisdiction over child custody could be based on a child's domicile, residence, or temporary presence in the state. The drafters of the UCCJA described the problems caused by pre-UCCJA law:

> There is a growing public concern over the fact that thousands of children are shifted from state to state and from one family to another every year while their parents or other persons battle over their custody in the courts of several states. Children of separated parents may live with their mother, for example, but one day the father snatches them and brings them to another state where he petitions a court to award him custody while the mother starts custody proceedings in her state; or in the case of illness of the mother the children may be cared for by grandparents in a third state, and all three parties may fight over the right to keep the children in several states. These and many similar situations constantly arise in our mobile society where family members often are scattered all over the

United States and at times over other countries. A young child may have been moved to another state repeatedly before the case goes to court. When a decree has been rendered awarding custody to one of the parties, this is by no means the end of the child's migrations. It is well known that those who lose a court battle over custody are often unwilling to accept the judgment of the court. They will remove the child in an unguarded moment or fail to return him after a visit and will seek their luck in the court of a distant state where they hope to find—and—often do find a more sympathetic ear for their plea for custody. The party deprived of the child may then resort to similar tactics to recover the child and this "game" may continue for years, with the child thrown back and forth from state to state, never coming to rest in one single home and in one community. . . .

In this confused legal situation the person who has possession of the child has an enormous tactical advantage. Physical presence of the child opens the doors of many courts to the petitioner and often assures him of a decision in his favor. It is not surprising then that custody claimants tend to take the law into their own hands, that they resort to self-help in the form of child stealing, kidnapping, or various other schemes to gain possession of the child. The irony is that persons who are good, law-abiding citizens are often driven into these tactics against their inclinations; and that lawyers who are reluctant to advise the use of maneuvers of

> doubtful legality may place their clients at a decided disadvantage.

(Commissioner's Comment to UCCJA, 9 *Uniform Laws Annotated* 116–117 (1988)).

To understand child custody jurisdiction *before* the UCCJA and why it was important to create the UCCJA, consider three cases. First, Mom and Dad marry in Washington State and have a child. The marriage breaks down and mom files for divorce. Dad is afraid the court will award custody to mom, so one night, without telling mom, he packs the car, plops junior in the car seat, and leaves for Missouri where he has family. Once in Missouri he files an action for custody. Does Missouri have jurisdiction? Yes, because the child is physically present in Missouri. Second, Mom and Dad divorce in Georgia. After a custody battle, Mom is awarded custody of the kids. Dad relocates to North Dakota. A year later, dad puts the kids on an airplane and takes them to North Dakota where he files a custody modification action. Does North Dakota have jurisdiction? Yes. Third, Mom and Dad divorce in Nevada and dad gets custody. Mom moves to Utah where she grew up and went to college. According to the divorce decree, Mom gets a month visitation in the summer in Utah with the kids. At the end of a summer visit, mom refuses to return the kids to Nevada and mom commences custody modification proceedings in Utah. Does Utah have jurisdiction? Yes. While Mom isn't looking, Dad spirits the kids back to Nevada and returns to court there. Nevada has jurisdiction because it issued the initial custody order and because the kids are located in Nevada. The kids go back and forth like ping pong balls.

The UCCJA was designed to bring uniformity to interstate child custody determinations and to reduce parental child snatching and forum shopping. Although the UCCJA worked reasonably well, states had slightly different versions of the UCCJA and the law had loopholes. The result was continued uncertainty. Congress stepped in in 1980 with the PKPA. The UCCJA was updated in 1997 to achieve consistency with the PKPA. The new version of the UCCJA is the Uniform Child Custody Jurisdiction and Enforcement Act (UCCJEA).

The PKPA is not long. It is reproduced below. The UCCJEA, by contrast, is lengthy. The entire UCCJEA is reproduced in Appendix A at the end of this Chapter. Key sections of the UCCJEA are reproduced and explained below.

§ 7–17 FEDERAL PARENTAL KIDNAPPING PREVENTION ACT: 28 U.S.C. § 1738A (PKPA)

Full faith and credit given to child custody determinations

(a) The appropriate authorities of every State shall enforce according to its terms, and shall not modify except as provided in subsections (f), (g), and (h) of this section, any custody determination or visitation determination made consistently with the provisions of this section by a court of another State.

(b) As used in this section, the term—(1) "child" means a person under the age of eighteen; (2) "contestant" means a person, including a parent or grandparent, who claims a right to custody or visitation of a child; (3) "custody determination" means a judgment, decree, or other order of a court providing for the custody of a child, and includes permanent and temporary orders, and initial orders and modifications; (4) "home State" means the State in which, immediately preceding the time involved, the child lived with his parents, a parent, or a person acting as a parent, for at least six consecutive months, and in the case of a child less than six months old, the State in which the child lived from birth with any of such persons. Periods of temporary absence of any of such persons are counted as part of the six-month or other period; (5) "modification" and "modify" refer to a custody or visitation determination which modifies, replaces, supersedes, or otherwise is made subsequent to, a prior custody or visitation determination concerning the same child, whether made by the same court or not; (6) "person acting as a parent" means a person, other than a parent, who has physical custody of a child and who has either been awarded custody by a court or claims a right to custody; (7) "physical custody" means actual possession and control of a child; (8) "State" means a State of the United States, the District of Columbia, the Commonwealth of Puerto Rico, or a territory or possession of the United States; and (9) "visitation determination" means a judgment, decree, or other order of a court providing for the visitation of a child and includes permanent and temporary orders and initial orders and modifications.

(c) A child custody or visitation determination made by a court of a State is consistent with the provisions of this section only if—(1) such court has jurisdiction under the law of such State and (2) one of the following conditions is met: (A) such State (i) is the home State of the child on the date of the commencement of the proceeding, or (ii) had been the child's home State within six months before the date of the commencement of the proceeding and the child is absent from such State because of his removal or retention by a contestant or for other reasons, and a contestant continues to live in such State; (B) (i) it appears that no other State would have jurisdiction under subparagraph (A), and (ii) it is in the best interest of the child that a court of such State assume jurisdiction because (I) the child and his parents, or the child and at least one contestant, have a significant connection with such State other than mere physical presence in such State, and (II) there is available in such State substantial evidence concerning the child's present or future care, protection training, and personal relationships; (C) the child is physically present in such State and (i) the child has been abandoned, or (ii) it is necessary in an emergency to protect the child because the child, a sibling or parent of the child has been subjected to or threatened with mistreatment or abuse; (D)(i) it appears that no other State would have jurisdiction under subparagraph (A), (B), (C), or another State has declined to exercise jurisdiction on the ground that the such court assume jurisdiction; or (E) the court has continuing jurisdiction pursuant to subsection (d) of this section.

(d) The jurisdiction of a court of a State which has made a child custody or visitation determination consistently with the provisions of this section continues as long as the requirement of subsection (c)(1) of this section continues to be met and such State remains the residence of the child or of any contestant.

(e) Before a child custody or visitation determination is made, reasonable notice and opportunity to be heard shall be given to the contestants, any parent whose parental rights have not been previously terminated and any person who has physical custody of a child.

(f) A court of a State may modify a determination if the custody of the same child made by a court of another State, if—(1) it has jurisdiction to make such a child custody determination; and (2) the court of the other State no longer has jurisdiction, or it has declined to exercise such jurisdiction to modify such determination.

(g) A court of a State shall not exercise jurisdiction in any proceeding for a custody or visitation determination commenced during the pendency of a proceeding in a court of another State where such court of that other State is exercising jurisdiction consistently with the provision of this section to make a custody or visitation determination.

(h) A court of a State may not modify a visitation determination made by a court of another State unless the court of the other State no longer has jurisdiction to modify such determination or has declined to exercise jurisdiction to modify such determination.

Three observations about the PKPA will help unravel its meaning. First, when it comes to child custody, there are *initial* custody determinations and there are efforts in court to *modify* custody rulings. The PKPA limits the ability of one state to *modify* a custody determination made by another state. (28 U.S.C. 1738A(a)). As the introduction to the PKPA states, the statute requires states to give full faith and credit to—*i.e.*, to enforce—custody determinations of sister states.

Second, although the PKPA does not directly govern jurisdiction to make initial custody rulings, the statute has a profound impact on which state should make the initial ruling. The PKPA provides that a custody determination is only entitled to enforcement under the PKPA if it is consistent with the provisions of the PKPA. (28 U.S.C. 1738A(a) & (c)). To be consistent with the PKPA the initial custody determination must be made in the child's home state if the child has a home state (Most kids have a home state). Thus, the PKPA creates are strong preference for initial custody determinations in the child's home state. (*See Sherrill v. Sherrill*, 373 P.3d 486 (Alaska 2016)).

Third, the PKPA and the UCCJEA are carefully crafted to be consistent with each other. This means that if you comply with the UCCJEA regarding jurisdiction, you comply with the PKPA.

§ 7-18 UCCJEA

The UCCJEA governs two things: (1) Subject matter jurisdiction to make an initial custody determination, and (2) subject matter jurisdiction to modify a custody determination of *another state*. A state that makes a custody determination retains continuing jurisdiction to modify its *own* determination.

The UCCJEA defines a custody determination as a court ruling that provides for legal custody, physical custody, or visitation. The term includes permanent, temporary, initial, and modification orders. The term does not include child support orders. Thus, the UCCJEA does not apply to child support. (UCCJEA § 102(3)).

The UCCJEA determines what state has jurisdiction over child custody. The UCCJEA does not deal with which parent should have custody. In other words, the UCCJEA does not concern the best interest of the child. Indeed, the words "best interest of the child" are nowhere to be found in the UCCJEA.

In *Loeb v. Vergara*, 313 So. 3d 346 (La. Ct. App. 2021), the court ruled that the UCCJEA does not apply to embryos or unborn children.

§ 7–18[A] JURISDICTION TO RENDER AN INITIAL CUSTODY DETERMINATION

Section 201 of the UCCJEA deals with jurisdiction to make an initial custody determination. Section 201 describes four bases for subject matter jurisdiction. Section 201 provides:

201. Initial Child-Custody Jurisdiction.

(a) Except as otherwise provided in Section 204 [Section 204 deals with emergency jurisdiction], a court of this State has jurisdiction to make an initial child-custody determination only if: (1) this State is the home State of the child on the date of the commencement of the proceeding, or was the home State of the child within six months before the commencement of the proceeding and the child is absent from this State but a parent or person acting as a parent continues to live in this State; (2) a court of another State does not have jurisdiction under paragraph (1), or a court of the home State of the child has declined to exercise jurisdiction on the ground that this State is the more appropriate forum under Section 207 [inconvenient forum] or 208 [unclean hands], and: (A) the child and the child's parents, or the child and at least one parent or a person acting as a parent, have a significant connection with this State other than mere physical presence; and (B) substantial evidence is available in this State concerning the child's care, protection, training, and personal relationships; (3) all courts having jurisdiction under paragraph (1) or (2) have

> declined to exercise jurisdiction on the ground that a court of this State is the more appropriate forum to determine the custody of the child under Section 207 or 208; or (4) no court of any other State would have jurisdiction under the criteria specified in paragraph (1), (2), or (3). (b) Subsection (a) is the exclusive jurisdictional basis for making a child-custody determination by a court of this State.

At first blush, it might appear that Section 201 allows four alternative bases for subject matter jurisdiction to make an initial custody determination. Not so. Section 201 is structured to give jurisdiction regarding initial custody determinations to the child's home state. (*See A.M. v. Superior Court,* 63 Cal. App. 5th 343, 277 Cal. Rptr. 3d 594 (2021); *Seekins v. Hamm,* 129 A.3d 940 (Me. 2015); *Garba v. Ndiaye,* 227 Md. App. 162, 132 A.3d 908 (2016); *Delima v. Tsevi*, 301 Neb. 933, 921 N.W.2d 89 (2018); *Matter of V.B.N.S.*, 368 Or. 516, 495 P.3d 1245 (2021)). As the Colorado Court of Appeals put it in *In re B.C.B.,* 411 P.3d 926 (Colo. Ct. App. 2015), "The UCCJEA prioritizes home state jurisdiction over all other jurisdictional bases for initial parental responsibilities orders." The Florida Court of Appeal adds in *Miller v. Mitchell*, 328 So.3d 1067 (Fla. Ct. App. 2021), "The state with home state jurisdiction over the child has jurisdictional priority under the UCCJEA." In this regard, Section 201 of the UCCJEA is in harmony with the PKPA, which prefers home state jurisdiction. A child's home state "means the State in which a child lived with a parent or a person acting as a parent for at least six consecutive months immediately before the commencement of a child-custody proceeding. In the case of a child less than six months of age, the term means the State in which the child lived from birth with any of the persons mentioned. A period of temporary absence of any of the mentioned persons is part of the period." (UCCJEA § 102(7)). Only if a child does not have a home state is it permissible to select from the three other bases for jurisdiction.

The UCCJEA definition of home state mentions "a period of temporary absence," but does not clarify the meaning of "temporary." In *Garba v. Ndiaye,* 227 Md. App. 162, 132 A.3d 908 (2016), the Maryland Court of Special Appeals explained, "Courts have developed three tests to determine whether absences are temporary or permanent: duration, intent, and totality of the circumstances. Some courts focus solely on the length of the absence. Other courts consider the intent of the parties, specifically whether parties intended to be away for a limited amount of time and which state they viewed as their place of permanent domicile." The Maryland court approved the more flexible approach of considering the totality of circumstances shedding light on the issue.

As mentioned above, the basic policy of the UCCJEA—and the PKPA—is that litigation to establish an initial custody determination should occur in a child's home state. (*Shandera v. Schultz,* 23 Neb. App. 521, 876 N.W.2d 667 (2016)). If a child has no home state it is permissible to select from the other jurisdictional bases in Section 201. When a child has no home state it is possible (although not common) for more than one state to have jurisdiction to make an initial custody determination. In other words, in rare cases there is concurrent initial jurisdiction.

§ 7–18[B] EXCLUSIVE, CONTINUING JURISDICTION

After a state renders a custody determination, Section 202 of the UCCJEA states that the rendering state retains *exclusive* continuing jurisdiction to modify the determination unless one of two events occurs. The UCCJEA is structured so that only one state at a time has jurisdiction to modify a custody determination. Over time, the state that has modification jurisdiction may switch, but only one state at a time has modification jurisdiction. There is *no such thing as concurrent modification jurisdiction*. Section 202 states:

202. Exclusive, Continuing Jurisdiction.

(a) Except as otherwise provided in Section 204 [emergency jurisdiction], a court of this State which has made a child-custody determination consistent with Section 201 [jurisdiction to make initial determination] or 203 [jurisdiction to modify] has exclusive, continuing jurisdiction over the determination until: (1) a court of this State determines that neither the child, the child's parents, and any person acting as a parent do not have a significant connection with this State and that substantial evidence is no longer available in this State concerning the child's care, protection,

> training, and personal relationships; or (2) a court of this State or a court of another State determines that the child, the child's parents, and any person acting as a parent do not presently reside in this State.
>
> (b) A court of this State which has made a child-custody determination and does not have exclusive, continuing jurisdiction under this section may modify that determination only if it has jurisdiction to make an initial determination under Section 201.

Under Section 202, a state that makes a custody determination has exclusive modification jurisdiction until one of two things happens. First, a court of the state that made the custody determination decides that the connection between the child and the state has become so attenuated that a different state should take over jurisdiction. (UCCJEA § 202(a)(1)). This usually happens when the child and at least one parent moves to another state and lives there for a considerable time. When this happens, the "fresh" evidence that is relevant to the child's best interests is in the new state. A judge in the state that made the custody determination can decide that the other state—the state that has the fresh evidence, and, typically, the state where the child lives and goes to school—should take over jurisdiction. (*See Ball v. McGowan,* 497 S.W.3d 245 (Ky. Ct. App. 2016)). Second, if the child and *both* parents have left the state that rendered the custody determination, then a judge of the rendering state *or* a judge of the new state can decide that the new state should take over jurisdiction. (UCCJEA § 202(a)(2)) (*See A.M. v. Superior Court,* 63 Cal. App. 5th 343, 277 Cal. Rptr. 3d 594 (2021); *Marriage of Nurie,* 176 Cal. App. 4th 478, 500–501, 98 Cal. Rptr. 3d 200 (2009); *De Almeida-Kennedy v. Kennedy,* 207 Conn. App. 244, 262 A.3d 872 (2021).

§ 7–18[C] JURISDICTION TO MODIFY A CUSTODY DETERMINATION OF ANOTHER STATE

As stated above, the UCCJEA provides that only one state at a time has jurisdiction to modify a custody determination. The state that rendered a custody determination retains exclusive continuing jurisdiction until that jurisdiction ends pursuant to Section 202. Whether a state can modify a custody determination rendered in another state is determined by Section 203, which provides:

203. Jurisdiction to Modify Determination.

Except as otherwise provided in Section 204 [emergency jurisdiction], a court of this State may not modify a child-custody determination made by a court of another State unless a court of this State has jurisdiction to make an initial determination under Section 201(a)(1) [home state] or (2) [significant connection] and: (1) the court of the other State determines it no longer has exclusive, continuing jurisdiction under Section 202 or that a court of this State would be a more convenient forum under Section 207; or (2) a court of this State or a court of the other State determines that the child, the child's parents, and any person acting as a parent do not presently reside in the other State.

Under Section 203, a state can exercise modification jurisdiction if (1) the state would have jurisdiction to render an *initial* custody determination because the state is the child's home state or the child has significant connections to the state, *and* (2) the state that had exclusive continuing jurisdiction determines it no longer has jurisdiction, or it declines to exercise its continuing jurisdiction, or the child and both parents have left the state that had exclusive continuing jurisdiction. (*See Plummer v. Plummer*, 823 S.E.2d 258 (Ga. 2019)).

§ 7–18[D] EMERGENCY JURISDICTION

A state that does not have jurisdiction can nevertheless assume temporary emergency jurisdiction to keep a child safe until jurisdiction is sorted out. (UCCJEA § 204). (*See In re J.W.*, 263 A.3d 143 (D.C. 2021); *Gorup v. Brady*, 46 N.E.3d 832, 299 Ill. Dec. 513 (Ct. App. 2015); *In re Alger*, 169 A.D.3d 1415 (N.Y. 2019); *Matter of V.B.N.S.*, 368 Or. 516, 495 P.3d 1245 (2021)).

§ 7–18[E] RACE TO THE COURTHOUSE

In some cases there is an incentive to get to the courthouse first. (*T.L.B. v. M.A.B.*, 272 P.3d 1148 (Colo. Ct. App. 2012)). If a proceeding is already underway in one state that has UCCJEA jurisdiction, the parent who started the first proceeding won the race to the courthouse and another state must not proceed. (UCCJEA § 206).

§ 7–18[F] INCONVENIENT FORUM

A state that has jurisdiction under the UCCJEA can decide that another state is in a better position to decide custody, usually because the other state has more evidence that is relevant to the child's best interests. (UCCJEA § 207). In *Hogan v. McAndrew*, 131 A.3d 717, 724 (R.I. 2016), the Rhode Island Supreme Court stated that before a trial court declines its jurisdiction on grounds of *forum non conveniens,* the court "must engage in a two-part inquiry. . . . The Family Court justice must conclude both that the court is an inconvenient forum under the circumstances *and* that a court of another state [or a foreign tribunal] is a more appropriate forum." (emphasis in original).

§ 7–18[G] UNCLEAN HANDS

A state that has jurisdiction under the UCCJEA can decline to exercise that jurisdiction because the parent asking the court to assert its jurisdiction has engaged in unethical or inappropriate behavior (UCCJEA § 208).

§ 7–18[H] COURTS COMMUNICATE

The UCCJEA encourages judges in different states to communicate in order to decide which state has jurisdiction, and which state is the best forum to determine custody. (UCCJEA §§ 110, 307). Pursuant to the UCCJEA, judges talk on the phone across state lines.

§ 7–18[I] REGISTER OUT OF STATE CUSTODY DETERMINATION

A parent can register an out-of-state custody determination and the court of the registering state will enforce it. (UCCJEA §§ 305, 306). *See Nadimpali v. Byrraju*, 326 Mich. App. 73 (Mich. Ct. App. 2018).

§ 7–18[J] CUSTODY DETERMINATION OF FOREIGN COUNTRY

Section 105 of the UCCJEA provides that a state court "shall treat a foreign country as if it were a State of the United States for the purpose of" applying the UCCJEA. Thus, an American court will typically recognize and enforce a custody determination of another nation. (*Marriage of Margain*, 239 Ariz. 369, 372 P.3d 313 (2016)).

§ 7–18[K] NOTICE AND OPPORTUNITY TO BE HEARD

Personal jurisdiction is not required to adjudicate child custody. However, notice and an opportunity to be heard is necessary, and the UCCJEA so provides in Section 205. (*W.M. v. V.A.*, 30 Cal. App. 5th 64, 241 Cal. Rptr. 3d 170 (2019)).

§ 7–18[L] EXAMPLES OF CHILD CUSTODY JURISDICTION UNDER THE UCCJEA LITIGATION

The UCCJEA is a complex statute. A useful way to understand it is to study examples.

1. Mom and Dad live in California and have 2 kids, ages 6 and 8. Mom separates from Dad and returns with the kids to New Mexico where she grew up. After living in New Mexico for 9 months, Mom commences a divorce action in New Mexico and seeks custody of the children. Does New Mexico have jurisdiction to adjudicate custody?

This case involves an initial custody determination. New Mexico has jurisdiction because it has become the children's home state. (UCCJEA § 102(7)). It is not necessary for New Mexico to have personal jurisdiction over Dad, although it is necessary that he be given notice of the proceeding. (UCCJEA § 205). If Dad wants the proceeding to take place in California, Dad can file a motion with the New Mexico judge asking the judge to rule that New Mexico is an inconvenient forum to decide custody because more evidence about the kids is in California. If Mom snuck away from California with the kids and remained hidden in New Mexico until six months passed so that she could file in New Mexico, Dad might convince a New Mexico judge to decline jurisdiction based on Mom's conduct—the unclean hands provision of Section 208.

2. Mom and Dad live in New York. They have two kids. They divorce in New York and Mom gets custody. Two years later, Dad moves to Kentucky for a new job. When the children are in Kentucky for a visit, Dad refuses to return them to New York. The kids remain in Kentucky for seven months, when Dad starts a custody modification proceeding in

Kentucky. Mom wants the children returned to New York. What result?

Example 2 deals with modification of custody. New York retains exclusive continuing jurisdiction to modify custody (UCCJEA § 202). The fact that the children have been in Kentucky long enough for Kentucky to become their home state (seven months) does not matter. Only one state at a time has modification jurisdiction. Mom still lives in New York and seven months is not long enough to make a meaningful claim that New York has lost jurisdiction. Once Dad is made aware of the law, he may return the children to New York voluntarily. If not, Mom should register the New York custody order in Kentucky and enforce it in Kentucky. Additionally, Mom may wish to contact child abduction authorities, including the F.B.I., because parental child abduction is a crime, and abduction across state lines is a federal crime.

3. Mom and Dad divorce in Michigan. The judge approves joint physical and legal custody of the children, who are two and three. Dad moves to Oregon. The kids go back and forth every 3 months according to an agreed upon schedule that is part of the divorce decree. When the older child is ready for kindergarten, Mom believes the older child should remain in Michigan during the school year. Dad insists that the parties follow the original custody arrangement. Mom files a motion in Michigan to modify custody. Does the Michigan court have jurisdiction? Suppose that while Mom's motion is pending, the children are in Oregon and Dad files a

motion in Oregon to change custody to him. Does the Oregon court have jurisdiction?

Only one state at a time has modification jurisdiction. Michigan rendered the initial custody determination and Michigan retains exclusive, continuing modification jurisdiction. Oregon lacks jurisdiction to modify custody. Mom may ask the Oregon judge to dismiss Dad's motion for want of subject matter jurisdiction.

Note that when the Michigan and Oregon courts are working out jurisdiction, they do not get into the merits of child custody. They do not consider whether to modify the custody order. The best interests analysis occurs *after* jurisdiction is settled.

4. Mom and Dad are from Kansas. They married in Kansas. They have two kids. They begin law school together in Texas. During their third year of law school in Texas they divorce in Texas. In the divorce, Mom gets primary custody. Upon graduation, Mom moves back home to Kansas with the children. Dad takes a job in Dallas. The children visit Dad in Texas four or five times a year. The kids live full time in Kansas with Mom where they go to school. Four years after the divorce, dad files a motion in a Texas court to modify custody. Does the Texas have jurisdiction to modify?

Texas made the initial custody determination. Dad still lives in Texas. Texas retains exclusive, continuing jurisdiction over custody. Because the kids have lived four years in Kansas, most of the evidence about their welfare is in Kansas (*e.g.*, schools, activities, friends, doctors, etc.). If Mom believes it would be better to litigate in Kansas, she needs to file a motion with the Texas court asking the Texas court to defer to Kansas as the more appropriate forum. (UCCJEA § 207). On the facts of this case, a Kansas judge would not have authority to rule that Texas has lost its exclusive, continuing jurisdiction. (*See* UCCJEA § 202(a)(1)).

5. Mom and Dad marry in Tennessee and have a child there. They divorce in Tennessee, and Mom gets custody of junior. Not long after the divorce, Dad moves to Arizona. A year later, Mom and Dad agree that junior will live in Arizona with Dad. After junior has been living in Arizona for 8 months, Mom insists that junior return to Tennessee. Dad says no, and files a petition in Arizona to modify the Tennessee custody decree. Does Arizona have jurisdiction?

Tennessee retains exclusive, continuing modification jurisdiction. The parties cannot confer or end subject matter jurisdiction by agreement. Dad's best course of action is probably to file a motion in Tennessee asking a Tennessee judge to rule that Arizona is a more convenient forum to determine custody. The Tennessee and Arizona judges can communicate with each other by phone. Dad can ask the Tennessee judge to consider the parents' agreement. The current problem could have been avoided if, before the child's move to Arizona, Mom and Dad signed a written agreement about their plans and asked a Tennessee judge to approve the agreement and make it an order.

6. Mom and Dad have lived in California many years. They divorced in California and Dad was awarded sole physical and legal custody of their child. Following the divorce, Mom moved to Washington State. A year after the divorce, Mom becomes concerned about the care afforded the child by Dad in California. While the child is visiting Mom in Washington, Mom brings an action in Washington seeking to modify custody and to award custody to her. Dad asks the Washington court to dismiss the proceeding. What should the Washington court do?

California has exclusive, continuing modification jurisdiction. A Washington court could assume temporary emergency jurisdiction under Section 204 if there is evidence the child is in danger in Dad's custody. However, once the issue of danger is resolved, the Washington court will dismiss Mom's case and defer to California's continuing jurisdiction.

7. Mom and Dad live in Idaho, and have one child. They divorce in Idaho, and Mom receives custody. Dad receives visitation. Mom and the kids move to Maryland and live there 8 years. Mom brings an action in Maryland to modify dad's visitation. Dad asks the Maryland court to dismiss the matter.

After eight years, it seems the more appropriate forum is Maryland. Nevertheless, Idaho retains exclusive continuing modification jurisdiction because Dad still lives in Idaho. Mom should file a motion in Idaho asking an Idaho judge to rule that Maryland is the more appropriate forum. Assuming the Idaho judge agrees, Maryland will have jurisdiction under Section 203 because Maryland is the children's home state, and because the Idaho judge ruled that Maryland is the more convenient forum.

8. Mom and dad meet and marry in Kansas where they attend the University of Kansas at Lawrence. They have two kids in Kansas. While in grad school, mom and dad divorce and agree on joint custody. Upon graduation, mom gets a job in Joplin, Missouri, while dad finds employment in Miami, Oklahoma. The drive time between Joplin and Miami is just 30 minutes. The kids live most of the time with mom in Missouri but spend alternating weekends with dad in Oklahoma. Five years later, mom decides she needs to modify the custody arrangement. Dad won't agree, so mom decides to go to court. Can mom file in Missouri, or does she need to file in Kansas?

In this case, the children and both parents have left Kansas, the state that made the initial custody determination. Missouri is the children's home state. If mom files her modification petition in Missouri, the Missouri judge can utilize § 203 to assume modification jurisdiction.

§ 7–18[M] PARENTAL CHILD ABDUCTION

States have statutes designed to deter and remedy parental child abduction. (*See, e.g.,* Cal. Penal Code § 277). A family court judge can issue orders to prevent or remedy parental child abduction. Fifteen states have adopted the Uniform Child Abduction Prevention Act, promulgated in 2006 by the National Conference of Commissioners on Uniform States Laws.

§ 7–19 HAGUE CONVENTION ON CIVIL ASPECTS OF INTERNATIONAL CHILD ABDUCTION

Imagine you are married. You have two kids, 9 and 11. One day you arrive home to find the children gone and the following note from your spouse, "I can't handle this relationship. I'm going to Germany to stay with my parents, and I'm taking the children with me. We won't be back. I'll e-mail you when we arrive. I'm sorry, but I have to do this." Once you recover from the initial shock, you wonder to yourself, "What can I do about the kids? I want them here. This is their home. This is nuts."

The Hague Convention on the Civil Aspects of International Child Abduction was promulgated to deal with international parental child abduction. The Colorado Court of Appeals explained in *T.L.B. v. M.A.B.*, 272 P.3d 1148, 1154 (Colo. Ct. App. 2012), "The purpose of the Hague Convention is to return promptly, children who are wrongfully removed from their place of habitual residence, unless one of the narrow exceptions to return applies." Just over one hundred countries, including the United States, have adopted the Convention. The Convention applies to children under age sixteen. Congress implemented the Convention with the International Child Abduction Remedies Act (22 U.S.C. §§ 9001 et seq.). Actions to enforce the Convention may be brought in state and federal court. (42 U.S.C. § 11603(a)). The Convention is reproduced at Appendix B.

Before describing the Convention, it should be mentioned that in some cases the enforcement remedies of the UCCJEA work as well as the Convention to secure the proper outcome. A useful law review article on the subject is Robert G. Spector, International Abduction of Children: Why the UCCJEA is Usually a Better Remedy Than the Abduction Convention, 49 *Family Law Quarterly* 385 (2015).

§ 7–19[A] COURT DOES NOT CONDUCT BEST INTEREST ANALYSIS

When a court applies the Convention, the court does *not* conduct a best interest analysis. (Article 19). As the Fifth Circuit Court of Appeals put it in *Berezowsky v. Ojeda*, 765 F.3d 456, 465 (5th Cir. 2014), "Our inquiry is limited to determining whether or not the child has been wrongfully removed from their country of habitual residence." You can think of the Convention as an elaborate venue statute. The Convention determines which country should examine the child's best interests.

§ 7–19[B] WRONGFUL REMOVAL AND WRONGFUL RETENTION

The Convention addresses two types of parental child abduction: Wrongful removal and wrongful retention. Wrongful removal occurs when a parent removes a child from the child's country of "habitual residence" without the consent of the other parent. The example in the opening paragraph of this section is a removal case. Wrongful retention occurs when a parent, with the agreement of the other parent, takes a child to another country, often for a visit, and then refuses to return the child to the child's habitual residence.

§ 7–19[C] PRIMA FACIE CASE

A parent seeking to invoke the Convention files a petition in court. The petitioner must establish a prima facie case of wrongful removal or retention. (*See Souratgar v. Lee*, 720 F.3d 96 (2d Cir. 2013)). The parent's burden of proof is a preponderance of the evidence. (*See Pfeiffer v. Bachotet,* 913 F.3d 1018 (11th Cir. 2019); *Calixto v. Lesmes,*, 909 F.3d 1079 (11th Cir. 2018); *Maurizio R. v. L.C.,* 201 Cal. App. 4th 616, 633 (2011); *In re Marriage of Eaddy*, 144 Cal. App. 4th 1202 (2006)). The Ninth Circuit Court of Appeal's decision in *Mozes v. Mozes,* 239 F.3d 1067 (9th Cir. 2001) describes the petitioner's prima facie case under the Convention:

> A court applying the Convention must therefore answer a series of four questions: (1) When did the removal or retention take place? (2) Immediately prior to the removal or retention, in which state was the child habitually resident? (3) Did the removal or retention breach the rights of custody attributed to the petitioner under the law of the habitual residence? (4) Was the petitioner exercising those rights at the time of the removal or retention? (239 F.3d at 1070).

§ 7–19[D] HABITUAL RESIDENCE

The concept of a child's "habitual residence" is central to the Convention. Yet, neither the

Convention nor the Child Abduction Remedies Act defines habitual residence. Habitual residence is not the same as domicile. Nor is habitual residence coterminous with home state in the UCCJEA.

In 2020, the United States Supreme Court provided guidance on the meaning of habitual residence. In *Monasky v. Taglieri*, 140 S. Ct. 719 (2020), the Court wrote:

> A child "resides" where she lives. . . . Her residence in a particular country can be deemed "habitual," however, only when her residence there is more than transitory. "Habitual" implies '[c]ustomary, usual, of the nature of a habit.' The Hague Convention text alone does not definitively tell us what makes a child's residence sufficiently enduring to be deemed "habitual." . . .
>
> The place where a child is at home, at the time of removal or retention, ranks as the child's habitual residence. . . .
>
> For older children capable of acclimating to their surroundings, courts have long recognized facts indicating acclimatization will be highly relevant. Because children, especially those too young or otherwise unable to acclimate, depend on their parents as caregivers, the intentions and circumstances of caregiving parents are relevant considerations. No single factor, however, is dispositive across all cases. . . .
>
> [A] child's habitual residence depends on the specific circumstances of the particular case. . . .

> The signatory nations sought to afford courts charged with determining a child's habitual residence "maximum flexibility" to respond to the particular circumstances of each case. . . . The aim: to ensure that custody is adjudicated in what is presumptively the most appropriate forum—the country where the child is at home. . . .
>
> The bottom line: There are no categorical requirements for establishing a child's habitual residence . . . .

The Supreme Court acknowledged that the intent of parents is sometimes a factor in determining habitual residence. That said, the approach to habitual residence taken by the Ninth Circuit Court of Appeals in *Mozes v. Mozes,* 239 F.3d 1067 (9th Cir. 2001) has some continued vitality. According to *Mozes,* habitual residence is determined by the parents' last shared, settled intent. The Ninth Circuit's "shared intent" approach is employed by other courts. (*See Mauvais v. Herisse*, 772 F.3d 6, 12 (1st Cir. 2014); *Sanchez-Londono v. Gonzalez,* 752 F.3d 533, 540 (1st Cir. 2014); *Hollis v. O'Driscoll,* 739 F.3d 108, 112 (2d Cir. 2014); *Marriage of Eaddy*, 144 Cal. App. 4th 1202, 1213, 51 Cal. Rptr. 3d 172 (2006)).

Decisions from the Sixth Circuit Court of Appeals focus primary attention on the child rather than the parents' intent.

If a child is habitually resident in Country A, how long can the child remain abroad in Country B before

Country B becomes the new habitual residence? The answer, as mentioned above, turns on the facts of each case. In *Sanchez-Londono v. Gonzalez,* 752 F.3d 533, 540 (1st Cir. 2014), the court ruled that the United States was a child's habitual residence despite an absence of two-and-a-half years. In *Murphy v. Sloan,* 764 F.3d 1144 (9th Cir. 2014), the United States remained a child's habitual residence despite the fact that the family lived in Ireland for three years. On the other hand, if parents intend to abandon a previous home and adopt a new permanent home in another country, a child's habitual residence can change relatively quickly, in a matter of months.

May a parent abscond with children to another country and hide there so long that the absconded-to country becomes the children's habitual residence? Tolerating such treachery would undermine the Convention, and the answer is no. "A parent cannot create a new habitual residence by wrongfully removing and sequestering a child." *Miller v. Miller,* 240 F.3d 392, 400 (4th Cir. 2001). On the other hand, an innocent parent must not "sit on their rights" because the Convention provides that after a child lives in a new place for a year, a judge may decline to return a wrongfully removed or retained child. (Article 12).

In *Calixto v. Lesmes,* 909 F.3d 1079 (11th Cir. 2018), the Eleventh Circuit considered whether habitual residence changes if conditions must be fulfilled before a move to the new country becomes final. In some cases, for example, a parent's ability to stay in a new country depends on whether immigration authorities approve the move. As the Court put it, "[W]e have considered whether a parent's relocation with a child from one country to another was conditioned upon the occurrence of certain events, and whether the first country would remain the child's habitual residence if those events did not come to pass." (909 F.3d at 1089). The Court concluded, "[T]he intent to change the habitual residence of a child from one country to another can be conditioned on the ability of one parent to be able to live in the new country with the child." (*Id.* at 1091).

§ 7–19[E] RIGHTS OF CUSTODY AND EXERCISE OF CUSTODY RIGHTS

The second key issue under the Convention is whether the petitioning parent has "rights of custody" under the law of the child's habitual residence, and, if so, whether the petitioning parent was exercising those rights (Article 3) (*See Ogawa v. Kang,* 946 F.3d 1176 (10th Cir. 2020) (father did not have rights of custody under law of Japan).

Custody rights can arise from a custody decision by a court or by operation of law. (Article 3). A parent does not need a court order to have custody rights. Normally, parents have rights of custody by operation of law.

For purposes of the Convention, a parent exercises custody rights if the parent plays a meaningful role in the child's life. The child need not live with a parent in order for the parent to exercise custody rights. The Fifth Circuit Court of Appeals wrote in *Rodriguez v. Yanez,* 817 F.3d 466 (5th Cir. 2016), "This Court, like many others, has adopted the expansive interpretation of 'exercise' articulated by the Sixth Circuit in *Friedrich v. Friedrich*, [78 F.3d 1060 (6th Cir. 1996)]. Under this standard, when a parent has custody rights under the laws of that country, even occasional contact with the child constitutes 'exercise' of those rights. To show failure to exercise custody rights, the removing parent must show the other parent has abandoned the child. Once it determines that the parent exercised custody rights in any manner, the court should stop—completely avoiding the question whether the parent exercised the custody rights well or badly." In *In re ICJ*, 13 F.4th 753, 762 (9th Cir. 2021), the Ninth Circuit wrote, "The Hague Convention does not explain how one 'exercises' custodial rights. But federal circuit courts in the United States have consistently required a showing that a parent has clearly and unequivocally abandoned a child before ruling that that parent is *not* actually exercising his custody rights." (emphasis in original). (*Accord, In re ICJ,* 13 F.4th 753, 764 (9th Cir. 2021) ("the test [Mother] had to meet to show that [Father] had clearly and unequivocally abandoned [the child] is 'stringent.' ").

For the practicing lawyer in the United States, one of the greatest challenges in Convention cases is determining the law of child custody in the child's country of habitual residence. For example, how does one research child custody law in France, China, or Brazil? Do you understand French, Chinese, or

Portuguese? Even if you understand the language, where do you turn for the relevant statutes? Google? Maybe. The U.S. State Department's Office of Children's Issues often has useful information. A family law lawyer in the other nation can be consulted. It is good advice to start early researching the custody law of the child's habitual residence. In *Garcia v. Pinelo,* 808 F.3d 1158 (7th Cir. 2015), the Seventh Circuit ruled that, for purposes of determining rights of custody under the Convention, proof of foreign law is a question of law rather than a question of fact. The court is free to "find the law" itself. In the main, however, responsibility to track down the custody law of the child's habitual residence falls to the attorney.

§ 7–19[F] DEFENSES TO RETURN OF CHILD

If the petitioning parent establishes a prima facie case of wrongful removal or retention, the court orders the child returned to the habitual residence unless the other parent establishes one of the defenses to return of the child to the habitual residence. In *Berenguela-Alvardo v. Castanos*, 950 F.3d 1352 (11th Cir. 2020) the Eleventh Circuit discussed the "consent defense" to return of a child: "The consent defense requires the retaining/ removing parent to prove by a preponderance of the evidence that the petitioning parent consented to the removal or retention. The petitioning parent's consent needn't be formal, but it is important to consider what the petitioner actually contemplated and agreed to in allowing the child to travel outside his home country. The focus of the court's inquiry should be on the petitioning parent's subjective intent, and should take into account the nature and scope of the petitioner's consent, and any conditions or imitations on that consent." The Federal District Court's opinion in *Trudrung v. Trudrung,* 686 F. Supp. 2d 570 (M.D. N.C. 2010) discussed defenses:

> Upon a showing of wrongful removal or retention, return of the child is required unless the Respondent establishes one of several affirmative defenses. Two of the defenses must be supported by clear and convincing evidence: (1) that return would expose the child to a "grave risk" of "physical or psychological harm or otherwise place the child in an intolerable situation" and (2) that return of the child would not be permitted by "fundamental principles of the United States relating to the protection of human rights and fundamental freedoms." The other three defenses may be supported by a preponderance of the evidence: (1) that the petition for return was not filed within one year of the removal and the child is now well-settled in another country; (2) that the petitioner was not actually exercising his custodial rights at the time of the removal or had consented to or acquiesced in the removal; and (3) the child objects to being returned and has attained an age and degree of maturity at which it is appropriate to take account of his or her views. These defenses, or exceptions, are to be narrowly construed so that their application does not undermine the purposes of the Convention. Even if a respondent meets the burden of

proving one of the defenses, the court retains the discretion to order the return of the child if it would further the aim of the Convention which is to provide for the return of a wrongfully removed child.

§ 7-19[F](1) Grave Risk of Physical or Psychological Harm; Intolerable Situation

Parents opposing return of a child sometimes argue that returning the child poses a grave risk to the child or will place the child in an intolerable situation. Courts construe this defense narrowly. (*Mauvais v. Herisse*, 772 F.3d 6 (1st Cir. 2014)). The parent seeking to invoke this defense to return must "show that the risk to the child is grave, not merely serious. . . . Only evidence directly establishing the existence of a grave risk that would expose the child to physical or psychological harm or otherwise place the child in an intolerable situation is material to the court's determination." (Hague International Child Abduction Convention: Text and Legal Analysis, 51 Fed. Reg. 10401, 10510 (1986)). The risk must be of harm immediately upon return, not the remote potential for future harm. (*In re ICJ*, 14 F.4th 753, 765 (9th Cir. 2021)).

In *Noergaard v. Noergaard,* 244 Cal. App. 4th 76, 84, 197 Cal. Rptr. 3d 546 (2015), the California Court of Appeal noted, "Domestic violence or child abuse constitutes a grave risk to the child." In *Gomez v. Fuenmayor*, 812 F.3d 1005 (11th Cir. 2016), the child's parents were embroiled in a custody battle in Venezuela. The child's mother threatened physical violence against the father and actually perpetrated violence. Father fled to the United States with the child. In refusing to return the child to Venezuela, the American court ruled that the violence directed at the father posed an immediate risk of harm to the child. In *Colchester v. Lazaro,* 16 F.4th 712 (9th Cir. 2021), the Ninth Circuit ruled that when domestic violence or child abuse are alleged, the trial judge can order a psychological evaluation to assist the court in reaching the correct decision.

The fact that the parent who wrongfully removed a child to the United States has more money than the left-behind-parent is not a reason to deny return. If the law were otherwise, rich parents could wrongfully bring children to America with impunity, thwarting the rights of innocent parents in poorer countries. In *Cuellar v. Joyce,* 596 F.3d 505 (9th Cir. 2010), the Ninth Circuit Court of Appeals noted that billions of perfectly competent parents live in poverty. If poverty "amounted to a grave risk of harm, parents in more developed countries would have unchecked power to abduct children from countries with a lower standard of living. At the time the Convention was adopted, the State Department took care to emphasize that grave risk doesn't encompass a home where money is in short supply, or where educational or other opportunities are more limited."

In *Ermini v. Vittori,* 758 F.3d 153 (2d Cir. 2014), the Second Circuit Court of Appeals grappled with an interesting issue. Could separating a wrongfully retained autistic child from the child's autism therapy in order to return the child to the habitual residence constitute a grave risk of psychological harm? The court answered "yes." In instructive language, the court wrote:

> We have in the past ruled that a "grave risk" of harm does not exist when repatriation might cause inconvenience or hardship, eliminate certain educational or economic opportunities, or not comport with the child's preferences. But we have also stressed that a grave risk of harm exists when repatriation would make the child face a real risk of being hurt, physically or psychologically. The potential harm must be severe, and there must be a probability that the harm will materialize.
>
> Domestic violence can satisfy the defense when the respondent shows by clear and convincing evidence a sustained pattern of physical abuse and/or a propensity for violent abuse. And we have concluded that a grave risk of harm from abuse had been established where the petitioning parent had actually abused, threatened to abuse, or inspired fear in the children in question. Spousal violence, in certain circumstances, can also establish a grave risk of harm to the child, particularly when it occurs in the presence of the child. We have also been careful to note that sporadic or isolated incidents of physical discipline directed at the child, or some limited incidents aimed at persons other than the child, even if witnessed by the child, have not been found to constitute a grave risk. (758 F.3d at 164–165).

As mentioned above and as discussed by the court in *Ermini v. Vittori*, intimate partner violence directed against a parent, or physical, sexual, or psychological abuse of a child, can constitute a sufficient reason to deny return of a wrongfully removed or retained child. (*See Acosta v. Acosta,* 725 F.3d 868 (2013); *Ortiz v. Martinez,* 789 F.3d 722 (7th Cir. 2015)).

When a court finds returning a child poses a serious risk to the child, the court may nevertheless require return if the parent seeking return establishes ameliorative measures to ensure the child's safety. (*See In re ICJ,* 13 F.4th 753, 764–765 (9th Cir. 2021) (trial court erred in failing to consider alternative remedies by means of which [the child] could be transferred back to [France] without placing her in an intolerable situation."); *Radu v. Shon,* 11 F. 4th 1080 (9th Cir. 2021); *Marriage of Emilie D.L.M. v. Carlos C.,* 64 Cal. App. 5th 876, 279 Cal. Rptr. 3d 330 (2021) (parent seeking return did not establish satisfactory ameliorative measures)).

§ 7–19[F](2) Return Is Inconsistent with Human Rights

In a rare case a judge concludes that returning a child to its habitual residence would be inconsistent with human rights. For example, it is difficult to imagine a judge returning a child to a country in the middle of a bloody civil war.

§ 7-19[F](3) Settled in the United States

A parent seeking return of a child must act promptly. The parent must find the child and file a petition for return in the court where the child is located. (*Fernandez v. Bailey*, 909 F.3d 353, 359 (11th Cir. 2018)). If the parent files within one year of the wrongful removal or retention, the court is required to return the child unless a defense to return applies. (Article 12). If more than a year separates the wrongful removal or retention from filing the petition, return is not automatic. The court determines whether the child has become settled in the new country. The Eleventh Circuit explained in *Fernandez v. Bailey*, 909 F.3d 353, 359 (11th Cir. 2018), "The Convention treats petitions filed in the first year differently from those filed more than one year after a child is removed . . . . [A]fter a year has passed, the abducting parent may prevent return by showing upon a preponderance of the evidence that the abducted child is 'now settled' in their new country. This exception [to return] accounts for the reality that 'at some point a child may become so settled in a new environment that return is no longer in the child's best interests.' "

In *Lozano v. Montoya Alvarez*, 572 U.S. 1, 134 S. Ct. 1224 (2014), the Supreme Court ruled that the one year period is not subject to equitable tolling.

In *In re B. Del C.S.B.*, 559 F.3d 999, 1009 (9th Cir. 2009), the Ninth Circuit discussed factors to consider in evaluating whether a child is settled: "(1) the child's age; (2) the stability and duration of the child's residence in the new environment; (3) whether the child attends school or day care consistently; (4) whether the child has friends and relatives in the new area; (5) the child's participation in community or extracurricular school activities, such as team sports, youth groups, or school clubs; (6) the respondent's employment and financial stability." Even if the court concludes a child is settled, the judge may order the wrongfully removed or retained child returned. (*See Yaman v. Yaman,* 730 F.3d 1 (1st Cir. 2013) *See also, Silva v. De Aredes*, 953 F.3d 67 (1st Cir. 2020)).

§ 7–19[F](4) Mature Child Objects to Return

A judge will listen to an older child's wishes about returning to the child's habitual residence, and in the right case, accede to the child's desires. In *Avendano v. Balza,* 985 F.3d 8 (1st Cir. 2021), the First Circuit wrote: "[The Convention] does not set an age at which a child is considered to be sufficiently mature; rather, the determination is to be made on a case by case basis." The child in *Avendano v. Balza* was nearly 12, and wished to remain in the United States.

§ 7–19[G] STAY OF RETURN ORDER

When a parent loses a Convention case and is ordered to return a child to the parent in the child's habitual residence, the losing parent may ask a court to stay the return pending appeal. In *Chafin v. Chafin*, 568 U.S. 165, 133 S. Ct. 1017, 1027 (2013), the Supreme Court discussed factors to consider regarding a stay: "Courts should apply the four traditional stay factors in considering whether to stay a return order: (1) whether the stay applicant has made a strong showing that he is likely to succeed on the merits; (2) whether the applicant will be irreparably injured absent a stay; (3) whether issuance of the stay will substantially injure the other parties interested in the proceeding; and (4) where the public interest lies."

§ 7–20 VISITATION/PARENTING TIME

If parents have joint physical custody, the child typically spends substantial time with both parents. However, if one parent has sole or primary physical custody, the other parent has the right to visitation, or as it is increasingly called, parenting time. Visitation is automatic unless the non-custodial parent forfeited the right through misconduct. (*Taylor v. Taylor*, 282 Ga. 113, 646 S.E.2d 238 (2007); *Williams v. Williams,* 264 So. 3d 722 (Miss. 2019)). In *McCartney v. McCartney*, 149 So. 3d 894 (La. Ct. App. 2014), the trial court did not err in denying visitation for an incarcerated father who barely knew the children. In *Huml v. Huml,* 826 S.E.2d 532 (N.C. Ct. App. 2019), the North Carolina Court of Appeals approved a trial judge's order denying visitation to a mentally ill father who had threatened to kill the child's mother and who refused to get needed psychological help for himself. The case of *In re T.M.*, 4 Cal. App. 5th 1214, 209 Cal. Rptr. 3d 391 (2016) dealt with visitation in juvenile court rather than family court. The child's father regularly beat the child, called him names, abused substances, and did little to control his anger. The child was afraid of his father, and did not want to see him. The juvenile court judge denied visitation, and the Court of Appeal affirmed.

A court order regarding visitation can be modified.

§ 7–21 VISITATION WITH GRANDPARENTS AND OTHER NON-PARENTS

Statutes and case law authorize courts to order visitation for grandparents and other adults who have a close relationship with a child. (*In re Kelly S.*, 139 A.D.3d 90, 28 N.Y.S.3d 714 (2016)). In *McAllister v. McAllister,* 779 N.W.2d 652 (N.D. 2010), the North Dakota Supreme Court approved visitation for a step-parent who was a child's psychological parent. A Wisconsin statute authorizes visitation for a "grandparent, greatgrandparent, stepparent, or person who has maintained a relationship similar to a parent-child relationship with the child." (Wis. Stat. § 767.43(1)). Illinois law is similar (Illinois Stats. § 750 ILCS 5/602.9).

The issue of grandparent visitation reached the U.S. Supreme Court in *Troxel v. Granville,* 530 U.S. 57, 120 S. Ct. 2054 (2000). The Court affirmed the right of parents to make decisions regarding their children, including decisions about visitation with grandparents and other adults. The Court ruled that the decision whether to allow grandparents to visit "is for the parent in the first instance. And, if a fit parent's decision of the kind at issue here becomes subject to judicial review, the court must accord at least some special weight to the parent's own determination." (*See Patten v. Ardis*, 304 Ga. 140, 816

S.E.2d 633 (2018) (Georgia Supreme Court holds grandparent visitation statute unconstitutional)).

In *Marriage of Deuel,* 2007 WL 2318744 (Cal. Ct. App. 2007) (not reported), the California Court of Appeal discussed *Troxel v. Granville*:

> The due process clause protects the fundamental right of custodial parents to make decisions concerning the care, custody, and control of their children. A presumption exists that fit parents act in the best interests of their children. *Troxel* held that a Washington statute, under which grandparents were given visitation over the parent's objection, was unconstitutional as applied, since the trial court gave no special weight to the parent's determination of her daughters' best interest and thus violated the parent's fundamental constitutional right to make decisions for her children. *Troxel* essentially affirmed the cardinal rule, as stated by the Supreme Court, that "the custody, care and nurture of the child reside first in the parents, whose primary function and freedom include preparation for obligations the state can neither supply nor hinder." Encompassed within this well-established fundamental right of parents to raise their children is the right to determine with whom their children should associate.
>
> Thus, a court may not disregard and overturn the decisions of fit custodial parents whenever a third party affected by the decision files a visitation petition. As to grandparents, however,

> a court is not precluded from granting visitation over the objection of a "fit" parent. The decision of fit parents regarding grandparent visitation is entitled to special weight, but not necessarily immunity from judicial review.
>
> A court does not have any inherent jurisdiction or equitable power to entertain a nonparent's visitation request. Instead, grandparents' rights to court-ordered visitation with their grandchildren are purely statutory.

Illinois law provides, "There is a rebuttable presumption that a fit parent's actions and decisions regarding grandparent, great-grandparent, sibling, or step-parent visitation are not harmful to the child's mental, physical, or emotional health. The burden is on the party filing a petition under this Section [for visitation] to prove that the parent's actions and decisions regarding visitation will cause undue harm to the child's mental, physical or emotional health." (750 ILCS 5/602.9).

A common scenario in which grandparents seek court ordered visitation follows: Mother and Father are married and have a child. Mother dies at a young age and Father refuses to allow the maternal grandparents to visit the child at all, or as often as they would like. If the grandparents have an established, healthy, nurturing relationship with the child, and the judge gives the Father's wishes the proper deference, the judge may order grandparent visitation. (*See Reid v. Lindsey,* 823 S.E.2d 359 (Ga. Ct. App. 2019); *Petition of Lundquist*, 134 A.3d 951

(N.H. 2016); *Marriage of Meister*, 876 N.W.2d 746 (Wis. 2016)).

§ 7-22 GUARDIANSHIP

Every state has guardianship laws that authorize courts to appoint a guardian for a child who has no parents or whose parents are not able to care for the child. The court issues "letters of guardianship." The guardian acquires the rights and responsibilities normally exercised by parents.

Appointing a guardian over the objections of parents is a major infringement on parental rights, and courts proceed cautiously. Only if the parents are deceased, unavailable, have abandoned the child, or are not competent to provide for the child will a guardian be appointed. (*Guardianship of JR*, 368 P.3d 910 (Wyo. 2016)).

After a guardian is appointed, the parent may petition the court to end the guardianship. States employ various standards to determine when a guardianship is no longer necessary. In *Guardianship of W.L.*, 467 S.W.3d 129 (Ark. 2015), the Arkansas Supreme Court ruled that when a fit parent agrees to guardianship, the fit parent can withdraw consent and terminate the guardianship. In *In re M.F.*, 298 Ga. 138, 780 S.E.2d 291 (2015), the Georgia Supreme Court ruled that a guardianship may be modified or cancelled upon a showing by clear and convincing evidence that there has been a material change of circumstances, and that it is in the child's best interest to end the guardianship.

In California, the fact that a parent whose problems necessitated guardianship has overcome those problems is not a sufficient reason to end guardianship. In *In re Guardianship of L.V.*, 136 Cal. App. 4th 481, 488–489 (2006), the California Court of Appeal explained, "The parents claim that because they are fit parents—*i.e.,* they can provide adequate food, clothing, shelter, and guidance for the minor—they are entitled to have the guardianship terminated and the minor returned to their custody. This is not the statutory standard in California law." The California Court of Appeal explained in *Guardianship of Kassandra H.*, 64 Cal. App. 4th 1228–1239, 75 Cal. Rptr. 2d 668 (1998), "Manifestly the legal criteria are not as simple as just whether the singular circumstances leading to the guardianship has been eliminated—as if the child has been a chattel who needed to be temporarily stored someplace. . . . Any new circumstances justifying the termination of a guardianship must be sufficient to overcome the inherent disruption of tearing a child away from a guardian who is doing a good job caring for and nurturing the child."

APPENDIX A

UNIFORM CHILD CUSTODY JURISDICTION AND ENFORCEMENT ACT

ARTICLE 1

GENERAL PROVISIONS

101. Short Title.

This Act may be cited as the Uniform Child-Custody Jurisdiction and Enforcement Act.

102. Definitions.

In this Act:

(1) "Abandoned" means left without provision for reasonable and necessary care or supervision.

(2) "Child" means an individual who has not attained 18 years of age.

(3) "Child-custody determination" means a judgment, decree, or other order of a court providing for the legal custody, physical custody, or visitation with respect to a child. The term includes a permanent, temporary, initial, and modification order. The term does not include an order relating to child support or other monetary obligation of an individual.

(4) "Child-custody proceeding" means a proceeding in which legal custody, physical custody, or visitation with respect to a child is an issue. The term includes a proceeding for divorce, separation, neglect, abuse,

dependency, guardianship, paternity, termination of parental rights, and protection from domestic violence, in which the issue may appear. The term does not include a proceeding involving juvenile delinquency, contractual emancipation, or enforcement under Article 3.

(5) "Commencement" means the filing of the first pleading in a proceeding.

(6) "Court" means an entity authorized under the law of a State to establish, enforce, or modify a child-custody determination.

(7) "Home State" means the State in which a child lived with a parent or a person acting as a parent for at least six consecutive months immediately before the commencement of a child-custody proceeding. In the case of a child less than six months of age, the term means the State in which the child lived from birth with any of the persons mentioned. A period of temporary absence of any of the mentioned persons is part of the period.

(8) "Initial determination" means the first child-custody determination concerning a particular child.

(9) "Issuing court" means the court that makes a child-custody determination for which enforcement is sought under this Act.

(10) "Issuing State" means the State in which a child-custody determination is made.

(11) "Modification" means a child-custody determination that changes, replaces, supersedes, or is otherwise made after a previous determination

concerning the same child, whether or not it is made by the court that made the previous determination.

(12) "Person" means an individual, corporation, business trust, estate, trust, partnership, limited liability company, association, joint venture, government; governmental subdivision, agency, or instrumentality; public corporation; or any other legal or commercial entity.

(13) "Person acting as a parent" means a person, other than a parent, who:

(A) has physical custody of the child or has had physical custody for a period of six consecutive months, including any temporary absence, within one year immediately before the commencement of a child-custody proceeding; and

(B) has been awarded legal custody by a court or claims a right to legal custody under the law of this State.

(14) "Physical custody" means the physical care and supervision of a child.

(15) "State" means a State of the United States, the District of Columbia, Puerto Rico, the United States Virgin Islands, or any territory or insular possession subject to the jurisdiction of the United States.

(16) "Tribe" means an Indian tribe or band, or Alaskan Native village, which is recognized by federal law or formally acknowledged by a State.

(17) "Warrant" means an order issued by a court authorizing law enforcement officers to take physical custody of a child.

103. Proceedings Governed by Other Law.

This Act does not govern an adoption proceeding or a proceeding pertaining to the authorization of emergency medical care for a child.

104. Application to Indian Tribes.

(a) A child-custody proceeding that pertains to an Indian child as defined in the Indian Child Welfare Act, 25 U.S.C. §§ 1901 et seq., is not subject to this Act to the extent that it is governed by the Indian Child Welfare Act.

(b) A court of this State shall treat a tribe as if it were a State of the United States for the purpose of applying Articles 1 and 2.

(c) A child-custody determination made by a tribe under factual circumstances in substantial conformity with the jurisdictional standards of this Act must be recognized and enforced under Article 3.

105. International Application of Act.

(a) A court of this State shall treat a foreign country as if it were a State of the United States for the purpose of applying Articles 1 and 2.

(b) Except as otherwise provided in subsection (c), a child-custody determination made in a foreign country under factual circumstances in substantial conformity with the jurisdictional standards of this Act must be recognized and enforced under Article 3.

(c) A court of this State need not apply this Act if the child custody law of a foreign country violates fundamental principles of human rights.

106. Effect of Child-Custody Determination.

A child-custody determination made by a court of this State that had jurisdiction under this Act binds all persons who have been served in accordance with the laws of this State or notified in accordance with Section 108 or who have submitted to the jurisdiction of the court, and who have been given an opportunity to be heard. As to those persons, the determination is conclusive as to all decided issues of law and fact except to the extent the determination is modified.

110. Communication Between Courts.

(a) A court of this State may communicate with a court in another State concerning a proceeding arising under this Act.

(b) The court may allow the parties to participate in the communication. If the parties are not able to participate in the communication, they must be given the opportunity to present facts and legal arguments before a decision on jurisdiction is made.

(c) Communication between courts on schedules, calendars, court records, and similar matters may occur without informing the parties. A record need not be made of the communication.

(d) Except as otherwise provided in subsection (c), a record must be made of a communication under this section. The parties must be informed promptly of the communication and granted access to the record.

ARTICLE 2

JURISDICTION

201. Initial Child-Custody Jurisdiction.

(a) Except as otherwise provided in Section 204, a court of this State has jurisdiction to make an initial child-custody determination only if:

(1) this State is the home State of the child on the date of the commencement of the proceeding, or was the home State of the child within six months before the commencement of the proceeding and the child is absent from this State but a parent or person acting as a parent continues to live in this State;

(2) a court of another State does not have jurisdiction under paragraph (1), or a court of the home State of the child has declined to exercise jurisdiction on the ground that this State is the more appropriate forum under Section 207 or 208, and:

A. the child and the child's parents, or the child and at least one parent or a person acting as a parent, have a significant connection with this State other than mere physical presence; and

B. substantial evidence is available in this State concerning the child's care, protection, training, and personal relationships;

(3) all courts having jurisdiction under paragraph (1) or (2) have declined to exercise jurisdiction on the ground that a court of this State is the more appropriate forum to determine the custody of the child under Section 207 or 208; or

(4) no court of any other State would have jurisdiction under the criteria specified in paragraph (1), (2), or (3).

(b) Subsection (a) is the exclusive jurisdictional basis for making a child-custody determination by a court of this State.

(c) Physical presence of, or personal jurisdiction over, a party or a child is not necessary or sufficient to make a child-custody determination.

202. Exclusive, Continuing Jurisdiction.

(a) Except as otherwise provided in Section 204, a court of this State which has made a child-custody determination consistent with Section 201 or 203 has exclusive, continuing jurisdiction over the determination until:

(1) a court of this State determines that neither the child, the child's parents, and any person acting as a parent do not have a significant connection with this State and that substantial evidence is no longer available in this State

concerning the child's care, protection, training, and personal relationships; or

(2) a court of this State or a court of another State determines that the child, the child's parents, and any person acting as a parent do not presently reside in this State.

(b) A court of this State which has made a child-custody determination and does not have exclusive, continuing jurisdiction under this section may modify that determination only if it has jurisdiction to make an initial determination under Section 201.

203. Jurisdiction to Modify Determination.

Except as otherwise provided in Section 204, a court of this State may not modify a child-custody determination made by a court of another State unless a court of this State has jurisdiction to make an initial determination under Section 201(a)(1) or (2) and:

(1) the court of the other State determines it no longer has exclusive, continuing jurisdiction under Section 202 or that a court of this State would be a more convenient forum under Section 207; or

(2) a court of this State or a court of the other State determines that the child, the child's parents, and any person acting as a parent do not presently reside in the other State.

204. Temporary Emergency Jurisdiction.

(a) A court of this State has temporary emergency jurisdiction if the child is present in this State and the child has been abandoned or it is necessary in an emergency to protect the child because the child, or a sibling or parent of the child, is subjected to or threatened with mistreatment or abuse.

205. Notice; Opportunity to Be Heard; Joinder.

(a) Before a child-custody determination is made under this Act, notice and an opportunity to be heard in accordance with the standards of Section 108 must be given to all persons entitled to notice under the law of this State as in child-custody proceedings between residents of this State, any parent whose parental rights have not been previously terminated, and any person having physical custody of the child.

(b) This Act does not govern the enforceability of a child-custody determination made without notice or an opportunity to be heard.

206. Simultaneous Proceedings.

(a) Except as otherwise provided in Section 204, a court of this State may not exercise its jurisdiction under this Article if, at the time of the commencement of the proceeding, a proceeding concerning the custody of the child has been commenced in a court of another State having jurisdiction substantially in conformity with this Act, unless the proceeding has been terminated or is stayed by the court of the other State because a court of this State is a more convenient forum under Section 207.

207. Inconvenient Forum.

(a) A court of this State which has jurisdiction under this Act to make a child-custody determination may decline to exercise its jurisdiction at any time if it determines that it is an inconvenient forum under the circumstances and that a court of another State is a more appropriate forum. The issue of inconvenient forum may be raised upon motion of a party, the court's own motion, or request of another court.

(b) Before determining whether it is an inconvenient forum, a court of this State shall consider whether it is appropriate for a court of another State to exercise jurisdiction. For this purpose, the court shall allow the parties to submit information and shall consider all relevant factors, including:

(1) whether domestic violence has occurred and is likely to continue in the future and which State could best protect the parties and the child;

(2) the length of time the child has resided outside this State;

(3) the distance between the court in this State and the court in the State that would assume jurisdiction;

(4) the relative financial circumstances of the parties;

(5) any agreement of the parties as to which State should assume jurisdiction;

(6) the nature and location of the evidence required to resolve the pending litigation, including testimony of the child;

(7) the ability of the court of each State to decide the issue expeditiously and the procedures necessary to present the evidence; and

(8) the familiarity of the court of each State with the facts and issues in the pending litigation.

(c) If a court of this State determines that it is an inconvenient forum and that a court of another State is a more appropriate forum, it shall stay the proceedings upon condition that a child-custody proceeding be promptly commenced in another designated State and may impose any other condition the court considers just and proper.

(d) A court of this State may decline to exercise its jurisdiction under this Act if a child-custody determination is incidental to an action for divorce or another proceeding while still retaining jurisdiction over the divorce or other proceeding.

208. Jurisdiction Declined by Reason of Conduct.

(a) Except as otherwise provided in Section 204 or by other law of this State, if a court of this State has jurisdiction under this Act because a person seeking to invoke its jurisdiction has engaged in unjustifiable conduct, the court shall decline to exercise its jurisdiction unless:

(1) the parents and all persons acting as parents have acquiesced in the exercise of jurisdiction;

(2) a court of the State otherwise having jurisdiction under Sections 201 through 203 determines that this State is a more appropriate forum under Section 207; or

(3) no court of any other State would have jurisdiction under the criteria specified in Sections 201 through 203.

209. Information to be Submitted to Court.

(a) In a child-custody proceeding, each party, in its first pleading or in an attached affidavit, shall give information, if reasonably ascertainable, under oath as to the child's present address or whereabouts, the places where the child has lived during the last five years, and the names and present addresses of the persons with whom the child has lived during that period.

ARTICLE 3

ENFORCEMENT

302. Enforcement Under Hague Convention.

Under this Article a court of this State may enforce an order for the return of the child made under the Hague Convention on the Civil Aspects of International Child Abduction as if it were a child-custody determination.

303. Duty to Enforce.

A court of this State shall recognize and enforce a child-custody determination of a court of another State if the latter court exercised jurisdiction in substantial conformity with this Act or the determination was made under factual circumstances meeting the jurisdictional standards of this Act and the determination has not been modified in accordance with this Act.

305. Registration of Child-Custody Determination.

(a) A child-custody determination issued by a court of another State may be registered in this State.

306. Enforcement of Registered Determination.

(a) A court of this State may grant any relief normally available under the law of this State to enforce a registered child-custody determination made by a court of another State.

(b) A court of this State shall recognize and enforce, but may not modify, except in accordance with Article 2, a registered child-custody determination of a court of another State.

307. Simultaneous Proceedings.

If a proceeding for enforcement under this Article is commenced in a court of this State and the court determines that a proceeding to modify the determination is pending in a court of another State having jurisdiction to modify the determination under Article 2, the enforcing court shall immediately communicate with the modifying court. The proceeding for enforcement continues unless the enforcing court, after consultation with the modifying court, stays or dismisses the proceeding.

311. Warrant to Take Physical Custody of Child.

(a) Upon the filing of a petition seeking enforcement of a child-custody determination, the petitioner may file a verified application for the issuance of a warrant to take physical custody of the child if the child is immediately likely to suffer serious physical harm or be removed from this State.

APPENDIX B

HAGUE CONVENTION ON THE CIVIL ASPECTS OF INTERNATIONAL CHILD ABDUCTION

CHAPTER I—SCOPE OF THE CONVENTION

Article 1

The objects of the present Convention are—

(a) to secure the prompt return of children wrongfully removed to or retained in any Contracting State; and

(b) to ensure that rights of custody and of access under the law of one Contracting State are effectively respected in other Contracting States.

Article 3

The removal or the retention of a child is to be considered wrongful where—

(a) it is in breach of rights of custody attributed to a person, an institution or any other body, either jointly or alone, under the law of the State in which the child was habitually resident immediately before the removal or retention; and

(b) at the time of removal or retention those rights were actually exercised, either jointly or alone, or would have been so exercised but for the removal or retention.

The rights of custody mentioned in sub-paragraph (a) above, may arise in particular by operation of law or by reason of a judicial or administrative decision, or by reason of an agreement having legal effect under the law of that State.

Article 4

The Convention shall apply to any child who was habitually resident in a Contracting State immediately before any breach of custody or access rights. The Convention shall cease to apply when the child attain the age of 16 years.

Article 5

For the purposes of this Convention—

(a) "Rights of custody" shall include rights relating to the care of the person of the child and, in particular, the right to determine the child's place of residence;

(b) "Rights of access" shall include the right to take a child for a limited period of time to a place other than the child's habitual residence.

CHAPTER II—CENTRAL AUTHORITIES

Article 6

A Contracting State shall designate a Central Authority to discharge the duties which are imposed by the Convention upon such authorities.

Article 7

Central Authorities shall co-operate with each other and promote co-operation amongst the competent authorities in their respective States to secure the prompt return of children and to achieve the other objects of this Convention.

CHAPTER III—RETURN OF CHILDREN

Article 8

Any person, institution or other body claiming that a child has been removed or retained in breach of custody rights may apply either to the Central Authority of the child's habitual residence or to the Central Authority of any other Contracting State for assistance in securing the return of the child.

The application shall contain [all information relevant to the case].

Article 10

The Central Authority of the State where the child is shall take or cause to be taken all appropriate measures in order to obtain the voluntary return of the child.

Article 11

The judicial or administrative authorities of Contracting States shall act expeditiously in proceedings for the return of children.

If the judicial or administrative authority concerned has not reached a decision within six weeks from the date of commencement of the proceedings, the applicant or the Central Authority of the requested State, on its own initiative or if asked by the Central Authority of the requesting State, shall have the right to request a statement of the reasons for the delay. If a reply is received by the Central Authority of the requested State, that Authority shall transmit the reply to the Central Authority of the requesting State, or to the applicant, as the case may be.

Article 12

Where a child has been wrongfully removed or retained in terms of Article 3 and, at the date of the commencement of the proceedings before the judicial or administrative authority of the Contracting State where the child is, a period of less than one year has elapsed from the date of the wrongful removal or retention, the authority concerned shall order the return of the child forthwith.

The judicial or administrative authority, even where the proceedings have been commenced after the expiration of the period of one year referred to in the preceding paragraph, shall also order the return of the child, unless it is demonstrated that the child is now settled in its new environment.

Where the judicial or administrative authority in the requested State has reason to believe that the child has been taken to another State, it may stay the proceedings or dismiss the application for the return of the child.

Article 13

Notwithstanding the provisions of the preceding Article, the judicial or administrative authority of the requested State is not bound to order the return of the child if the person, institution or other body which opposes its return establishes that—

(a) the person, institution or other body having the care of the person of the child was not actually exercising the custody rights at the time of removal or retention, or had consented to or subsequently acquiesced in the removal of retention; or

(b) there is a grave risk that his or her return would expose the child to physical or psychological harm or otherwise place the child in an intolerable situation.

The judicial or administrative authority may also refuse to order the return of the child if it finds that the child objects to being returned and has attained an age and degree of maturity at which it is appropriate to take account of its views.

In considering the circumstances referred to in this Article, the judicial and administrative authorities shall take into account the information relating to the social background of the child provided by the Central Authority or other competent authority of the child's habitual residence.

Article 16

After receiving notice of a wrongful removal or retention of a child in the sense of Article 3, the judicial or administrative authorities of the Contracting State to which the child has been removed or in which it has been retained shall not decide on the merits of rights of custody until it has been determined that the child is not to be returned under this Convention or unless an application under the Convention is not lodged within a reasonable time following receipt of the notice.

Article 19

A decision under this Convention concerning the return of the child shall not be taken to be determination on the merits of any custody issue.

Article 20

The return of the child under the provision of Article 12 may be refused if this would not be permitted by the fundamental principles of the requested State relating to the protection of human rights and fundamental freedoms.

CHAPTER VI—RIGHTS OF ACCESS

Article 21

An application to make arrangements for organizing or securing the effective exercise of rights of access may be presented to the Central Authorities of the Contracting States in the same way as an application for the return of a child.

The Central Authorities are bound by the obligations of co-operation which are set forth in Article 7 to promote the peaceful enjoyment of access rights and the fulfillment of any conditions to which the exercise of such rights may be subject. The central Authorities shall take steps to remove, as far as possible, all obstacles to the exercise of such rights. The Central Authorities, either directly or through intermediaries, may initiate or assist in the institution of proceedings with a view to organizing or protecting these rights and securing respect for the conditions to which the exercise of these rights may be subject.

Article 26

Each Central Authority shall bear its own costs in applying this Convention.

Central Authorities and other public services of Contracting States shall not impose any charges in relation to applications submitted under this Convention. In particular, they may not require any payment from the applicant towards the costs and expenses of the proceedings or, where applicable, those arising from the participation of legal counselor advisers. However, they may require the payment of the expenses incurred or to be incurred in implementing the return of the child.

Upon ordering the return of a child or issuing an order concerning rights of access under this Convention, the judicial or administrative authorities may, where appropriate, direct the person who removed or retained the child, or who prevented the exercise of rights of access, to pay necessary expenses incurred by or on behalf of the applicant, including travel expenses, any costs incurred or payments made for locating the child, the costs of legal representation of the applicant, and those of returning the child.

CHAPTER 8

CHILD SUPPORT

Parents have a moral and legal responsibility to support their minor children. Arizona law provides, "Every person has the duty to provide all reasonable support for that persons' natural and adopted minor, unemancipated children" (Ariz. Rev. Stat. § 25–501.A). California law states, "A parent's first and principle obligation is to support his or her minor children according to the parent's circumstances and station in life." (Cal. Family Code § 4053(a)). In Pennsylvania, "A parent has an absolute duty to support one's children." (*In re Ciotti*, 448 B.R. 694, 703 n.7 (W.D. Pa. 2011)).

When children reach the age of majority, the parents' duty of support ends. (*Estate of Wolfe,* 915 A.2d 1197 (Pa. Super. 2006)). As well, the duty of support generally ends when a child joins the military or marries.

The duty of child support applies whether or not parents marry. A parent can bring a civil action for child support in the appropriate court, and failure to pay court-ordered support is punishable by sanctions and contempt. As well, chronic failure to support one's children is a crime. (*See Commonwealth v. Marshall*, 345 S.W.3d 822 (Ky. 2011)). A parent who fails to pay child support can lose their driver's license, passport, or professional license. Child support enforcement officials seize tax refunds, garnish wages, attach bank accounts, and take lottery winnings.

Stepparents have no duty to continue supporting stepchildren when marriage ends. In *A.S. v. I.S.*, 130 A.3d 763 (Pa. 2015), the Pennsylvania Supreme Court discussed an exception to this rule known as parentage by estoppel. When a stepparent affirmatively holds himself out as a child's parent, the stepparent cannot disavow that status and the support duty that comes with it.

Most divorcing parents agree on the custody arrangement that is best for the children and on child support. The court will not second guess the child support amount agreed between parents unless the amount is not in the children's best interests. Parents cannot bind the court regarding child support. As the Pennsylvania appellate court put it in *Morgan v. Morgan*, 99 A.3d 554, 557 (Pa. Super. 2014), "They have no power, however, to bargain away the rights of their children."

§ 8–1 FEDERAL LEADERSHIP REGARDING CHILD SUPPORT

In 1935, during the height of the Great Depression, Congress passed the Social Security Act. Part of the Act created the program called Aid to Families with Dependent Children (AFDC). This program supplied federal funds to states to help support low income parents and children. Over the decades, AFDC provided a financial lifeline to millions of children. In 1996, AFDC was replaced with Temporary Assistance for Needy Families (TANF).

In addition to providing federal money to low income parents through AFDC and then TANF,

Congress was interested in finding ways to enforce the obligation parents have to support their children. Federal efforts to enforce child support grew into what is today a major federal commitment to funding child support enforcement. (*See* 45 CFR Parts 301 et seq.). At the federal level, the effort is led by the Office of Child Support Enforcement in the Administration for Children and Families in the Department of Health and Human Services.

At state and local levels, counties and parishes have a child support agency that establishes parentage, locates noncustodial parents, obtains and enforces child support orders, modifies child support orders, and collects and pays support to payees. Local child support enforcement offices are often referred to as Title IV-D agencies, after Title IV-D of the Social Security Act that authorizes and supports their work. Individuals receiving TANF are required to assign their right to child support to the local Title IV-D child support agency, which then pursues the obligor parent. In many counties, the child support agency assists parents who are not on TANF.

§ 8-2 UNIFORM INTERSTATE FAMILY SUPPORT ACT

States have the Uniform Interstate Family Support Act (UIFSA). The UIFSA works in tandem with the federal Full Faith and Credit for Child Support Orders Act (FFCCSOA) (28 U.S.C. § 1738B). The two laws establish procedures and jurisdictional rules regarding the creation and enforcement of child support orders across state lines. Only one state at a time has jurisdiction to make or modify child support. (*Hayes v. Hayes*, 49 N.E.3d 1030 (Ind. Ct. App. 2016); Margaret Campbell Haynes & Susan Friedman Paikin, "Reconciling" FFCCSOA and UIFSA, 49 *Family Law Quarterly* 331 (2015)).

A state that issues a child support order retains continuing, exclusive jurisdiction over support until and unless the court loses jurisdiction. The issuing state retains continuing jurisdiction so long as one of the parents or the child lives in the issuing state. The North Carolina Court of Appeals observed in *Lacarrubba v. Lacarrubba,* 202 N.C. App. 532, 688 S.E.2d 769 771 (2010), "Together, UIFSA and the Full Faith and Credit for Child Support Orders Act (FFCCSOA), 28 U.S.C. § 1738B, have severely limited the circumstances under which a state may modify a child support order issued by another state." For decisions explaining UIFSA, *see Chalmers v. Burrough,* 494 P.3d 128 (Kan. 2021); *Monteith v. Monteith,* 255 A.3d 1030 (Me. 2021); *Cohen v. Cohen,* 470 Mass. 708, 25 N.E.3d 840 (2015).

If both parents and the child have moved from the issuing state, another state may gain jurisdiction over support. Even though the issuing state has lost jurisdiction, its child support order is valid unless it is modified by the state that assumes jurisdiction.

A child support order from the state that issued the order (issuing state) may be registered and enforced in another state (responding state). The responding state may enforce the order but cannot modify it unless the state that issued the order no longer has jurisdiction. During the time the issuing state retains continuing jurisdiction, only it can modify support. However, multiple other states may enforce the issuing state's order.

To secure enforcement of a child support order in another state, the order is registered with the court of the responding state. The law of the responding state determines enforcement procedures, but the law of the issuing state controls the amount of child support owed, the duration of the support obligation, and the amount of any arrears.

§ 8-3 HOW MUCH CHILD SUPPORT?

In the first half of the twentieth century, the amount of child support in individual cases was left to the discretion of the judge. The judge looked at the number and ages of children, at which parent had custody, and at the income and wealth of the parents. The judge selected a child support amount that was fair under the circumstances. We may assume this system worked reasonably well. Yet, because there were few standards to guide decision making, and because no two judges are exactly alike, it was difficult to predict what judges would do. Given the same set of facts, one judge might set support at $100 per week, while the judge in the next courtroom might double that amount. Gradually, a consensus emerged that child support decisions should be more predictable. Today, states use formulas or guidelines to set child support.

Although child support formulas/guidelines differ somewhat from state to state, similarities outnumber differences. The formula/guideline considers parental income, which is defined broadly. (*In re Doherty*, 137 A.3d 393 (N.H. 2016)). The Florida statute, for example, defines income to include: salary or wages, bonuses, commissions, overtime, tips, all types of business income, disability benefits, worker's compensation, unemployment compensation, pensions, annuity payments, Social Security benefits, spousal support from a previous marriage, interest, dividends, rental income, income from royalties, trusts, or estates, reimbursements of any kind, reduced living expenses (*e.g.*, free rent), and any gains from property. (Fla. Stat. Ann. § 61.30(2)).

Most states employ a child support formula based on the Income Shares Model, which calculates support based on the income of both parents, coupled with consideration of how much time the children spend with each parent. (*See, e.g., McKeon v. Lennon*, 321 Conn. 323, 138 A.3d 242 (2016)). The income shares approach is based on the idea that both parents should contribute to child support. A small number of states use the Percent of Income Model, which considers primarily the income of the non-custodial parent. (*See* Laura W. Morgan, *Child Support Guidelines: Interpretation and Application*). In *Grabe v. Hokin*, 341 Conn. 360, 267 A.3d 145 (2021), the Connecticut Supreme Court wrote, "a noncustodial parent is not entitled to a child support award."

Indian tribes have their own rules regarding support. (*State v. Central Council of Tlingit and Haida Indian Tribes of Alaska*, 371 P.3d 255 (Alaska

2016)). For example, the Navajo Nation Child Support Guidelines are based on the Income Shares Model.

With income established, a limited number of deductions are allowed. In Florida, deductions include: income tax deductions, self-employment tax, mandatory union dues, mandatory retirement payments, health insurance payments, court-ordered support for other children (that is actually paid) and spousal support paid to a previous spouse. (Fla. Stat. Ann. § 61.30(2)(c)).

§ 8-4 IMPUTING INCOME

In some circumstances, judges impute or attribute income to a parent that the parent does not actually have. (*Damask v. Ryabchenko*, 329 So.3d 759 (Fla. Ct. App. 2021) ("A party's loss of employment due to misconduct is sufficient to support a finding that the termination of income was voluntary."); (*Mack v. Mack,* 169 A.D.3d 1214 (N.Y. 2019); *Pulham v. Kirsling*, 443 P.3d 1217 (Utah 2019)). Robert Rufus describes imputed income, "Earnings parents should have earned (*i.e.*, probable income) had they diligently pursued reasonable employment opportunities, or reasonably utilized, applied, or invested assets. Factors often considered by the courts when attributing income include, but are not limited to, the parent's education, training, work history, occupational qualifications, and employment potential." (Robert J. Rufus, Voluntary Reduction of Child Support Income: When Does an Economic Self-Improvement Plan Preclude Income Attribution?, 30

American Journal of Family Law 1, 3 (2016)). (*See Brossett v. Brossett*, 195 So.3d 471 (La. Ct. App. 2015); *Lasecki v. Lasecki,* 786 S.E.2d 286 (N.C. Ct. App. 2016)). Some states have statutes on attributing income. (Pa. R. Civ. Pro. 1910.16–2(d)(4); W. Va. Code § 48–1–205).

The North Dakota Supreme Court wrote in *Brouillet v. Brouillet,* 875 N.W.2d 485 (N.D. 2016), "When a child support obligor is underemployed, the district court may impute income to the obligor." The relevant Florida statute typifies the approach of most states. The Florida statute provides: "Monthly income shall be imputed to an unemployed or underemployed parent if such employment or underemployment is found by the court to be voluntary on that parent's part. . . . In the event of such voluntary unemployment or underemployment, the employment potential and probable earnings level of the parent shall be determined based upon his or her recent work history, occupational qualifications, and prevailing earnings level in the community if such information is available." (Fla. Stat. Ann. § 61.30(2)(b)). The Texas Supreme Court wrote, "A parent who is qualified to obtain gainful employment cannot evade his or her child support obligation by voluntarily remaining unemployed or underemployed." (*Iliff v. Iliff*, 339 S.W.3d 74 (Tex. 2011)).

Suppose a parent with a duty to pay child support decides to go to college or graduate school. The parent quits work or reduces work hours in order to devote time to school. May the student ask a judge to reduce child support because of the changed circumstance of school? In *Little v. Little*, 193 Ariz. 518, 975 P.2d 108 (1999), an Air Force officer resigned his commission, left the service, and entered law school. He sought a reduction of child support because he was a full time law student. The Arizona Supreme Court ruled against him.

In *Andrews v. Andrews*, 217 N.C. App. 154, 719 S.E.2d 154 (2011), John was employed as an engineer, earning more than $100,000 a year. John and Becky were divorced with two kids, and John was ordered to pay monthly child support of $1,496. John quit his high-paying job to "follow Jesus Christ," and start a church. When the church was up and running, John's salary as pastor was $52,800, approximately a 70% decrease in income. John filed a motion to reduce his child support. The trial court reduced his support, but the North Carolina Court of Appeals reversed. The appellate court wrote, "If a trial court determines that the party seeking the reduction of child support has acted in a manner that evidences a disregard for the child support obligation, the court may refuse to modify the support obligation. . . ." (719 S.E.2d at 157). Although the court did not question the sincerity of John's religious beliefs, the court ruled John's financial obligations to his children came first.

May a parent quit a high paying job to take a lower paying job that may eventually lead to more money? Courts take a case-by-case approach, always bearing in mind that a parent's first duty is to support her or his children. (*Melinda H. v. William R.*, 230 W. Va.

731, 742 S.E.2d 419 (2013); *Porter v. Bego*, 200 W. Va. 168, 488 S.E.2d 443 (1997)).

§ 8–5 HIGH INCOME PARENTS

Child support guidelines sometimes do not work well with wealthy parents. (*Doscher v. Doscher,* 137 A.D.3d 962, 27 N.Y.S.3d 231 (2016)). In *Smith v. Smith,* 786 S.E.2d 12 (N.C. Ct. App. 2016), the North Carolina Court of Appeals wrote, "For cases with higher combined monthly adjusted income, child support should be determined on a case-by-case basis." *See* Charles J. Meyer, Justin W. Soulen & Ellen Goldberg Weiner, Child Support Determinations in High Income Families—A Survey of the Fifty States, 28 *Journal of the American Academy of Matrimonial Lawyers* 483 (2016).

§ 8–6 CHILD SUPPORT INCLUDES HEALTH INSURANCE

Federal law requires states to include coverage for a child's health needs under the rubric of child support.

§ 8–7 DUTY TO SUPPORT DISABLED ADULT CHILD OR PARENT

Many states obligate parents to support adult disabled children. (*See Cutts v. Trippe,* 208 Md. App. 696, 57 A.3d 1006 (2012); *Guardianship of M.A.S.*, 363 Mont. 96, 266 P.3d 1267 (2011); Mo. Stat. Ann. § 452.340). Some states require children to support disabled parents.

Parents of seriously disabled children provide for their child when the child is young, and long after the child reaches the age of majority. Prince and Oliverio describe the considerable costs involved, including therapy, medications, various professional services, equipment, special diets, and respite care, just to name the most obvious. (Margaret S. Price & Ponzio Oliverio, The Costs of Raising a Special Needs Child After Divorce, 30 *American Journal of Family Law* 25 (2016)). Courts take such costs into consideration in ordering child support.

§ 8-8 PRIVATE SCHOOL AND COLLEGE TUITION

Parents are free as part of their marriage settlement contract to agree that they will pay for private school and/or college tuition. Courts enforce such agreements. It is one thing for a court to enforce a voluntary agreement to pay for private school or college. It is another to force an unwilling divorcing parent to pay such expenses. Some states have statutes authorizing judges to order such payments. In *Short v. Short*, 77 So. 3d 405 (La. Ct. App. 2011), the Louisiana Court of Appeals wrote, "A trial court may award child support for expenses of tuition, registration, books, and supply fees required for attending a special or private elementary or secondary school to meet the needs of the child. La. R.S. 9:315.6(1)." The Appellate Division of the New York Supreme Court wrote in *Maybaum v. Maybaum*, 89 A.D.3d 692, 933 N.Y.S.2d 43 (2011), "The court may direct a parent to contribute to a child's education, even in the absence of special circumstances or a voluntary agreement of the parties." The South Carolina Supreme Court wrote in *Burch v. Burch,* 395 S.C. 318, 717 S.E.2d 757 (2011), that child support "may include contributing to private school expenses where appropriate." The court noted that relevant factors include: (1) Is it in the child's best interest to attend private school? (2) Can the paying parent afford it? (3) Was the child attending private school before the divorce? (4) Would private schooling have continued in the absence of divorce? In *Smith v. Smith,* 786 S.E.2d 12 (N.C. Ct. App. 2016), the North Carolina Court of Appeals approved a trial court order that children continue attending private school in part because the children had been consistently enrolled in private school.

Turning from elementary and secondary school to college, may a court order divorcing parents to pay for college? Normally, the duty to pay child support ends when a child turns eighteen. States vary on whether parents can be ordered to pay for college. *See,* Mo. Stat. Ann. § 452.340(5) (support can continue for child enrolled in college and getting passing grades). In *McLeod v. Starnes,* 396 S.C. 647, 723 S.E.2d 198 (2012), the South Carolina Supreme Court ruled divorced parents can be ordered to pay college expenses. In *Marriage of Goodman,* 690 N.W.2d 279 (Iowa 2004), the Iowa Supreme Court wrote, "We have recently interpreted [Iowa Code Ann. § 598.21F] as not limiting college expenses to only tuition, room, and books."

§ 8–9 ARE CHILD SUPPORT AND VISITATION LINKED?

Millions of noncustodial parents who *could* pay child support don't. Many parents who refuse to support their children nevertheless insist on visiting them. Consider Sue and Tom. In their divorce, Sue got custody; Tom got visitation and a child support order. Tom has the money to pay support, but refuses to pay. Yet, Tom says, "I won't pay child support, but I insist on visitation."

On the other side of the coin, some custodial parents deliberately frustrate the noncustodial parent's visitation with the children. Examples range from last minute cancelled visits, at one end of the spectrum, to spiriting the kids out of the country, at the other. Consider Beth and Mike. In their divorce, Mike got custody. Beth has visits and must pay child support. Without telling Beth, Mike moves the children three thousand miles away. He does so *in order to* frustrate Beth's relationship with the kids. From his new home on the other side of the country, Mike insists that Beth pay child support.

The law has remedies for intentional failure to pay child support, and intentional interference with visitation. Injured parents can seek court orders enforcing their rights. In extreme cases, the court can hold a disobedient parent in contempt.

May a judge suspend the visitation rights of a noncustodial parent who deliberately withholds support? May a judge suspend or alter receipt of child support until a custodial parent stops interfering with visitation? In most states, the answer to both questions is "no." (*See* M.L. Cross, *Violation of Custody or Visitation Provision of Agreement or Decree as Affecting Child Support Payment Provision, and Vice Versa*, 95 A.L.R.2d 118 (1964); Edward L. Raymond, Jr., *Withholding Visitation Rights for Failure to Make Alimony or Support Payments*, 65 A.L.R. 4th 1155 (1988)). In most states, child support and visitation are independent; they are not linked. A parent who intentionally refuses to pay child support nevertheless is entitled to visitation. A parent who intentionally thwarts visitation is entitled to child support. In *Marriage of Popa*, 995 N.E.2d 521, 522, 374 Ill. Dec. 382 (Ct. App. 2013), the Illinois Court of Appeal wrote, "Child support payments cannot be linked to a custodial parent's violation of visitation terms." The West Virginia Supreme Court wrote in *Ledsome v. Ledsome*, 171 W. Va. 602, 301 S.E.2d 475, 477 (1983), "Ordinarily, a father's visitation rights may not be denied merely for nonpayment of child support."

Several states have statutes codifying the rule. In California, for example, the Family Code specifies that the duty to pay child support is not affected by the custodial parent's refusal to facilitate visitation. (Cal. Family Code § 3556). Kentucky is to the same effect: The duty to pay support "is not suspended" by a custodial parent's thwarting of visitation. (Ky. Rev. Stat. Ann. § 403.240(1)).

The majority rule is well established in California case law. (*In re Marriage of Damico,* 7 Cal. 4th 673, 872 P.2d 126, 29 Cal. Rptr. 2d 787 (1994); *Moffat v.*

Moffat, 27 Cal. 3d 645, 612 P.2d 967, 165 Cal. Rptr. 877 (1980)). The California Court of Appeals' decision in *Camacho v. Camacho,*173 Cal. App. 3d 214, 218 Cal. Rptr. 810 (1985), is a good illustration. An unwed father brought an action to establish paternity and obtain visitation. The trial court conditioned visitation on father's timely payment of child support. The Court of Appeal reversed. The appellate court noted statutory law that *requires* trial courts to grant visitation to noncustodial parents unless visitation would be detrimental to the child. The court acknowledged that the child's best interest is the most important consideration in determining visitation. The court concluded that the rule de-linking support and visitation preserves the parent-child relationship, thus furthering the child's interests. On the other hand, a parent who deliberately conceals a child from the other parent can be estopped from collecting child support arrearages. (*Stanislaus County Department of Child Support Services v. Jensen*, 112 Cal. App. 4th 453, 5 Cal. Rptr. 3d 178 (2003)).

In *Stevens v. Stevens,* 729 S.W.2d 461 (Ky. Ct. App. 1987), Nancy and Tom Stevens divorced. They were frequently in family court fighting over visitation and child support. Eventually, a trial judge relieved Tom of his child support duty until Nancy cooperated with visitation. The Court of Appeal reversed because a Kentucky statute provided: "If a party fails to comply with a provision of a decree or temporary order or injunction, the obligation of the other party to make payments for support or maintenance or to permit visitation is not suspended; but he may move the court to grant an appropriate order." The appellate court wrote that the statute "codifies the common law position that a failure of one party in a divorce action to fulfill his obligation does not relieve the other party of his obligation with respect to either child support or visitation rights. . . . [T]he public policy behind the statute is to insure that the child in question is adequately supported."

The majority rule has critics who argue that in cases of willful failure to support children and intentional interference with visitation, judges should have discretion to limit or suspend visitation or support. (*See* John E.B. Myers, "I won't pay child support, but I insist on Visitation." Should Visitation and Child Support Be Linked?, 45 *McGeorge Law Review* 695 (2014)).

In an occasional case, one parent's conduct is so egregious that a judge takes action. In *Coull v. Rottman*, 131 A.D.3d 964, 15 N.Y.S.2d 834 (2015), a child refused to visit his dad. The trial judge concluded that mother was deliberately alienating the child from the father. On several occasions, mother said she would never allow the father to see the child. The judge stopped the father's child support obligation, and the Appellate Division approved.

§ 8–10 MODIFICATION OF CHILD SUPPORT

States allow judges to modify child support on a showing of substantial changed circumstances. The parent seeking modification files a motion with the court setting forth the changed circumstances and asking for modification. The moving party has the burden of persuasion. (*Cheney v. Cheney*, 86 A.D.3d 833, 927 N.Y.S.2d 696, 699 (2011)). If the moving party carries the burden of proof, the judge looks at support anew. As the North Carolina Court of Appeal put it in *Meehan v. Meehan*, 166 N.C. App. 369, 602 S.E.2d 21, 28 (2004), "Modification of a child support order involves a two-step process. The court must first determine a substantial change of circumstances has taken place; only then does it proceed to . . . calculate the applicable amount of support."

Often, the parent seeking lower child support lost a job, and loss of employment can constitute substantial changed circumstances. In *Cheney v. Cheney*, 86 A.D.3d 833, 927 N.Y.S.2d 696, 699–700 (2011), the Appellate Division of the New York Supreme Court wrote, "A substantial change in circumstances may be shown when, despite diligent efforts, a party fails to find new employment after a job loss."

In *McCall v. McCall,* 2019 WL 350628 (Miss. Ct. App. 2019), the Mississippi Court of Appeals outlined some of the circumstances that can justify modification of child support: children's increased needs as they mature, inflation, the relative financial circumstances of the parents, and the health and special needs of children.

CHAPTER 9

SPOUSAL SUPPORT

This chapter addresses spousal support or as it is called in some states, maintenance or alimony. Historically, alimony arose from the fact that a husband controlled all property, including the wife's property. A husband was obliged to support the wife during marriage and afterward if the marriage ended in divorce. Originally, only husbands could be ordered to pay spousal support. In *Orr v. Orr,* 440 U.S. 268, 99 S. Ct. 1102 (1979), the U.S. Supreme Court ruled this gender-based approach unconstitutional.

§ 9-1 PURPOSE OF SPOUSAL SUPPORT

Spousal support is based on one spouse's need for financial support and the other spouse's ability to pay. (*Varty v. Varty,* 923 N.W.2d 131 (N.D. 2019); *Sweeny v. Sweeny,* 826 S.E.2d 299 (N.C. 2019) (ability of pay includes investment income); *Leaver v. Leaver,* 499 P.3d 222 (Wash. Ct. App. 2021) (a person's mental health issues can be relevant to need for support)). Spousal support is intended to allow the supported spouse to maintain the station in life that she or he enjoyed during marriage. (*Oudheusden v. Oudheusden,* 338 Conn. 761, 259 A.3d 598 (2021); *Marriage of Madden,* 923 N.W.2d 688 (Minn. Ct. App. 2019); *Putnam v. Putnam,* 863 S.E.2d 291 (N.C. Ct. App. 2021); *Miner v. Miner,* 496 P.3d 242 (Utah Ct. App. 2021); *Gildersleeve v. Gildersleeve,* 386 Wis. 2d 629, 927 N.W.2d 926 (2019). In *Dickert v. Dickert,* 387 S.C. 1, 691 S.E.2d 448 (2010), the South Carolina

Supreme Court described spousal support as "a substitute for the support that is normally incidental to the marital relationship. Generally, alimony should place the supported spouse, as nearly as is practical, in the same position he or she enjoyed during the marriage." In a similar vein, the Wisconsin Supreme Court wrote in *McReath v. McReath*, 800 N.W.2d 399, 412 (Wis. 2011), "There are two objectives that an award of maintenance seeks to meet. The first objective is support of the payee spouse. This objective may not be met by merely maintaining the payee spouse at a subsistence level. Rather, maintenance should support the payee spouse at the pre-divorce standard. This standard should be measured by the lifestyle that the parties enjoyed in the years immediately before the divorce and could anticipate enjoying if they were to stay married. The second objective is fairness, which aims to compensate the recipient spouse for contributions made to the marriage, give effect to the parties' financial arrangements, or prevent unjust enrichment of either party."

§ 9–2 TYPES OF SPOUSAL SUPPORT

In *Gnall v. Gnall*, 222 N.J. 414, 119 A.3d 891 (2015), the New Jersey Supreme Court described four kinds of spousal support. First, permanent support, which is intended to support the dependent spouse at the same lifestyle as during the marriage. Second, limited duration support following a relatively short marriage. Third, rehabilitative support, which is provided for a limited term to support a spouse while she or he prepares to re-enter the workforce. Fourth, reimbursement support to assist a spouse who sacrificed to allow the other to obtain an advanced degree.

The Illinois Appellate Court described rehabilitative support in *Marriage of S.D.*, 980 N.E.2d 1151, 366 Ill. Dec. 792 (Ct. App. 2012), as providing "a spouse with an opportunity to adjust to life after a divorce and become self-sufficient."

When a divorce case begins, the judge can order temporary spousal support while the case proceeds. (*Marriage of Pletcher,* 68 Cal. App. 5th 906, 283 Cal. Rptr. 3d 728 (2021)).

§ 9-3 CASE-BY-CASE APPROACH TO SPOUSAL SUPPORT

Courts take a case-by-case approach to requests for spousal support. The judge has broad discretion to award appropriate spousal support. (*Carter v. Oliver*, 201 A.3d 582 (D.C. 2019); *Connor v. Benedict*, 481 Mass. 567, 118 N.E.3d 96 (2019); *Matter of Henry*, 163 N.H. 175, 37 A.3d 320 (2012)). As the Wisconsin Supreme Court put it in *McReath v. McReath*, 800 N.W.2d 399, 412–413 (Wis. 2011), "It is within the circuit court's discretion to determine the amount and duration of maintenance."

States have statutes listing factors to consider in awarding spousal support. The California statute is typical: "In ordering spousal support . . . , the court shall consider all of the following circumstances: (a) The extent to which the earning capacity of each party is sufficient to maintain the standard of living established during the marriage, taking into account all of the following: (1) The marketable skills of the supported party; the job market for those skills; and the time and expenses required for the supported party to acquire the appropriate education or training to develop those skills; and the possible need for retraining or education to acquire other, more marketable skills or employment. (2) The extent to which the supported party's present or future earning capacity is impaired by periods of unemployment that were incurred during the marriage to permit the supported spouse to devote time to domestic duties. (b) The extent to which the supported party contributed to the attainment of an education, training, a career position, or a license by the supporting party. (c) The ability of the supporting party to pay spousal support, taking into account the supporting party's earning capacity, earned and unearned income, assets, and standard of living. (d) The needs of each party based on the standard of living established during the marriage. (e) The obligations and assets, including the separate property, of each party. (f) The duration of the marriage. (g) The ability of the supported party to engage in gainful employment without unduly interfering with the interests of dependent children in the custody of the party. (h) The age and health of the parties. (i) Documented evidence of any history of domestic violence . . . between the parties, including, but not limited to, consideration of emotional distress resulting from domestic violence perpetrated against the supported party by the supporting party, and consideration of any history of violence against the supporting party by the supported party. (j) The immediate and specific tax consequences to each party. (k) The balance of hardships to each party. (*l*) The goal that the supported party shall be self-supporting within a reasonable period of time. Except in the case of a marriage of long duration [10 years], a "reasonable period of time" for purposes of this section shall be one-half the length of the marriage. However, nothing in this section is intended to limit the court's discretion to order support for a greater or lesser length of time, based on any of the other factors listed in this section . . . and the circumstances of the parties. (m) The criminal conviction of an abusive spouse shall be considered in making a reduction or elimination of a spousal support award [to an abusive spouse]. (n) Any other factors the court determines are just and equitable." (Cal. Family Code § 4320).

Length of marriage is a factor in awarding spousal support. (*O'Neill v. O'Neill*, 209 Conn. App. 165 (2021)). Massachusetts deals explicitly with this factor. For marriages less than five years in length, spousal support cannot be longer than half the number of months married. The percent goes up with the length of the marriage. In Massachusetts, the judge can add the length of premarital cohabitation to the length of the marriage. (*Connor v. Benedict*, 481 Mass. 567, 118 N.E.3d 96 (2019)).

If divorcing spouses are relatively young and able to work, the judge may award no spousal support. If support is awarded, it may be limited to a number of years with the idea that the supported spouse should become financially self-sufficient. In *McReath v. McReath*, 800 N.W.2d 399, 413 (Wis. 2011), the Wisconsin Supreme Court explained, "The payment of maintenance is not to be viewed as a permanent annuity. Rather, maintenance is designed to maintain a party at an appropriate standard of living, under the facts and circumstances of the individual case, until the party exercising reasonable diligence has reached a level of income where maintenance is no longer necessary." The Appellate Division of the New York Supreme Court explained in *Wheeler v. Wheeler,* 12 A.D.3d 982, 983, 785 N.Y.S.2d 170 (2004), "It is settled that the purpose of maintenance is to provide temporary support while the recipient develops the skills and experience necessary to become self-sufficient." The Florida Court of Appeal added in *Demont v. Demont,* 67 So.3d 1096 (Fla. Ct. App. 2011), "Even if a spouse is employable, an alimony award effectively rehabilitating the spouse in making the transition from married life to single status can be justified as a 'bridge-the-gap measure.'" The North Dakota Supreme Court wrote in *Nuveen v. Nuveen*, 795 N.W.2d 308, 316 (N.D. 2011), "A district court may award a spouse either rehabilitative or permanent spousal support. Rehabilitative spousal support is awarded to equalize the burdens of divorce or to restore an economically disadvantaged spouse to independent status by providing a disadvantaged spouse with an opportunity to acquire an education, training, work skills, or experience to become self-supporting. Rehabilitative support is appropriate when one spouse has bypassed opportunities or lost advantages as a consequence of the marriage or when one spouse has contributed during the marriage to the other's increased earning capacity or moved to further the other's career."

Divorcing spouses may agree to gradually decreasing spousal support, often called step-down support. (*Marriage of Khera and Sameer*, 206 Cal. App. 4th 1467, 143 Cal. Rptr. 3d 81 (2012)).

Permanent spousal support usually is reserved for long marriages, especially marriages in which the supported spouse has not worked at all or in decades. The North Dakota Supreme Court explained in *Nuveen, supra,* "Permanent spousal support is appropriate when the economically disadvantaged spouse cannot be equitably rehabilitated to make up for the opportunities and development she lost during the course of the marriage. Permanent spousal support is awarded to provide traditional maintenance for a spouse incapable of adequate rehabilitation or self-support. Permanent spousal support may be appropriate if there is a substantial disparity in earning capacity and a substantial income disparity that cannot be adjusted through property division or rehabilitative support." (795 N.W.2d at 316).

§ 9-4 FAULT AND SPOUSAL SUPPORT

During the fault era of divorce prior to the 1970s (*See* Chapter 3), spousal support was generally not available to a spouse whose fault led to breakup of the marriage. Today, there is less emphasis on fault. Yet, in some states fault remains a factor in determining spousal support. (*McCarron v. McCarron,* 168 So. 3d 68 (Ala. Civil App. 2015); *Diggs v. Diggs*, 6 So.3d 1030 (La. Ct. App. 2009); *Hammond v. Hammond*, 327 So. 3d 173 (Miss. Ct. App. 2021)). The California statute quoted above lists domestic violence as a factor influencing an award of support. The South Carolina statute provides, "In making an award of alimony . . . , the court must consider and give weight in such proportion as it finds appropriate [to] marital misconduct or fault of either or both parties." (S.C. Code Ann. § 20–3–130(C)(10). *See Weller v. Weller*, 863 S.E.2d 835 (S.C. Ct. App. 2021)). In *Giraldi v. Giraldi,* 64 Va. App. 676, 771 S.E.2d 687, 691 (2015), the Virginia Court of Appeals wrote, "Adultery is a fault ground for divorce . . . , and, therefore, a finding that a party has committed adultery generally is an absolute bar to the adulterous party from receiving spousal support. . . ."

§ 9–5 IMPUTING INCOME

An award of spousal support depends on need and ability to pay. In appropriate circumstances, a judge can "impute" income to a supporting or a supported spouse. (*Brendle v. Roberts-Brendle,* 169 A.D.3d 752 (N.Y. 2018); *Miner v. Miner,* 496 P.3d 242 (Utah Ct. App. 2021)). Thus, when a supported spouse is able to work but chooses to remain unemployed or underemployed, the judge may impute income to the supported spouse, and decrease support accordingly. The same is true for a supporting spouse—the judge may impute income that would be available for support if the supporting spouse applied her or himself. In *Hartvigsen v. Hartvigsen,* 437 P.3d 1257

(Utah Ct. App. 2018), the Utah Court of Appeals observed, "Imputation, by definition, contemplates a degree of speculation. Indeed, the statute allows courts to impute income based upon employment potential and probable earnings." The Appellate Division of New York Supreme Court wrote in *Matter of Rubley v. Longworth*, 35 A.D.3d 1129, 1130, 825 N.Y.S.2d 839 (2006) that the trial judge is "not bound by a [spouse's] account of his or her own finances, and may impute income based upon prior employment experience, as well as such [spouse's] future earning capacity in light of that [spouse's] educational background." (*See* Utah Code Ann. § 78B–12–203; *Fish v. Fish*, 242 P.3d 787 (Utah 2010); David W. Griffin, Earning Capacity and Imputing Income for Child Support Calculations: A Survey and Outline of Practice Tips, 26 *Journal of the American Academy of Matrimonial Lawyers* 365 (2014)).

Can a spouse be forced to take a higher paying job in order to pay more spousal support? No. Consider the following facts, based on *Marriage of Kochan*, 193 Cal. App. 4th 420, 122 Cal. Rptr. 3d 61 (2011). Elizabeth has been a judge on the family court bench for 15 years and is regarded as a superb judge. Elizabeth's salary as a judge is $195,000 per year. Elizabeth and her husband Dan are divorcing. Dan is a teacher, with an annual salary of $60,000. In the divorce, Dan seeks spousal support, joint custody of their fifteen-year-old daughter, and child support. Dan argues that Elizabeth could double her income by resigning from the bench and becoming a "private judge." People hire "private judges" to help them resolve disputes without formal litigation. Assume

Dan is right, Elizabeth could double her income by becoming a private judge. Elizabeth, however, has no interest in resigning, and plans to remain on the bench until retirement which is at least five years in the future. In the divorce case, Dan argues that when setting spousal and child support the judge should use what Elizabeth *could* earn as a private judge, not what she does earn as a sitting judge. Dan's argument will be rejected.

When an older couple divorces, one or both spouses may be old enough to begin receiving Social Security retirement. The federal government does not automatically send Social Security checks when a person reaches the age at which Social Security becomes available. A person must apply for benefits. John, who is 68, and Joan, who is 60, are divorcing after a long marriage. Joan seeks spousal support, and argues that John should be ordered to apply for Social Security so he will have more income to pay support. John argues that he does not intend to apply for Social Security until later in life, when his monthly checks will be greater. Can the judge order John to apply for Social Security? There is little law on this question, but the answer seems to be no. (*McKernan v. McKernan*, 135 A.3d 1116 (Pa. Super. 2016)). Nor would it be proper to impute Social Security income to John.

§ 9–6 VOCATIONAL EVALUATION

In an appropriate case a court may order a vocational evaluation. The evaluator interviews the person, administers vocational tests, examines the person's work history and education as well as the person's health. The evaluator researches job opportunities. (Brett R. Turner, Earning Capacity and Spousal Support: The Uses and Abuses of Vocational Evidence in Divorce Cases, 14 *Divorce Litigation* 213 (2002); Martin A. Kranitz, Understanding the Vocational Evaluation, 35 *Family Advocate* 38 (2012)).

§ 9–7 DEATH, COHABITATION, OR REMARRIAGE

Generally, spousal support ends if a supported spouse remarries or cohabits with an intimate partner. (*Schaffeld v. Schaffeld*, 824 S.E.2d 735 (Ga. Ct. App. 2019); *McQuarrie v. McQuarrie*, 496 P.3d 44 (Utah 2021)). As well, spousal support ends if the supported or supporting spouse dies. (*Quinn v. Quinn*, 225 N.J. 34, 137 A.3d 423 (2016)). California law is typical, providing: "Except as otherwise agreed by the parties in writing, the obligation of a party under an order for the support of the other party terminates upon the death of either party or the remarriage of the other party." (Cal. Family Code § 4337). The parties are free in their divorce to agree otherwise. (*Marriage of Martin*, 32 Cal.App.5th 1195 (2019)).

§ 9–8 LIFE INSURANCE TO GUARANTEE SPOUSAL SUPPORT

As mentioned above, spousal support typically ends when the supporting spouse dies. A divorcing couple can agree that spousal support will continue after the supporting spouse dies and in these circumstances the couple may agree that the supporting spouse will purchase life insurance with the supported spouse named as the beneficiary. (*See, e.g., Brown v. Brown,* 348 N.J. Super. 792 A.2d 463, 474 (2002); *DiLascio v. DiLascio,* 170 A.D.3d 804 (N.Y. A.D. 2019)).

§ 9–9 MODIFICATION OF SPOUSAL SUPPORT

Spousal support can be modified on a showing of substantial changed circumstances. (*Zink v. Zink,* 147 A.3d 75 (Vt. 2016)). Perhaps the supporting spouse is laid off. (*Nielsen v. Nielsen,* 73 Va. App. 370, 860 S.E.2d 397 (2021)). Perhaps the supported spouse wins the lottery. The party seeking modification files a motion for modification. The moving party has the burden of proving substantial changed circumstances that warrant a fresh look at support.

§ 9–10 PLANNING FOR RETIREMENT AT TIME OF DIVORCE

Couples divorcing in their twenties or thirties probably think little about retirement, decades in the future. For these couples, by the time retirement rolls around, the kids will be grown and child support will be a faded memory. Property is divided at the time of divorce. It is true that pension issues can re-surface at retirement, but pensions, like other property, are largely settled at divorce. In many short marriages there is no spousal support order. Even if spousal support is ordered, the typical order is not for lifetime support. It is not surprising that many young divorcing couples do not plan specifically for retirement. Beyond taking care of pensions, retirement planning is often unnecessary.

But what about couples who marry later in life? It is not uncommon today for people to get married in their fifties or sixties. In addition to couples who marry later in life, thousands of divorcing couples have been married 30 or 40 years. When older couples divorce, planning for retirement needs to be part of the equation. An obvious example concerns spousal support. With long marriages, permanent or indeterminate spousal support orders are common. What happens when the supporting spouse retires and experiences decreased income? May the supporting spouse return to court and seek lower spousal support? Suppose it is the supported spouse who retires? May the supported spouse return to court and seek increased spousal support? (*See Valitutto v. Valitutto,* 137 A.D.3d 1526, 28 N.Y.S.3d 472 (2016) (in this case, the court awarded spousal support that was to continue until the husband retired)).

Courts generally hold that retirement at normal retirement age can constitute a change of circumstances justifying adjustment of spousal support. (*Landers v. Landers*, 444 N.J. Super. 315, 133 A.3d 637 (2016); *Marriage of Reaves*, 236 Or. App. 313, 236 P.3d 803 (2010); *McKernan v. McKernan*, 135 A.3d 1116 (Pa. Super. 2016)). The Colorado Court of Appeals observed in *Marriage of*

Swing, 194 P.3d 498, 501 (Colo. Ct. App. 2008), "The majority rule appears to be that reduced income due to a spouse's objectively reasonable decision to retire, made in good faith and not with the intention of depriving the other spouse of support, should be recognized as a basis for modifying maintenance." In a similar vein, the California Court of Appeal wrote in *Marriage of Shimkus*, 244 Cal. App. 4th 1262, 1277, 198 Cal. Rptr. 3d 799 (2016), "A prerequisite to modification or termination of spousal support is a material change of circumstances. . . . Where there is a bona fide retirement, it may be considered a material change of circumstances justifying a modification of spousal support. Just as a married couple may expect a reduction in income due to retirement, a divorced spouse cannot expect to receive the same high level of support after the supporting spouse retires."

Massachusetts has a statute dealing directly with retirement and spousal support. Massachusetts provides that alimony "shall terminate upon the payor attaining the full retirement age. The payor's ability to work beyond the full retirement age shall not be a reason to extend alimony." (Mass. Laws. Ch. 208, § 49(f)). Despite the law, a divorcing couple may agree to alimony beyond retirement. The Massachusetts statute allows a judge to extend support in limited circumstances.

§ 9–11 TRUST INCOME AND CHILD AND SPOUSAL SUPPORT OBLIGATIONS

A trust is a three way fiduciary relationship in which one person holds legal title to property for the benefit of another. The person who creates and funds a trust is the settlor or trustor. The person or entity holding legal title is the trustee. The beneficiary is the person(s) for whose benefit the trust is established.

Divorcing couples sometimes agree that the spouse with support duties will establish a trust to ensure payment of spousal or child support. In most states, the judge has authority to order such a trust. (*Spicer v. Spicer*, 168 N.C. App. 283, 607 S.E.2d 678 (2005) (trial court ordered dad to create a child support trust)).

A spendthrift is someone who is financially irresponsible. A spendthrift trust is set up (often by the spendthrift's parents) to protect the spendthrift from her or himself. With a spendthrift trust, the beneficiary—the spendthrift—cannot sell or give away trust property. Nor can the spendthrift's creditors attach the trust property to satisfy the spendthrift's debts. Of course, not all beneficiaries of spendthrift trusts are financially irresponsible—most are not. Nevertheless, spendthrift clauses are a common tool to protect trust assets from creditors.

When a former spouse who has child or spousal support obligations is the beneficiary of a spendthrift trust, and the beneficiary fails to make support payments, the supported spouse is a creditor.

Normally, creditors cannot invade a spendthrift trust to secure payment. A supported former spouse, however, is not a "normal" creditor. Most states place limits on the extent to which spendthrift trusts can defeat child or spousal support duties. (*See* Cal. Probate Code § 15305; Wis. Stat. Ann. § 701.06(4)). In some states, a supported spouse can satisfy support obligations from a spendthrift trust so long as non-trust assets are first exhausted. (*Mason v. Mason*, 798 So. 2d 895 (Fla. Ct. App. 2001); M.L. Cross, Trust Income or Assets as Subject to Claim Against Beneficiary for Alimony, Maintenance, or Child Support, 91 A.L.R.2d 292 (1963)).

The California Court of Appeal, in *Ventura County Department of Child Support Services v. Brown*, 117 Cal. App. 4th 144, 154–155 11 Cal. Rptr. 3d 489 (2004), considered the "deadbeat dad" of six children by three women. Dad did not support any of his kids. Dad's mother established a spendthrift trust for her son. The trustee refused to disburse trust income to pay dad's child support obligations. The Court of Appeal disapproved, writing, "Even if the trust instrument contains a spendthrift clause applicable to claims for child support, it is against public policy to give effect to the provision. As a general rule, the beneficiary should not be permitted to have the enjoyment of the interest under the trust while neglecting his or her dependents." In a similar vein, the Michigan Court of Appeals held in *Hurley v. Hurley*, 107 Mich. App. 249, 254, 309 N.W.2d 225 (1981) that the public policy requiring parents to support their children "outweighs the public policy that an owner of property, such as the settlor of a trust, may dispose of it as he pleases and may impose spendthrift restraints on the disposition of income."

A discretionary support trust is a trust set up to support/benefit a beneficiary. For example, grandparents might create discretionary support trusts for their grandkids, naming themselves—grandpa and grandma—as trustees. As described by the Iowa Supreme Court in *Emmet County Board of Supervisors v. Ridout*, 692 N.W.2d 821, 826 (Iowa 2005), "A settlor creates a discretionary support trust when the purpose of the trust is to furnish the beneficiary with support, and the trustee has the discretion to pay the income or principal to the beneficiary, as the trustee deems necessary for the support of the beneficiary." Discretionary support trusts nearly always contain a spendthrift clause. Guided by the terms of the trust, the trustee has broad discretion to make payments from the trust for the benefit of the beneficiary. Generally, the beneficiary cannot insist on payment from the trust. It is up to the trustee to decide when, why, and how much to pay.

Suppose Hank is divorcing Sally. Some years back, Hank's parents created a discretionary support trust for Hank, containing a spendthrift provision. Hank's parents are the trustees. At the time of the divorce, Hank is not receiving any money from the trust. In the divorce, Sally seeks spousal support. Sally asks the family court judge to include in Hank' income the amount Hank *could* receive from the trust *if* the trustees decided to pay. Hank responds, "I'm not getting *any* money from the trust. I have no income from the trust, and I can't force the trustees to give me any. My income for spousal support purposes does not include money I don't have and can't get." Sally asks the judge to impute income from the trust to Hank. Hank is likely to prevail.

Most cases dealing with trusts and duties of support involve a trust beneficiary with a duty of support. (*See, e.g., Pfannenstiehl v. Pfannenstiehl*, 475 Mass. 105, 55 N.E.3d 933 (2016); *In re Goodlander and Tamposi*, 161 N.H. 490, 20 A.3d 199 (2011)). But what if the trust beneficiary is the party *seeking* support? Should income from a trust be considered in calculating the need for spousal or child support? If a trustee actually distributes income to a beneficiary, the money is income. But what if the trustee of a discretionary support trust with a spendthrift provision is not distributing available income to a beneficiary? The money is sitting in the trust and *could* be distributed, but the trustee decides not to let go of the money. As long as the trustee is carrying out the terms of the trust, the beneficiary cannot compel the trustee to distribute money. Is money that a trustee *could but doesn't* disburse income? In *Marriage of Rhinehart*, 704 N.W.2d 677, 681 (Iowa 2005), the supported spouse, Deborah, was the beneficiary of a trust. The Iowa Supreme Court wrote, "Deborah has no right to the allocated, but undistributed, income from the trust. Consequently, it would not be appropriate to treat the *undistributed* income from the trust as a current source of financial support that would alleviate Deborah's need for alimony."

The Connecticut Appellate Court grappled with this issue in *Taylor v. Taylor,* 117 Conn. App. 229, 978 A.2d 538 (2009). Marvin and Elinor Taylor divorced after forty years of marriage. Marvin was ordered to pay Elinor $5,000 per month alimony. Five years later, Marvin filed a motion in family court to reduce alimony because Elinor had become a beneficiary of a discretionary support trust with a spendthrift provision. The trial judge found that the trust earned more than enough income to support Elinor, and reduced alimony from $5,000 per month to $1 per year. Elinor appealed. The trustees were not actually paying trust income to Elinor—she didn't need it because she was getting alimony! In virtually eliminating Marvin's alimony obligation, the trial court considered income the trustees *could* give to Elinor *if* they decided to pay her. In essence, the trial court imputed trust income to Elinor. The Appellate Court reversed, ruling that the trial court had no authority to enter an order that basically compelled the trustees to make distributions to Elinor or leave her out in the cold. The Appellate Court wrote, "The well-settled rule in this state is that the exercise of discretion by the trustee of a spendthrift trust is subject to the court's control only to the extent that an abuse has occurred. There has been no claim raised that the trustees have abused their discretion in not making any distributions to [Elinor]. The court improperly interpreted the provisions of the trust agreement when, in effect, it assumed that the trustees were obligated to distribute the income to [Elinor]. . . . Until [Elinor] receives a distribution from the supplemental spendthrift trust, the undistributed income from the trust itself cannot be considered as income to [Elinor]. . . . We conclude, therefore, that it was an abuse of discretion for the court to consider the undistributed trust assets as income to [Elinor] when the court . . . reduced [Marvin's] alimony obligation to [Elinor] to $1 per year." (978 A.2d at 543–544).

§ 9–12 RELATIONSHIP BETWEEN SPOUSAL SUPPORT AND PROPERTY DIVISION: THE PROBLEM OF DOUBLE DIPPING

Property division and spousal support serve different yet interrelated purposes. (*Sampson v. Sampson*, 62 Mass. App. 366, 816 N.E.2d 999, 1002–1003 (2004)). An issue at the intersection of property and support is whether income from income producing property awarded to one spouse in the divorce should be considered income for purposes of determining support. (*See Marriage of Dahm-Schell and Schell,* 2021 IL 126802 (Ill. 2021); *Grunfeld v. Grunfeld*, 94 N.Y.2d 696, 731 N.E.2d 142, 709 N.Y.S.2d 486 (2000); *Sieber v. Sieber*, 37 N.E.3d 776 (Ohio Ct. App. 2015)). In *Sampson v. Sampson,* 62 Mass. App. 366, 816 N.E.2d 999, 1006 (2004), the Massachusetts Appeals Court wrote, "Commentators use the phrase 'double dipping' to describe the seeming injustice that occurs when property is awarded to one spouse in an equitable distribution of marital assets and is then also considered as a source of income for purposes of imposing support obligations. Courts and commentators have often disagreed, as to what constitutes double-dipping, whether double-dipping ought to be prohibited as a matter of law, and if not so prohibited, whether it is inequitable in the circumstances of the particular divorce settlement." (*See* Laura W. Morgan (Note) "Double Dipping": A Good Theory Gone Bad, 25 *Journal of the American Academy of Matrimonial Lawyers* 133 (2012)).

Consider Sue and Tom who were married 20 years. They divorced five years ago. During the marriage, Sue worked for the Acme Company for 15 years, and had a defined benefit pension through Acme. On divorce, the pension, which was marital/community property, was valued at $100,000, and was awarded to Sue. Tom received $50,000 in other marital/community property to equalize the property division. In the divorce, Sue was ordered to pay spousal support to Tom in the amount of $500 per month. Sue recently retired from Acme after twenty years' service, and started drawing her pension. Because Sue retired, her income decreased, and Sue filed a motion in family court seeking to eliminate her $500/month spousal support obligation. In reply, Tom argues that Sue's pension is income, and when her pension income is combined with other income, Sue has enough income to continue paying $500/month spousal support. Sue argues that it would be wrong to count her pension as income because she had been awarded the pension in the division of property, five years earlier. To count her pension as income would unfairly count the pension twice, once at the time of divorce, and again as income at retirement.

Wisconsin courts have grappled with double counting pension awards in divorce. (*McReath v. McReath,* 800 N.W.2d 399 (Wis. 2011)). One solution employed in Wisconsin is to allow the retired spouse to receive the value of the pension assigned to the spouse in the divorce—in Sue's case, $100,000—before the pension is considered income in determining support. California courts reject the double dipping argument in most scenarios. In *Marriage of White*, 192 Cal. App. 3d 1022, 1027, 237 Cal. Rptr. 764 (1987), for example, husband received his entire pension in the divorce, while wife got the family home. It was proper to consider husband's retirement income for purposes of determining spousal support. The Court of Appeal wrote, "Double counting of a pension occurs only on those occasions when jurisdiction is reserved over the pension, and it is divided in kind as payments fall due. Then each spouse is, properly speaking, an owner of a portion of those benefits and it would be incorrect to attribute the whole to either spouse for alimony determination purposes. When, however, all marital property division is effected at divorce and one spouse is awarded the entire pension, it is not in any way improper to consider the pension benefits as entirely [the supporting spouse's] income for purposes of alimony determination."

In an article title "The Validity of 'Double Dipping,'" Gene Trevino writes, "In the case of pensions, the double-dipping argument is valid. . . . In the case of income-producing real estate, the double dipping argument is not valid." *American Journal of Family Law*, vol. 30, pp. 145–149, at 145

(2016). Trevino points out that the double-dipping issue becomes complex in the context of closely held businesses.

§ 9-13 IS SPOUSAL SUPPORT JUSTIFIABLE TODAY?

Why should spousal support *ever* be awarded? Why should one former spouse be required to support the other former spouse? The marriage is over. The parties have gone separate ways. Shouldn't each former spouse provide for her or himself? If you live with someone in a non-marital romantic relationship for ten years and the relationship ends, you do not have a legal duty to support your former lover. Why should it be different if it was a ten year marriage?

This short treatise is not the place to debate spousal support. The interested reader is referred to the following resources: Mary Kay Kisthardt, Re-Thinking Alimony, 21 *Journal of the American Academy of Matrimonial Lawyers* 61 (2008); Cynthia Lee Starnes, Alimony Theory, 45 *Family Law Quarterly* 271 (2011).

CHAPTER 10

PROPERTY ISSUES IN FAMILY LAW

This chapter discusses property issues in family law. The subject is vast and the law varies from state to state. In addition to state property law, federal law, in particular tax law, law governing pensions, and bankruptcy law, play roles in family law cases. Much of the day-to-day work of family law attorneys focuses on property.

§ 10–1 CONTRACTS REGARDING PROPERTY; FIDUCIARY DUTIES

Individuals in intimate relationships can contract with each other regarding property. (*Oshinaike v. Oshinaike*, 140 A.3d 1206 (D.C. 2016); *Steele v. Steele*, 467 N.J. Super. 414, 253 A.3d 1190 (2021)). As the Kentucky Supreme Court put it in *Davis v. Davis*, 489 S.W.3d 225 (Ky. 2016), "Kentucky has a long history of enforcing contacts between spouses." Contracts between unmarried cohabitants who are not planning to marry are called cohabitation agreements or *Marvin* agreements, after the California Supreme Court's decision in *Marvin v. Marvin*, 18 Cal. 3d 660, 557 P.2d 106, 134 Cal. Rptr. 815 (1976) (Chapter 4). Prior to marriage, a couple intending to marry may enter into a premarital contract (Chapter 3). During the course of an intact marriage, a married couple may agree to change ownership of some or all of their property, often called a transmutation agreement. A couple may contract regarding what happens to property when one or both dies. A married couple intending to divorce may enter a contract to settle issues related to property, support, and child custody, often called a marriage settlement agreement or MSA.

Married persons are in a fiduciary relationship and owe each other obligations of honesty and fair dealing. (*See* Ann Crawford McClure & John F. Nochols, Sr., Fraud, Fiduciaries, and Family Law, 43 *Texas Tech Law Review* 1801 (2011)). Remedies are available when one spouse gains an unfair financial advantage over the other.

§ 10–2 SYSTEMS OF MARITAL PROPERTY

In the United States, real and personal property acquired during marriage is either marital property belonging to both spouses, or separate/non-marital property belonging to one spouse. To oversimplify, on divorce, separate/non-marital property belongs to the spouse who owns the property. Marital property is divided, either equally or equitably, depending on the jurisdiction.

States employ one of two systems of marital property: equitable distribution or community property. In both systems the fundamental principle is the same: Property acquired or possessed during marriage through the time, effort, energy, or skill of one or both spouses is presumed to be marital/ community property, belonging to both spouses. (*See Succession of Barrois,* 184 So. 3d 230 (La. Ct. App. 2016); *Brozek v. Brozek,* 874 N.W.2d 17, 31 (Neb. 2016); *Silvers v. Silvers,* 197 A.D.3d 1195, 153 N.Y.S.3d 548 (2021); *Marroquin v. Marroquin,* 440

P.3d757 (Utah Ct. App. 2019); *Schwarz v. Schwarz,* 192 Wash. App. 180, 368 P.3d 173 (2016)).

Marital/community property is based on the idea that marriage is a partnership to which both spouses contribute. (*Contis v. Contis,* 789 S.E.2d 51 (S.C. Ct. App. 2016)). Thus, a married person's pay check is marital/community property. So are retirement benefits earned during marriage. (*Fleece v. Fleece,* 185 So. 3d 90 (La. Ct. App. 2016); *Cornwell v. Cornwell,* 309 Neb. 156, 959 N.W.2d 243 (2021)).

In equitable distribution states, marital property is divided equitably on divorce. (Del. Code Ann. Title 13, § 1513). Many equitable distribution states begin with the presumption that it is equitable to divide marital property equally. (*See Sinkovitz v. Sinkovitz,* 64 N.E.3d 382 (Ohio Ct. App. 2016); *In re Munson,* 169 N.H. 274, 146 A.3d 153 (2016)). In *Silvers v. Silvers,* 197 A.D.3d 1195, 153 N.Y.S.3d 548, 552 (2021), the New York Appellate Division wrote, "Equitable distribution of marital property does not necessarily mean equal distribution. Rather, the equitable distribution of marital assets must be based on the circumstances of the particular case and the considerations of a number of statutory factors. Those factors include: the income and property of each party at the time of marriage and at the time of commencement of the divorce action; the duration of the marriage; the age and health of the parties; the loss of inheritance and pension rights; any award of maintenance; any equitable claim to, interest in, or direct or indirect contribution made to the acquisition of marital property by the party not having title; and any other factor which the court shall expressly find to be just and proper. While equitable distribution does not necessarily mean equal division, when both spouses have made significant contribution to a marriage of long duration, the division of marital property should be as equal as possible."

The community property states are: Arizona, California, Idaho, Louisiana, Nevada, New Mexico, Texas, Washington, and Wisconsin. In community property states, community property is divided equally or equitably, depending on the state. In Texas, a family court judge divides the marital estate in a "just and right" manner. The division does not have to be equal. (*Marriage of Hardin,* 572 S.W.3d 310 (Tex. Ct. App. 2019); *Marriage of Bradshaw*, 487 S.W.3d 306 (Tex. Ct. App. 2016)). In Arizona, community property is divided equitably. (*Lehn v. Al-Thanayyan,* 438 P.3d 646 (Ariz. Ct. App. 2019)). A California family court judge must, with few exceptions, divide community property equally. (Cal. Fam. Code § 2550). In Louisiana, "The court shall divide the community assets and liabilities so that each spouse receives property of an equal net value." (*Keenan v. Keenan*, 186 So. 3d 289 (La. Ct. App. 2016)).

The two systems of marital property—equitable distribution and community property—are increasingly similar.

A divorce court has three responsibilities regarding property: (1) Characterize property as marital/community or separate; (2) Value the property (typically market value); and (3) Divide the property. (*Flory v. Flory,* 783 S.E.2d 122 (Ga. 2016); *Sellers v. Sellers,* 294 Neb. 346, 882 N.W.2d 705 (2016); *Mack v. Mack,* 169 A.D.3d 1214 (N.Y. 2019); *Sluder v. Sluder,* 826 S.E.2d 242 (N.C. Ct. App. 2019); *Eason v. Taylor,* 784 S.E.2d 200 (N.C. Ct. App. 2016); *Brouillet v. Brouillet,* 875 N.W.2d 485 (N.D. 2016); *McCulloch v. McCulloch,* 69 A.3d 810 (R.I. 2013)).

As mentioned above, most equitable distribution and community property states start with the presumption that marital/community property should be divided equally. (*Flom v. Flom,* 170 A.D.3d 440, 96 N.Y.S.3d 26 (2019)). New Hampshire law, for example, states, "When a dissolution of a marriage is decreed, the court may order an equitable division of property between the parties. The court shall presume that an equal division is an equitable distribution of the property." (N.H. Rev. Stat. § 458:16–a(II)). The New Hampshire statute provides that the judge may make an *un*equal division after considering the following factors:

> (a) The duration of the marriage. (b) The age, health, social or economic status, occupation, vocational skills, employability, separate property, amount and sources of income, needs and liabilities of each party. (c) The opportunity of each party for future acquisition of capital assets and income. (d) The ability of the custodial parent, if any, to engage in gainful employment without substantially interfering with the interests of any minor children in the custody of said party. (e) The need of the

custodial parent, if any, to occupy or own the marital residence and to use or own its household effects. (f) The actions of either party during the marriage which contributed to the growth or diminution in value of property owned by either or both of the parties. (g) Significant disparity between the parties in relation to contributions to the marriage, including contributions to the care and education of the children and the care and management of the home. (h) Any direct or indirect contribution made by one party to help educate or develop the career or employability of the other party and any interruption of either party's educational or personal career opportunities for the benefit of the other's career or for the benefit of the parties marriage or children (i) The expectation of pension or retirement rights acquired prior to or during the marriage. (j) The tax consequences for each party. (k) The value of property that is allocated by a valid prenuptial contract made in good faith by the parties. (*l*) The fault of either party . . . if said fault caused the breakdown of the marriage and: (1) Caused substantial physical or mental pain and suffering; or (2) Resulted in substantial economic loss to the marital estate or the injured party. (m) The value of any property acquired prior to the marriage and property acquired in exchange for property acquired prior to the marriage. (n) The value of any property acquired by gift, devise, or descent. (*o*) Any other factor that the court deems relevant. (N.H. Rev. Stat. § 458:16–a(II)).

New Hampshire's factors influencing unequal division are similar to factors in other states that allow unequal division of marital/community property. (*See, e.g.*, S.C. Code Ann. § 20–3–620(B)).

An equitable distribution is not always an equal distribution. (*Banks v. Banks*, 574 S.W.3d 187 (Ark. Ct. App. 2019); *Hamilton v. Hamilton*, 378 P.3d 185 (Hawai'i 2016); *Lacoste v. Lacoste*, 313 So. 3d 1097 (Miss. Ct. App. 2021); *Lewis v. Pagel*, 172 So. 3d 162 (Miss. 2015)). The Wyoming Supreme Court remarked in *Dane v. Dane*, 368 P.3d 914, 920 (Wyo. 2016), "We have held that an equitable distribution of property is as likely as not to be unequal."

Does marital fault—*e.g.*, adultery, mental cruelty—play a role in division of property on divorce? In some states, fault is relevant. (*See Fredrickson v. Schulze*, 785 S.E.2d 392 (S.C. Ct. App. 2016); *Marriage of Hardin*, 572 S.W.3d 310 (Tex. Ct. App. 2019)). In *Ewing v. Ewing*, 333 Ga. App. 766, 777 S.E.2d 56, 58 (2015), the Georgia Court of Appeals wrote, "In divorce cases . . . in which equitable division of property is at issue, the conduct of the parties, including evidence of a spouse's alleged adultery, is relevant and admissible. Accordingly, the wife is entitled to engage in discovery which might lead to admissible evidence of the husband's alleged adultery." In other states, for example, California, fault is irrelevant in the division of property. One type of fault is relevant in all states: Conduct by a spouse to hide or steal marital/community property from the other spouse. (*See Marriage of Bradshaw*, 487 S.W.2d 306 (Tex. Ct. App. 2016)).

§ 10-3 CHARACTERIZATION OF PROPERTY

One of the fundamental tasks in divorce cases is characterizing property as marital/community or separate/non-marital. As the Illinois Appellate Court put it in *In re Marriage of Faber*, 58 N.E.3d 52 (Ill. Ct. App. 2016), "Before a court may distribute property upon the dissolution of a marriage, it must first classify the property as either marital or nonmarital." (*See Williams v. Williams,* 264 So. 3d 722 (Miss. 2019); *Lewis v. Pagel,* 172 So. 3d 162, 172 (Miss. 2015)). Elaborate rules govern characterization, and the law of characterization varies somewhat from state to state. This section describes essential principles of characterization.

The most fundamental principle of characterization is that property—real or personal—that is acquired during marriage through the effort, energy, or skill of a married person belongs to both spouses, and is presumed to be marital/community property. (*Schwarz v. Schwarz,* 192 Wash. App. 180, 368 P.3d 173 (2016)). As the Appellate Division of the New York Supreme Court put it in *Mack v. Mack,* 169 A.D.3d 1214 (N.Y. 2019), "Property acquired during a marriage is presumed to be marital property . . . ." The Texas Court of Appeals wrote in *Battle v. Battle,* 2021 WL 5318160 (Tex. Ct. App. 2021), "In Texas, there is a rebuttable presumption that all property possessed by either spouse during or on dissolution of marriage is community property. When a challenging party asserts the separate character of property, they must prove its separate character by clear and convincing evidence." (*Baughman v. Baughman*, 173 N.E.3d 938 (Ohio 2021)).

Property acquired prior to marriage is separate/non-marital property. (*See* 750 Fla. Stat. § 61.075(6)(b)(1); ILCS 5/503(a)(6); *Dabo v. Sibblies*, 36 N.Y.S.3d 648, 142 A.D.3d 459 (2016); *Baughman v. Baughman*, 173 N.E.3d 938 (Ohio 2021)). In *Sellers v. Sellers*, 294 Neb. 346, 882 N.W.2d 705 (2016), for example, husband owned a cattle herd before marriage. The herd remained his separate property when the couple divorced a few years later. Property acquired during marriage by gift, decent, inheritance, devise, or bequest is separate/non-marital property. (*Marriage of Asta*, 404 Ill. Dec. 675 56 N.E.3d 1088 (Ct. App. 2016)). Once marriage ends, property acquired thereafter is separate/non-marital property. (*See* § 10–6, for discussion of when marriage ends for purposes of characterizing property). The Washington Court of Appeals wrote, "An asset is separate property if acquired before marriage; acquired during marriage by gift or inheritance; acquired during marriage with the traceable proceeds of separate property; or, in the case of earnings or accumulations, acquired during permanent separation." (*Schwarz v. Schwarz*, 192 Wash. App. 180, 368 P.3d 173 (2016)).

Income from a trust may be separate/non-marital property or marital/community property, depending on the circumstances. In *Pfannenstiehl v. Pfannenstiehl*, 475 Mass. 105, 55 N.E.3d 933 (2016), the Massachusetts Supreme Judicial Court considered a discretionary support trust with a spendthrift provision established by husband's father. Because the husband had no right to insist on income from the trust, the court ruled that the trust was a mere expectancy and not property to be "included in the parties' divisible marital estate." For information on discretionary support trusts and spendthrift provisions, see § 9–11.

As mentioned above, states utilize presumptions to characterize property. In California, for example, property acquired during marriage is presumed to be community property (Cal. Family Code § 760). Property acquired prior to marriage is presumed to be separate property (Cal. Family Code § 770). In New York, placing separate property money into a joint bank account raises a presumption the money is marital property. (*Valitutto v. Valitutto,* 137 A.D.3d 1526, 28 N.Y.S.3d 472 (2016)). In Texas, "there is a rebuttable presumption that all property possessed by either spouse during or on dissolution of marriage is community property." *Battle v. Battle,* 2021 WL 5318160 (Tex. Ct. App. 2021).

When property has a formal title, the title *sometimes* helps characterize the property. In California divorce cases, for example, taking title in one spouse's name alone during marriage does not help characterize property. By contrast, taking title as joint tenants with right of survivorship raises a presumption the property is community property on divorce. (Cal. Family Code § 2581).

Generally, a presumption that property is marital/community or separate/non-marital can be rebutted by tracing to the money used to purchase the property. Suppose, for example, that a married couple purchases a piece of real property and puts title in both their names. This may raise a presumption of marital/community property. However, if one spouse can trace the money used to make the purchase to the spouse's separate property, the marital/community presumption *may* be rebutted, characterizing the property as separate. States vary on when tracing is sufficient to rebut a marital/community property presumption.

During marriage, a couple may change the character of property from marital/community to separate/non-marital, and vice-a-versa. This change process is often called transmutation. States differ in the requirements for transmutations. Some states require transmutations to be in writing. (*See* Cal. Family Code § 852(c)).

Separate/non-marital property can be transmuted into marital/community property if it becomes so intermingled with marital/community property that it is no longer traceable to separate/non-marital property. (*Robirds v. Robirds,* 499 P.3d 431 (Idaho 2021); *Eis v. Eis,* 310 Neb. 243, 965 N.W.2d 19 (2021); *Contis v. Contis,* 789 S.E.2d 51 (S.C. Ct. App. 2016); *Brozek v. Brozek,* 874 N.W.2d 17, 31 (Neb. 2016) ("Separate property becomes marital property by commingling if it is inextricably mixed with marital property or with the separate property of the other spouse.").

§ 10-4 ORIGINS OF EQUITABLE DISTRIBUTION AND COMMUNITY PROPERTY SYSTEMS

To understand today's equitable distribution system of marital property it is useful to examine the law at the time of the nation's birth. After the Revolutionary War, the original states continued their adherence to much of the English law of domestic relations. In particular, states perpetuated English law that relegated married women to an inferior status vis à vie husbands. When a woman married, ownership of her personal property passed to her husband. The husband could sell the property, and his creditors could reach it to satisfy *his* debts. A married woman's real property fell under her husband's control as well, although he could not sell her real property without her consent. In many states, a married woman could not enter into binding contracts. A married woman could not make a will. For many legal purposes, women were placed in the same category as children and "idiots."

Over the years, mechanisms emerged to ameliorate a wife's subordinate position regarding property. Some states allowed a married couple to agree that the wife would retain control of her property. Sometimes, a woman's parents created a trust for their daughter, placing her property in the trust in order to remove the property from the control of the daughter's husband. In some states, married women who wished to go into business were authorized to transact business and enter contacts.

From early days, reformers agitated against inequitable treatment of married women. Finally, in 1839, Mississippi passed the first married women's property act. The act provided in part: "That any married woman may become seized or possessed of any property, real or personal, by direct bequest, demise, gift, purchase, or distribution, in her own name, and as of her own property. . . ." (Laws of Mississippi, Chapter 46, § 1, Feb. 15, 1839). Although the Mississippi law was a step forward, it by no means bestowed equality on women. Following Mississippi's lead, states across the country adopted married women's property acts, lessening, to varying degrees, the inequities of English law.

Divorce was relatively uncommon during the nineteenth century. When a divorce action was commenced, legal rules—only partially alleviated by married women's property acts—combined with common forms of property ownership to disadvantage women. By the old law, a married woman's property was controlled by her husband. Thus, a wife's property rested in the hands of the man she was divorcing. Add that it was common for title to property to be in the husband's name. Thus, the family home or farm often stood in the husband's name. Some courts ruled that the husband was presumed to be the owner of all non-titled personal property.

Throughout the nineteenth century, and into the twentieth, divorce courts in non-community property states generally assigned property based on title or ownership. Under the "title theory" of marital property, the judge's job was simple: Determine who held title or ownership, and assign property accordingly. It was often the case that husbands owned the lion's share of property. Consider Willodene and Henry, who married in 1920. Henry worked full time. Willodene stayed home to raise the children. They purchased a home and put title in Henry's name. All mortgage payments were from Henry's income from work. In 1930, Henry purchased a farm, putting title in his name. Mortgage payments on the farm were from Henry's earnings at work. They bought a car, a truck, and a tractor, putting title in Henry's name. Their bank account was in Henry's name. Under the title theory of marital property, when Willodene and Henry divorced, Henry owned everything! Willodene's only remedy was alimony.

Chinks in the title system developed in the first half of the twentieth century. In 1936, the Michigan Supreme Court wrote in *Robinson v. Robinson*, 275 Mich. 420, 266 N.W. 403 (1936), "There is no rigid rule of division of property in divorce proceedings, but the division must be equitable." Turner writes, "Legislatures began passing statutes permitting the court to award the wife a share of the property to which she had directly contributed. These statutes were passed not all at once, but rather gradually over a period of years. . . . None of these enactments were equitable distribution statutes in the modern sense." (Brett R. Turner, *Equitable Distribution of Property* § 1:3, pp. 8–9 (3d ed. 2005)). In 1970, the National Conference of Commissioners on Uniform State Laws took a major step forward with promulgation of the *Uniform Marriage and Divorce Act* (UMDA).

Although the UMDA is most famous for introducing no-fault divorce, the UMDA also recommended abandonment of the title theory of property and adoption of equitable distribution. By the 1980s, all non-community property states had some form of equitable distribution.

Switching from equitable distribution to community property, the history is easier to tell. Today's community property system derives not from England, but from continental Europe. Louisiana's community system devolved from France. Other community property states inherited their systems from Spain and Mexico.

The hallmark of the community property system is that property acquired through the effort or skill of either spouse during marriage belongs to the community. Property that is not community is separate.

§ 10–5 ALL PROPERTY STATES

In most equitable distribution and community property states, marital/community property is divided equitably/equally, while separate property belongs to the owner. A few states give judges authority to divide all property, including separate property. In Massachusetts, for example, "the court may assign to either husband or wife all or any part of the estate of the other." (Mass. Gen. Laws. Ann. Ch. 208, § 34) (*See Connor v. Benedict,* 118 N.E.3d 96 (Mass. 2019); *Pfannenstiehl v. Pfannenstiehl*, 475 Mass. 105, 55 N.E.3d 933 (2016)). Connecticut is an "all-property" state. A Connecticut family court "may assign to either the husband or wife all or any part of the estate of the other." (Conn. Gen. Stat. Ann. § 46b–81(a)). Indiana law provides, "In an action for dissolution of marriage, the court shall divide the property of the parties, whether: (1) owned by either spouse before marriage; (2) acquired by either spouse in his or her own right: (A) after the marriage; and (B) before final separation of the parties; or (3) acquired by their joint efforts." (Indiana Code Ann. § 31–15–7–4(a)). "South Dakota is an all property state: all property is subject to division regardless of its origins or title." (*Kolbach v. Kolbach*, 877 N.W.2d 822 (S.D. 2016)).

§ 10–6 BEGINNING AND END OF MARITAL/ COMMUNITY PROPERTY

The system of marital/community property comes into effect the moment the official presiding at the wedding says, "I now pronounce you married." Thus, the marital/community property system comes into operation automatically—by operation of law—when you say, "I do." Couples who do not want the marital/ community property system to apply to them can contract out of the system with a premarital agreement (*See* Chapter 3).

The beginning date for acquisition of marital/ community property is clear. But when does the acquisition of marital/community property end? The end date is critical because property acquired after that date is separate property. States differ on the end date. In California, the community ends when a couple separates and at least one of them believes the relationship is over. (Cal. Family Code §§ 70, 771). In Mississippi, "for purposes of classifying marital property, the marriage runs from the date of marriage until the final judgment of divorce," or until the parties obtain an order for separate maintenance or an order for temporary support. (*Wheat v. Wheat*, 37 So. 3d 632, 637 (Miss. 2010)). In Indiana, "the marital pot closes on the day the petition for dissolution is filed." (*Granzow v. Granzow*, 855 N.E.2d 680, 683 (Ind. Ct. App. 2006)). In New York, "the marital partnership ceases for the purposes of equitable distribution of property upon the commencement of a divorce action." (*DiLascio v. DiLascio*, 170 A.D. 3d 804, 95 N.Y.S.3d 588 (2019) (word order changed)).

§ 10–7 PROPERTY WORK OF THE FAMILY LAW LAWYER

Statutes describe how the court divides marital/community property. In most cases, however, the lion's share of work regarding property is carried out by attorneys for the parties, not judges. A great deal of attorney time is taken up with finding, valuing, and characterizing property as separate, marital/community, or, as often happens, part separate and part marital/community. The lawyer helps the client understand property rights on divorce. The lawyer negotiates with the other side to reach a settlement regarding property division. In most cases, the parties reach agreement on how to divide property. The attorneys memorialize the agreement in a contract called a separation agreement or a marriage settlement agreement (MSA). The parties and the attorneys sign the MSA and the MSA is submitted to the court for approval and/or merged into the judgment or decree of divorce. More is said about MSAs in Section 10–25.

Divorcing couples can divide their marital/community property however they like. Thus, a couple does not have to divide marital/community property equally or equitably. Of course, any agreement between parties to divide property must be fully informed and voluntary.

If the parties cannot agree on property division, a trial is necessary, and the court characterizes the property, values it, and divides it according to applicable law.

As mentioned above, family law attorneys devote considerable attention to finding assets. Sometimes, however, an asset that is subject to division on divorce is not discovered during the divorce process, and the asset comes to light only after the divorce is complete. States have court procedures to handle such "omitted assets." (*Hilton v. Hilton,* 496 P.3d 839 (Idaho 2021)).

§ 10–8 DEBTS

Most discussion of property division focuses on assets. Of course, many couples have debts as well as assets. States have complex rules on how debts are allocated on divorce, which party is responsible for payment, and what property creditors can attach following divorce. (*See Sluder v. Sluder,* 826 S.E.2d 242 (N.C. Ct. App. 2019)).

§ 10-9 PRO RATA APPORTIONMENT

It is common for married couples to purchase real or personal property partly with separate property and partly with marital/community property. If the relationship ends, how should the property be characterized? States vary in the treatment of this issue. (*See Stark v. Dinarany*, 73 Va. App. 733, 865 S.E.2d 440 (2021)).

A useful place to start is to ask whether an item of property has a written document of title. All real property and some personal property (car, boat, airplane, stock), has title documents, and the way title is held can impact characterization.

Many types of personal property have no title. For example, Hillary and Bill are married and living in Carmel-by-the-Sea, California. California is a community property state. Hillary and Bill are avid surfers. Hillary buys a surfboard for $1,000, paying $500 of community property and $500 of her separate property. If Hillary and Bill divorce and cannot agree about the surfboard, how will it be characterized? A surfboard has no title. The surfboard is half separate and half community. This manner of division is called pro rata apportionment. Characterization is tied to the relative contributions of separate and marital/community property to the purchase. (*See Flory v. Flory*, 783 S.E.2d 122 (Ga. 2016)).

The surfboard is easy: half and half. But what about the following? Before Hillary married Bill five years ago, Hillary purchased a home on Scenic Road in Carmel-by-the-Sea. The home is 100 feet from the

Pacific Ocean with an unobstructed view of the beach and the water—a view worth its weight in gold. Hillary purchased the small house for $7 million. (Yes, that is how much small houses cost on Scenic Drive!) She put $500,000 down, and financed the balance with a loan from the bank, secured by a mortgage. Before marriage, monthly mortgage payments were made with separate property. When Hillary and Bill married, mortgage payments were made with earnings from Hillary and Bill's employment—community property. If Hillary and Bill divorce, how should the Scenic Road home be characterized? Title is in Hillary's name alone because she was single when she acquired the property. At the time of divorce, the home is worth $10 million. Should the home be treated like the surfboard?—pro rata apportionment based on the relative contributions of community and separate property? That is the answer in California, where courts use a complicated formula to determine the separate and community shares. (*Marriage of Ramsey and Holmes,* 67 Cal. App. 5th 1043, 282 Cal. Rptr. 3d 622 (2021)). Many other states use a similar pro rata approach. Texas, by contrast, uses the "inception of title" approach. (*Blair v. Blair*, 2021 WL 5416244 (Tex. Ct. App. 2021)). In *Miller v. Evans*, 452 S.W.2d 426 (Tex. 1970), the Texas Supreme Court wrote, "Property acquired during marriage acquires its status of separate or community at the time of its acquisition." In Texas, there may be a right to reimbursement of community mortgage payments.

§ 10–10 BUSINESSES AS MARITAL PROPERTY

Businesses owned by one or both spouses can be martial/community property or separate property. (*Starrett v. Starrett,* 101 A.3d 435 (Me. 2014)). Special rules apply when a separate property business increases in value during marriage (*See* § 10–11).

How much is a marital/community business worth? Accountants play important roles regarding business valuation. Value has several meanings, the most common being "fair market value," defined as the price at which a business would change hands between a willing seller and a willing buyer, neither under any compulsion to sell or to buy, and both equally informed of all relevant facts. (*Kean v. Kean*, 189 So.3d 61 (Ala. Civil. App. 2015); *King v. King,* 313 So. 3d 887 (Fla. Ct. App. 2021); *Sparks v. Sparks*, 417 S.W.3d 269 (Mo. Ct. App. 2013)).

Accountants employ several methods to value businesses. As stated by the North Dakota Supreme Court in *Adams v. Adams*, 863 N.W.2d 232, 237 (N.D. 2015), "There is no set formula for valuation of a business." Moreover, valuation is not an exact science. (*Brown v. Brown*, 792 A.2d 463, 477 (N.J. Super. 2002)). The IRS has guidelines to assist in valuing businesses. (Revenue Rulings 59–60; 68–609). Accountants who are retained by opposing spouses often reach different values. The trial judge has broad discretion to adopt the value supported by evidence.

Some businesses are simple to value; others very complex. In his book titled *Investigative Accounting in Divorce* (2d ed. 2002), Kalman Barson observes that it can be particularly challenging to value professional practices (lawyer, doctor, dentist), sole proprietorships, and closely held corporations (p. xxvii). The Georgia Supreme Court remarked in *Sullivan v. Sullivan*, 295 Ga. 24, 757 S.E.2d 129, 132 (2014), "Three principle methods of determining the value of a closely-held corporation are: the income or capitalized earnings method; the market approach method; and the cost approach method. The trial court has the discretion to choose which valuation method it will employ." (*See Ward v. Ward,* 233 W. Va. 108, 755 S.E.2d 494 (2014)).

An accountant does not accept at face value the tax returns, financial records, and books of a small business or professional practice. The accountant digs below the surface and examines not only the financial records of the business but also the records of the spouse who owns the business. With many small businesses it is necessary to delve into the owner's personal finances because the owner's finances are intertwined with the business. If the business owner is less than enthusiastic about disclosing personal financial information, the lawyer employs discovery tools to unearth needed information.

Sometimes, a divorcing couple owns a minority interest in a closely held corporation. In the divorce, the spouse involved in the business generally keeps the interest and buys out the other spouse. But what is the value of a minority interest in a closely held business? (*See Marriage of Johnson,* 400 Ill. Dec. 96, 47 N.E.3d 1061 (Ct. App. 2016)). Shares of stock in a closely held corporation are not traded on a public exchange, and this makes selling the shares difficult or, in some cases, virtually impossible. As well, a minority owner lacks the ability to control corporate decision making. The spouse retaining the interest will argue that the value of the interest should be discounted. Specifically, the retaining spouse will seek a discount for lack of corporate control. As well, the retaining spouse will argue for a discount based on illiquidity. When such discounts are allowed, they can reduce a minority interest by up to half, which often advantages the retaining spouse. Not surprisingly, the non-retaining spouse argues against discounts. The majority position appears to be that discounts should not apply (*see Sieber v. Sieber,* 37 N.E.3d 776 (Ohio Ct. App. 2015)), although a number of cases approve discounts. When the buy-out amount is determined it generally bears interest. (*Adams v. Adams,* 863 N.W.2d 232 (N.D. 2015)).

Most spouses who own a business or professional practice are honest. On occasion, however, an owner spouse works hard to hide assets and undervalue the business. A forensic accountant can often determine that the numbers don't add up. For example, the owner of a business claims the business earns $100,000 a year, yet the business owner has homes in Palm Springs and New York City and an apartment in Paris. Each spouse drives a new Mercedes each year. The kids are in private schools. And husband maintains a mistress in a home of her own. All this on $100,000 a year? Again, the figures don't add up. Somewhere there are large quantities of unreported income. A forensic accountant can find the hidden money. The accountant examines reported income in light of lifestyle, expenses, cash flow, income generated by similar businesses, and other factors. Sometimes, it is necessary to hire private investigators. If deliberate fraud is going on, the court can remedy the situation.

When a couple has sizeable assets, an accountant should be retained early in the case rather than on the eve of trial. The accountant works with the attorney to locate assets, determine income, debts, and value, evaluate whether efforts have been made to hide assets, and plan the tax implications of divorce. In many instances, an accountant helps *avoid* trial by clarifying financial issues.

§ 10–11 INCREASED VALUE OF SEPARATE PROPERTY BUSINESS

Before Ann marries, she starts a business called Allied Electron Systems (AES). Five years *after* AES has become a profitable and expanding business, Ann meets and marries Noel. Because AES was owned by Ann prior to marriage, it is her separate property. During their ten year marriage, Ann devotes countless hours to AES, serving as its chief executive officer. Over the course of the marriage, AES triples in value. When the parties divorce, how should AES be characterized? Does AES remain entirely Ann's separate property? Is AES part separate and part marital/community? If AES is Ann's separate property, what about the increased value during marriage? Does the increased value belong in whole or part to the marital/community estate?

Consider Bill and Tamara. When they married 10 year ago, Bill owned a large and valuable stock portfolio that he inherited from his parents. The portfolio was separate property. During the marriage, Bill did very little to manage the portfolio. Bill entrusted the portfolio to a stock broker. Periodically, Bill met briefly with the stock broker, but apart from these meetings, Bill ignored the portfolio and simply enjoyed the checks sent to him by the stock broker. Between the marriage and the divorce, the portfolio doubles in value. Who owns the portfolio? What about the increased value during marriage? Change the facts. Bill managed the stock portfolio himself, devoting many hours a week to research and to trading stocks. Who owns the portfolio? The increased value?

When a spouse owns a separate property business or asset that increases in value during marriage due to the efforts of the owner spouse, many states provide that the increased value is marital/community property that should be divided on divorce. The American Law Institute's *Principles of the Law of Family Dissolution: Analysis and Recommendations,* address the issue, providing: "(1) A portion of any increase in the value of separate property is marital property whenever either spouse has devoted substantial time during marriage to the property's management or preservation. (2) The increase in value of separate property over the course of the marriage is measured by the difference between the market value of the property when acquired, or at the beginning of the marriage, if later, and the market value of the property when sold, or at the end of the marriage, if sooner. (3) The portion of the increase in value that is marital property under Paragraph (1) is the difference between the actual amount by which the property has increased in value, and the amount by which capital of the same value would have increased over the same time period if invested in assets of relative safety requiring little management." (§ 4.05, p. 663).

Florida law provides that "marital assets" includes, "The enhancement in value and appreciation of nonmarital assets resulting either from the efforts of either party during the marriage or from the contribution to or expenditure thereon of marital funds or other forms of marital assets, or both." (Fla. Stat. § 61.705(6)(a)).

In California, the business remains entirely separate property. At divorce, the focus is on the increased value of the business. If the increased value is due entirely to natural growth, then the entire increase is the separate property of the owner spouse. However, if the owner spouse expended more than *de minimus* effort on the business, and if at least part of the increased value is attributable to the owner spouse's efforts, then the increased value is divided between community property and separate property. When the increase in value is due primarily to the efforts of the owner spouse, the lion's share of the increase is community property. On the other hand, if the owner's efforts account for only a small portion of the increase—market forces account for most of the increase—most of the increase in separate property.

Two cases guide decision making in California: *Van Camp v. Van Camp,* 53 Cal. App. 17, 199 P. 885 (1921) and *Pereira v. Pereira,* 156 Cal. 1, 103 P. 488 (1909). If the trial judge concludes the increase in value is due primarily to the efforts of the owner spouse, the judge employs *Pereira.* The judge allocates a fair return on the owner spouse's business (typically the legal interest rate) as separate property and allocates the rest of the increased value as community property arising from the owner's efforts. On the other hand, if most of the increase is due to market forces, the judge uses *Van Camp.* With *Van Camp,* the judge determines the reasonable value of the owner spouse's services to the business and allocates that amount as community property. The remainder of the increase is separate property.

§ 10–12 GOODWILL

Sue graduates from law school, passes the bar, and enters practice. After a few years in the legal trenches, Sue realizes her true passion is not the courtroom but the kitchen. Sue hangs up her shingle, donates her fancy suits to charity, and moves to Paris. Sue gets a little apartment on the Left Bank, with a view of the Eifel Tower, wiles away the hours sipping coffee at quaint sidewalk cafes, mingles with artists, and enrolls in the famous Le Cordon Bleu school of French cooking. Upon graduation from Le

Cordon Bleu, Sue returns home to start her career as a chef. Most novice chefs take an entry level position at a restaurant, and work their way up. But not Sue! She buys a well-established and popular French restaurant. What will Sue pay? If the current owner owns the building, she will pay for that. Obviously, she will pay for the furniture and fittings of the restaurant—stoves, pots and pans, etc. But that's not all. A substantial portion of the purchase price is for "goodwill."

In *McReath v. McReath*, 800 N.W.2d 399, 408 (Wis. 2011), the Wisconsin Supreme Court described goodwill:

> In its broadest sense the intangible asset called good will may be said to be reputation; however, a better description would probably be that element of value which inheres in the fixed and favorable consideration of customers arising from an established and well-conducted business.
>
> The advantage or benefit which is acquired by an establishment beyond the mere value of the capital stock, funds, or property employed therein, in consequence of the general public patronage and encouragement which it receives from constant or habitual customers on account of its local position, or common celebrity, or reputation for skill or affluence, or punctuality, or from other accidental circumstances or necessities, or even from ancient partiality or prejudices.

> Goodwill is a business's reputation, patronage, and other intangible assets that are considered when appraising the business, especially for purchase; the ability to earn income in excess of the income that would be expected from the business viewed as a mere collections of assets.
>
> Simply stated, goodwill is an asset of recognized value beyond the tangible assets of a business.

The South Carolina Supreme Court provides an instructive analysis of goodwill in *Moore v. Moore,* 414 S.C. 490, 779 S.E.2d 533 (2015).

The goodwill of a traditional commercial business (*e.g.*, dry cleaner, restaurant) is often relatively easy for an accountant to value: What would a willing buyer pay for the business, including the goodwill? Commercial goodwill is often called enterprise goodwill. Beebe describes enterprise goodwill: "Enterprise goodwill attaches to a business entity and is associated separately from the reputation of the owners. Product names, business locations, and skilled labor forces are common examples of enterprise goodwill. The asset has a determinable value because the enterprise goodwill of an ongoing business will transfer upon sale of the business to a willing buyer." (Courtney E. Beebe, The Object of My Appraisal: Idaho's Approach to Valuing Goodwill as Community Property in *Chandler v. Chandler,* 39 *Idaho Law Review* 77, 83–84 (2002)). To the extent enterprise goodwill is acquired during marriage, it is marital/community property.

Professionals, including attorneys, accountants, physicians, dentists, engineers, and architects, can acquire goodwill. Is professional goodwill marital/ community property? This is a more challenging question than enterprise goodwill. Professional goodwill is uniquely tied to an individual. You hire an architect to build your dream home based on the architect's reputation, not simply because the person has a license to practice architecture. It is the unique style and taste of the individual you want, not just the person's ability to put a roof over your head. Because professional goodwill is so closely linked to a particular professional, what is it worth? For example, if someone is interested in purchasing your architect's business when the architect retires, what is the value of the business's goodwill? The difficulty is that the value of the goodwill is tied to the personal attributes of the architect, and the architect is retiring!

The Utah Court of Appeals addressed goodwill in *Marroquin v. Marroquin,* 440 P.3d 757 (Utah Ct. App. 2019). The Court wrote:

> When valuing a business in marriage dissolution cases, district courts must consider whether goodwill is institutional or personal to one spouse. Institutional, or enterprise, goodwill is based on the intangible, but generally marketable, existence in a business of established relations with employees, customers and suppliers, and may include factors such as business location, its name recognition and its business reputation.

> Personal goodwill is based on an individual's reputation for competency and is not subject to distribution upon divorce.

Despite the challenge of valuing professional goodwill, most courts agree that professional goodwill can be marital/community property. In *McReath v. McReath*, 800 N.W.2d 399, 410 (Wis. 2011), the Wisconsin Supreme Court wrote, "Originally, it was posited that goodwill did not inhere in professional businesses because professional businesses depend on the skill and reputation of the professional. However, courts and scholars now recognize goodwill in professional businesses."

Some courts divide professional goodwill into two components: personal goodwill and enterprise goodwill. (*Ahern v. Ahern*, 938 A.2d 35 (Me. 2008)). Enterprise goodwill is the goodwill of the professional practice itself. Personal goodwill is unique to the individual. In *May v. May*, 589 S.E.2d 536, 545–546 (W. Va. 2003), the West Virginia Supreme Court wrote: "There is a split of authority on whether enterprise goodwill and/or personal goodwill in a professional practice may be characterized as marital property and thus equitably distributed. Three different approaches have developed. A large number of courts make no distinction between personal and enterprise goodwill. These jurisdictions have taken the position that both personal and enterprise goodwill in a professional practice constitute marital property. . . . On the other hand, a minority of courts have taken the position that neither personal nor enterprise goodwill in a professional practice constitutes marital property. . . . The majority of states differentiate between enterprise goodwill and personal goodwill. Courts in these states take the position that personal goodwill is not marital property, but that enterprise goodwill is marital property."

The American Law Institute's *Principles of the Law of Family Dissolution* have this to say: "Professional goodwill earned during marriage [is] marital property to the extent [it has] value apart from the value of spousal earning capacity, spousal skills, or post-dissolution spousal labor." (§ 4.07(3), p. 694).

Do movies stars and professional athletes have goodwill?—celebrity goodwill? What is the value of a name like Serena or Venus Williams, David Beckham, Lebron James, Jennifer Lopez, Taylor Swift, or Matt Damon? Many millions to these star entertainers and athletes. But does a celebrity have goodwill that can be valued and divided on divorce? California is home to Hollywood, and given the divorce rate among actors, it may surprise you to learn that the issue of celebrity goodwill did not reach a California appellate court until 2006. In *Marriage of McTiernan and Dubrow,* 133 Cal. App. 4th 1090, 35 Cal. Rptr. 3d 287 (2006), the California Court of Appeal ruled celebrity goodwill is not property for purposes of divorce. Courts in New Jersey and New York have ruled celebrity goodwill can be property subject to equitable distribution. (*Piscopo v. Piscopo,*

232 N.J. Super. 559, 557 A.2d 1040 (1989); *Elkus v. Elkus*, 169 A.D.2d 134, 572 N.Y.S.2d 901 (2001)).

§ 10-13 RETIREMENT BENEFITS FROM EMPLOYMENT

Pension and retirement benefits are marital/community property to the extent they are earned from employment during marriage. (*Koelsch v. Koelsch*, 148 Ariz. 176, 713 P.2d 1234 (1986); *Hardy v. Hardy*, 273 So. 3d 448 (La. Ct. App. 2019); *Valitutto v. Valitutto*, 137 A.D.3d 1526, 28 N.Y.S.3d 472 (2016); *Marriage of Hardin*, 572 S.W.3d 310 (Tex. Ct. App. 2019)). Government employees at federal, state, and local levels have pension plans. Members of the armed forces have a retirement system. Workers in the private sector may or may not have a pension at work. For those without a work-related pension, pension-like savings plans are available (*e.g.*, 401(k)).

Most private sector pensions are governed by a federal law called the Employee Retirement Income Security Act (ERISA) and by the Internal Revenue Code (IRC). Government pensions are governed by the IRC, although government pensions are not, for the most part, regulated by ERISA.

Federal civilian employees participate in the Federal Employees' Retirement System (FERS). Employees of state and local governments have pensions governed by state law. State pensions often go by the acronym PERS—Public Employees' Retirement System.

§ 10–13[A] BASIC PENSION TERMINOLOGY

During the early years of employment, some pensions are unvested. If an employee leaves a job before a pension vests, the employee has no pension rights. Although an unvested pension may have little or no monetary value, it is nevertheless marital/community property to the extent earned during marriage.

After a period of time with an employer, a pension vests, which means the employee has rights even if the employee leaves or is fired or laid off before normal retirement age. When an employee is eligible to retire, the pension is mature. If the employee retires and draws on the pension, the mature pension is in pay status.

§ 10–13[B] DEFINED BENEFIT AND DEFINED CONTRIBUTION PLANS

Traditional pensions are divided into defined benefit plans and defined contribution plans. Both have many permutations. In a defined benefit plan, an employer agrees to provide pension benefits upon retirement. The pension amount for each employee is tied to a formula that typically includes length of employment with the employer and the employee's salary during the final years of employment. Every defined benefit plan is different.

With a defined contribution plan, each employee has a retirement account. Typically, the employee and the employer make regular contributions—*e.g.*, every payday—to the employee's account. At retirement, the employee's pension depends on the amount in the account. Typically, during the employee's working years, the money is invested according to the wishes of the employee.

With a defined contribution plan, it is easy at any given time to tell how much money is in an employee's retirement account. The employee or the plan administrator can tell at a glance the balance of the account. With a typical defined benefit plan, by contrast, the employee does not have an individual retirement account containing a set amount of money. Instead, the employee has a contractual promise that at retirement age the retirement plan will apply the applicable formula and determine, *at that time*, the amount of the pension. With defined benefit plans it is generally not possible to tell precisely the amount of a pension until the employee retires.

Most employers that offer defined benefit plans (*e.g.*, federal and state governments, unions), also offer defined contribution plans. Millions of Americans have both types of retirement plan.

§ 10–13[C] DETERMINING THE MARITAL/ COMMUNITY PROPERTY PORTION OF A PENSION

A pension is marital/community property to the extent it is acquired during marriage. Consider Mary, who enlisted in the Navy at age 18, right after high school. Mary served twenty years, and retired at age 38. At 39, Mary married Mike. Five years later, they divorce. Mary's Navy pension is entirely her separate property because it was acquired prior to marriage. The fact that Mary receives pension checks during marriage does not change the fact that the pension was acquired before marriage. Now consider Sue and Tom, who fell in love and married in college. Following graduation, Sue entered the Navy at age 22. After thirty years of service, Sue retired at age 52. Two years after retirement, Sue and Tom divorce. Sue's pension is entirely marital/community property because it was acquired entirely during marriage. Finally, consider John and Kim. Upon graduation from law school at age 26, Kim was commissioned an officer in the Navy Judge Advocate General's corps—a Navy lawyer. Five years into her Navy career, Kim married John, a Navy pilot. After twenty years' service, Kim retired from the Navy at age 46. A few years following retirement, Kim and John divorce. Kim's pension is partly her separate property and partly marital/community property because part of the pension was acquired prior to marriage and part during marriage. To be precise, 75% of the pension is marital/community, and 25% is Kim's separate property. In the divorce, Kim is entitled to the 25% that is separate plus half the marital/community portion of the pension.

When a defined contribution plan is part separate and part marital/community, the proportions are calculated at the time of the divorce based on the characterization of the funds that contributed to the pension account. Depending on the type of defined contribution pension, the divorce decree may order the administrator of the pension to create separate accounts for the employee and the non-employee.

From that time forward, each spouse owns the money in their respective account.

With defined benefit plans, when a pension is partly separate and partly marital/community, the division into separate and marital/community components is typically accomplished with the so-called "time rule" or "coverture fraction." (*See Morey v. Morey,* 49 N.E.3d 1065 (Ind. Ct. App. 2016); *Stark v. Dinarany,* 73 Va. App. 733, 865 S.E.2d 440 (2021)). The numerator of the fraction is years of service during marriage. The denominator is total years during which the pension was earned.

Consider, for example, Sue, who retired after twenty years with the highway patrol. The highway patrol has a defined benefit pension. During ten of Sue's years of service with the Patrol, Sue was married to Paul. The numerator of the fraction is 10; the denominator is 20. Half of Sue's pension is her separate property. Half is marital/community. Sue owns half of the marital/community portion. In the end, Sue is entitled to 75% of the pension and Paul has 25%.

In Sue's case, she was already retired at the time of the divorce. Thus, the denominator of the fraction—20—was established. In many divorces, the employee spouse is years from retirement. The employee may retire after 20 years of service or may continue working. The denominator of the fraction cannot be determined until the employee retires. In this scenario, the divorce decree contains the coverture fraction, with the proviso that the denominator will be filled in when the employee retires.

The time rule is not generally used with defined contribution plans. Turner explains, "Classification of defined contribution plans requires proration of funds, not proration of time." (Brett R. Turner, *Equitable Distribution of Property* § 6:24, p. 147 (3d ed. 2005)).

An important part of a lawyer's job in divorce is learning about all pension/retirement benefits of both parties. The lawyer determines whether pension benefits are separate or marital/community. The lawyer educates the client about the impact of family law on pensions.

§ 10–13[D] METHODS OF DIVIDING PENSIONS

In addition to learning about a couple's pensions, and calculating marital/community shares, attorneys help clients decide how to divide marital/community pension interests. There are many ways divorcing couples can handle pensions.

With a defined contribution plan, the parties determine what is in the pension account on the proper day (*e.g.*, date of separation, date marriage ends) and how much of the money is marital/community. This amount can be divided in the divorce, perhaps by creating separate accounts for each spouse. Alternatively, the employee spouse can keep the entire pension and cash out the non-employee spouse. A cash out can be accomplished by giving the non-employee spouse extra marital/community property to compensate for the interest in the pension. In some cases, the employee spouse takes out a loan or uses separate property to cash out the non-employee spouse.

Turning to defined benefit pensions, two techniques predominate. (*Cornwell v. Cornwell,* 309 Neb. 156, 959 N.W.2d 243 (2021)). First, the employee spouse keeps the entire pension and the non-employee spouse receives other property equal in value to the foregone pension—the cash out method. To use the cash out method it is necessary to determine the value of the defined benefit plan at the time of the divorce—present value—a subject discussed later. Second, at the time of the divorce, the court determines the marital/community interest in the pension using the coverture fraction or time rule. The non-employee spouse then waits to receive her or his share of the pension until the employee-spouse retires and the pension is paid—the wait and see method. With the wait and see method, it is not necessary at the time of the divorce to determine the present value of the defined benefit plan. The non-employee spouse waits until the employee retires to see, at that time, how much the pension pays based on the formula used by the pension and the time rule applied at the time of the divorce.

Consider, Rita and Juan who married while in college. Upon graduation Rita became a police officer. Juan became a teacher. Both have defined benefit pensions. After five years of marriage, Rita and Juan divorce. They are many years from retirement. For this couple, the best solution may be for each to keep her or his entire pension. If there is a difference in present value between the pensions, the spouse with the less valuable pension can receive other property to make up the difference. As mentioned above, if one spouse is to be cashed out it will be necessary to determine the present value of the pension.

It is important to understand that the law does not insist that Rita and Juan leave the marriage with exactly the same value in pension benefits. Divorcing couples are free to divide their property as *they* see fit. If Rita's public safety pension is worth more than Juan's teaching pension, Juan is a free to say, "Rita, you keep your pension. I'll keep mine. I don't care if yours is worth more than mine." Although many people getting a divorce are angry and hurt, many still care about their partner and desire what is best for them. If Juan wants to give up his portion of Rita's more valuable pension he is free to do so as long as his decision is voluntary and informed. (*See Oshinaike v. Oshinaike*, 140 A.3d 1206 (D.C. 2016)). It is the responsibility of Juan's attorney to explain to him the rights he has and what he is giving up. In the final analysis, the law allows divorcing couples to arrange their property according to their own lights.

One advantage of the employee spouse keeping her or his entire pension and the non-employee spouse taking other property is that the parties can make a clean break from each other. With this approach, all pension rights are disposed of at divorce. A second advantage of the employee spouse retaining the entire pension is that when retirement rolls around the employee has more money in pocket. Of course, this benefit for the employee spouse may disadvantage the non-employee ex-spouse.

When divorcing spouses use the wait and see method to divide a defined benefit plan, they remain entangled into the future, at least in so far as the pension is concerned.

§ 10–13[E] PENSION VALUATION

Defined contribution plans and defined benefit plans are described above. When a pension is marital/community property in whole or in part it is sometimes necessary to determine the value of the pension at the time of the divorce.

If the pension is a defined contribution plan, it is simple to value the asset. The plan administrator can tell the attorneys the value of the pension on the appropriate date.

If a defined benefit pension is in pay status because the employee is retired, it is easy to determine value. Difficulties arise in determining the value *today* of a defined benefit plan that is not in pay status because the employee is not retired. Recall that with defined benefit plans, unlike defined contribution plans, there typically is no individual account with a running balance. Rather, there is a promise of benefits in the future—benefits that are tied to variables that are impossible to predict with certainty years in advance of retirement. Determining the value *today* ("present value") of a defined benefit pension that is years away from maturity requires an expert, often an actuary. As explained in more detail below, the expert makes assumptions about when the employee will probably retire and what the employee's pension amount will likely be at retirement (this depends, of course, on the formula used by the retirement plan and assumptions about the employee's future salary, etc.). The likely pension amount is discounted to present value. Needless to say, determining present value of a defined benefit pension that will not materialize for years—if it ever materializes—is not an exact science.

Assume Mary has worked for the ABC Company for ten years and has a defined benefit retirement plan. Mary and her husband, Jan, have been married eleven years. They are divorcing. The portion of Mary's pension that was earned during marriage is marital/community property. Suppose Jan decides he wants to receive his share of Mary's pension at the time of the divorce. How do we figure out *today*, at the time of the divorce, what Mary's pension will be worth ten or more years in the future? The short answer, as mentioned above, is that it is not possible to determine the exact value of Mary's pension in the future because we don't know what factors will be plugged into the pension formula *at that future time*. To estimate present value, an actuary considers: (1) mortality tables that predict how long Mary will live—the mortality discount (women usually live longer than men); (2) the formula used by the pension; (3) the appropriate interest rate; (4) the probable tax rate; and (5) other relevant factors. The number derived from this assessment is reduced to present value and this number is considered the value of the defined benefit pension *at the time of the divorce*.

§ 10–13[F] SURVIVOR BENEFITS

Retirement plans generally have benefits for the surviving widow or widower of a worker who dies. ERISA mandates survivor benefits for pensions covered by ERISA. In *Ablamis v. Rober*, 937 F.2d 1450 (9th Cir. 1991), the Ninth Circuit described survivor benefits: "[ERISA] specifically afforded protection to widows (and widowers) by requiring pension plans to provide automatic survivor benefits. Once a participant becomes vested under the plan—that is, has earned a nonforfeitable right to any portion of his accrued benefit—his spouse is assured of receiving a survivor's annuity if her husband predeceases her; the plan administrator must pay the surviving spouse, on the participant's death, at least 50% of the participant's benefit. The survivor annuity may be waived only if the waiver is in writing and signed by the participant and the participant's spouse. On the death of the surviving spouse the survivor annuity terminates. It cannot be bequeathed." In divorce proceedings it is the responsibility of the non-employee spouse's attorney to make sure survivor benefits are assigned to the non-employee spouse.

§ 10–13[G] QUALIFIED DOMESTIC RELATIONS ORDER (QDRO)

Many private sector pensions are governed by ERISA and the Internal Revenue Code (IRC). Government pensions are governed by the IRC, but government pensions are not regulated by ERISA. (*Jones v. West Virginia Public Employees Retirement System*, 235 W. Va. 602, 775 S.E.2d 483, 493 (2015)). For federal civilian employees, complex statutes regulate pensions. States have similarly complex statutes regarding pensions of state employees, teachers, and employees of local governments (counties and cities).

ERISA provides that pension benefits of employees (participants) in ERISA covered pensions cannot be alienated by participants. (29 U.S.C. § 1056(d)(1)). This anti-alienation rule is sometimes called the spendthrift provision. Absent an exception to ERISA's anti-alienation provision, a participant's retirement benefit cannot be awarded (alienated) in a divorce to the non-employee spouse. In ERISA parlance, the non-employee spouse is an alternative or alternate payee.

ERISA creates the needed exception to the anti-alienation rule. This exception authorizes state courts to divide ERISA pensions, giving part of a pension to an alternate payee. The division is accomplished with a court order called a Qualified Domestic Relations Order (QDRO). The Texas Court of Appeal explained QDROs in *Quijano v. Quijano*, 347 S.W.3d 345, 353–354 (Tex. Ct. App. 2011), "The purpose of a QDRO is to create or recognize an alternate payee's right, or to assign an alternate payee the right, to receive all or a portion of the benefits payable to a participant under a retirement plan." (*See also, Marriage of Denning and Stokes,* 2021 WL 3577731 (Tex. Ct. App. 2021)).

Drafting a DRO is the responsibility of the attorneys; usually the attorney for the alternate payee. The attorney drafts a Domestic Relations Order (DRO) that meets the following federal requirements:

> A domestic relations order meets the requirements of this subparagraph only if such order clearly specifies—(i) the name and last known mailing address (if any) of the participant and the name and mailing address of each alternative payee covered by the order. (ii) the amount or percentage of the participant's benefits to be paid by the plan to each such alternative payee, or the manner in which such amount or percentage is to be determined. (iii) the number of payments or period to which such order applies, and (iv) each plan to which such order applies. A domestic relations order meets the requirements of this subparagraph only if such order—(i) does not require a plan to provide any type or form of benefit, or any option, not otherwise provided under the plan, (ii) does not require the plan to provide increased benefits (determined on the basis of actuarial value), and (iii) does not require payment of benefits to an alternate payee which are required to be paid to another alternative payee under another order

previously determined to be a qualified domestic relations order. (29 U.S.C. § 1056).

The DRO specifies the spouses' interests in the pension and describes how the interests are to be divided. Before the DRO is submitted to court for a judge's signature, many family law attorneys submit the DRO to the pension plan for pre-approval. Assuming everything is in order, the pension plan pre-approves the DRO. The pre-approved DRO is submitted to court and a judge signs it, making is an order. The signed DRO is then filed with the pension plan for qualification. The plan administrator approves, that is, qualifies, the DRO, rendering it a Qualified Domestic Relations Order. The pension plan then divides the pension according to the QDRO, and pays the appropriate amount to the alternate payee.

In some cases the DRO is filed with the court for signature during the divorce. In other cases the divorce decree specifies how the pension will be divided and a DRO is submitted to the court later.

It might seem that drafting a DRO should be straight forward. It is not difficult for a lawyer to obtain names and mailing addresses. Nor is it particularly challenging to specify "the amount or percentage of the participant's benefits to be paid by the plan to" the alternative payee. The tricky bit is ensuring that the DRO does not require the plan to pay any type of benefit that is not provided by the plan. The Indiana Court of Appeals explained in *Evans v. Evans,* 946 N.E.2d 1200, 1206 (Ind. Ct. App. 2011), "A QDRO must comply with ERISA. . . . A

QDRO cannot require the plan administrator to provide any type or form of benefit, or any option, not otherwise provided under the plan." The only way to make sure this requirement is satisfied is obtain the actual pension plan—perhaps hundreds of pages, and not always readily available—and to read and understand precisely what the plan does and does not provide. The difficulty with this requirement—reviewing the actual plan—is the reason many family law attorneys do not draft DROs, referring this task to DRO specialists.

The attorney for the non-employee spouse must be sure to (1) discover all pension benefits that are marital/community property (2) protect the non-employee spouse's right to cost-of-living increases in pension benefits; (3) secure survivor benefits for the non-employee spouse; (4) draft the proper QDRO; and (5) make sure to finalize the QDRO. Because the QDRO process can go on for months after the divorce is complete, is easy to forget to complete the process. (*See* David Carrad, *The Complete QDRO Handbook* (3dh ed. 2009); Patricia Shewmaker & James R. Lewis, *The Complete QDRO Handbook* (4th ed.)).

Overlooking a client's pension rights, and/or getting those rights wrong, is a fertile ground for legal malpractice. (*See Faber v. Herman*, 731 N.W.2d 1 (Iowa 2007)(malpractice claim related to pension); *McCoy v. Feinman*, 99 N.Y.2d 295, 785 N.E.2d 714, 755 N.Y.S.2d 693 (2002)(malpractice claim related to pension)).

QDROs are necessary to divide private sector pensions governed by ERISA. As mentioned earlier, government pensions are not governed by ERISA. Thus, government pensions are not divided with an ERISA-QDRO. The law governing each government pension specifies how the pension is divided. Although government pensions do not require ERISA-QDROs, government pensions generally require a division process—and a court order—very similar to an ERISA-QDRO. Indeed, many attorneys and judges use the term QDRO to describe division of government pensions.

A QDRO is only needed when a pension is divided. When an employee spouse keeps the entire pension, a QDRO is generally not required. Suppose that Mary and Sue are married. Each has a defined benefit pension at work. On divorce, Mary keeps her pension and Sue keeps hers. No QDRO is needed because the pensions are not divided.

When we think QDRO, we usually think pension. It should be mentioned that a QDRO can be used to enforce child and spousal support orders.

§ 10–13[H] MILITARY RETIREMENT

Members of the active duty military have a defined benefit retirement plan as well as a defined contribution plan. Members of the reserve and National Guard have a retirement system. In 1981, in *McCarty v. McCarty*, 453 U.S. 210, 101 S. Ct. 2728 (1981), the Supreme Court ruled that state family courts could not divide military pensions. Congress abrogated *McCarty* with passage of Uniformed Services Former Spouses' Protection Act (USFSPA; 10 U.S.C. § 1408). (*See Thayer v. Thayer*, 378 P.3d

1232 (Utah Ct. App. 2016); Congressional Research Services, *Military Benefits for Former Spouses: Legislation and Policy Issues* (2021)).

USFSPA allows family courts to divide military pensions on divorce. Sullivan writes, "State courts can order the direct pay of pension division awards through Defense Finance and Accounting Service (DFAS) when there is ten years' overlap between the marriage and creditable military service." (Mark E. Sullivan, *The Military Divorce Handbook: A Practical Guide to Representing Military Personnel and Their Families* 484 (2d ed. 2011)). When a marriage lasts less than ten years, the court can divide the pension but DFAS will not cut a separate check for the non-military former spouse. The former spouse has to collect from the military member.

In 2017, Congress amended USFSPA to limit the portion of military pensions available to spouses of servicemembers. The Maryland Court of Special Appeals explained in *Fulgium v. Fulgium*, 240 Md. App. 269, 203 A.3d 33 (2019):

> The amendment to § 1408 was intended to modify 'the division of military retired pay in a divorce decree to the amount the member would be entitled based upon the member's pay grade and years of service at the time of the divorce rather than at the time of retirement.' . . . Rather than dividing actual retired pay at the time of retirement, the benefit would be frozen at the time of divorce. The rationale for using a 'date of divorce' method for pension valuation was that a former spouse would not receive a

windfall benefit from promotions and other pay increases that accrued from the date of divorce to the date of retirement, to which the former spouse made no contribution.

§ 10–13[I] RAILROAD RETIREMENT

Employees of railroads have pensions under the federal Railroad Retirement Act (RRA). In *Hisquierdo v. Hisquierdo,* 439 U.S. 572, 99 S. Ct. 802 (1979), the Supreme Court ruled that state divorce courts could not divide RRA pension benefits. In 1983, Congress amended the RRA to allow divorce courts to divide certain components of RRA pensions.

§ 10–14 DISABILITY BENEFITS

Courts agree that retirement pension benefits acquired during marriage are marital/community property (*Marriage of Miller,* 966 N.W.2d 630 (Iowa 2021)). Characterization of disability benefits has proven a challenge. The Iowa Supreme Court's decision in *Marriage of Miller*, 966 N.W.2d 630 (Iowa 2021) provides guidance. The Iowa Court wrote, "Disability pensions or benefits . . . have been difficult to categorize as marital or separate property due to the multiple forms they may take and their different purposes." If the purpose of a disability benefit is to compensate a disabled person for loss of good health, or to replace post-marriage earnings lost due to disability, the benefit is separate property. On the other hand, when a benefit contains a retirement component that is analogous to a regular retirement pension, a court is likely to characterize the benefit as marital/community property. Courts agree that the label put on the policy does not control. The trial court examines the purposes of the "disability" benefit and rules accordingly.

In *Topolski v. Topolski*, 802 N.W.2d 482 (Wis. 2011), the Wisconsin Supreme Court described the difference between pension and disability benefits:

> The value of a spouse's interest in a retirement, pension, or deferred benefit account, although presenting valuation challenges, is generally classified as a divisible asset at divorce. Therefore, these assets generally must be considered in the circuit court's division of property at divorce.
>
> In contrast, a disability benefit is ordinarily viewed as distinct from a retirement, pension, or deferred benefit account. "Disability benefit" or "disability income," in ordinary parlance, commonly refers to a payment received when a person is unable to work, either in a chosen profession or totally, due to a physical or mental medical condition. Disability benefits are not ordinarily referred to as deferred compensation. Disability benefits are generally considered wage replacement, that is, compensation for lost future wages because a physical or mental condition prevents the person from being gainfully employed.
>
> Disability payments, such as Social Security disability payments or veteran's disability payments, replace the wages lost by the

individual due to the disability and are generally classified as income at divorce. As such, these payments are not assets divisible at dissolution of the marriage. . . .

A disabled spouse's disability benefit may in effect be an amalgam: a portion may be a replacement for lost wages and a portion may be a replacement for deferred compensation (that is, retirement or pension benefits).

Depending on the terms of a plan, a disability benefit may encompass both a wage replacement component and a deferred compensation replacement component. In other words, under a plan, a disability benefit may in substance be both a replacement for lost future wages and a replacement for deferred compensation. The disability benefit should be viewed in light of the totality of the circumstances to determine whether all or any part of the disability benefit received by the disabled spouse replaces post-divorce lost wages or replaces deferred compensation.

When and to the extent that a disability benefit replaces the disabled spouse's post-divorce wages, the benefit should be characterized as income and will be individual property not subject to property division at divorce. Alternatively, when and to the extent that the disability benefit replaces deferred compensation, the disability benefit should be characterized as deferred compensation and will be subject to property division at divorce.

In sum, pension benefits earned during marriage are marital/community property, whereas the characterization of disability benefits varies from case to case.

The United States military has three disability programs: (1) Military disability retired pay; (2) Veterans Administration (VA) disability; and (3) Combat-Related Special Compensation.

When a service member is sufficiently disabled that she or he can no longer perform assigned duties, the service member may receive disability retired pay.

Service members who are not sufficiently disabled to quality for military disability retired pay, or whose disability is detected after retirement, may qualify for VA disability benefits. The service member gives up a portion of regular retirement benefits to obtain VA disability benefits.

Combat-related Special Compensation (CRSC) is available to service members who are least 10% disabled and whose disability is related to the award of a Purple Heart or to combat.

CRSC is not divisible on divorce. CRSC is awarded entirely to the service member. When a service member is entitled to CRSC and is also entitled to a retirement pension, the member cannot receive both. Regular retirement is taxable. CRSC benefits are tax free. Understandably, most service members who are eligible for CRCS select tax free CRCS benefits over regular retirement. The member gives up the retirement pension—dollar for dollar—to receive

CRSC disability benefits. As a result, a former spouse who would receive part of a retirement pension loses the money when the ex-spouse service member replaces the pension with CRSC disability benefits. (*See Spruell v. Spruell,* 356 Ga. App. 722, 848 S.E.2d 896 (2020); *Foster v. Foster,* 505 Mich. 151, 949 N.W.2d 102 (2020); *Russ v. Russ,* 485 P.3d 223 (N.M. 2021)).

As with CRSC disability, state courts cannot divide VA disability or disability retirement. (Mark E. Sullivan, *The Military Divorce Handbook: A Practical Guide to Representing Military Personnel and Their Families* 509 (2d ed. 2011); *Williams v. Burks,* 2021 WL 5143756 (Ala. Civil. App. 2021); *Yourko v. Yourko,* 74 Va.App. 80 (Va. Ct. App. 2021)).

As mentioned above, state family courts cannot divide military disability in divorce cases. (*Howell v. Howell,* 137 S. Ct. 1400 (2017); *Jordan v. Jordan,* 480 P.3d 626 (Alaska 2021); *Fulgium v. Fulgium,* 203 A.3d 33 (Md. Spec. App. 2019)). When a service member gives up regular retirement in order to receive disability benefits, federal law mandates the entire amount be awarded to the service member.

§ 10–15 SOCIAL SECURITY RETIREMENT

Social Security retirement is available to workers who reach a pre-set age and who paid the required amount of payroll tax under the Federal Income Contributions Act (FICA). Federal Social Security retirement benefits are not subject to division on divorce. (*See, e.g., Marriage of Peterson,* 243 Cal. App.

4th 923, 197 Cal. Rptr. 3d 588 (2016); *Jackson v. Sollie*, 449 Md. 165, 141 A.3d 1122 (2016)).

If a court cannot divide Social Security retirement, may the court offset Social Security benefits by awarding additional property to the other spouse to compensate for the "lost" Social Security? Courts divide on this question. (*Jackson v. Sollie*, 449 Md. 165, 141 A.3d 1122 (Md. 2016)). Some courts rule that it is improper to offset Social Security with other property. (*See Marriage of Peterson*, 243 Cal. App. 4th 923, 197 Cal. Rptr. 3d 588 (2016)). Other courts hold that Social Security can be factored into an overall division of property. (*Jackson v. Sollie*, 449 Md. 165, 141 A.3d 1122 (2016)). In *Smith v. Smith,* 381 Mont. 1, 358 P.3d 171 (2015), the Montana Supreme Court wrote:

> We adopt the rule that social security benefits may be considered as a factor, among others, when dividing marital property. By not allowing a district court to divide the benefits in substance or form, this approach adheres to federal law, and, at the same time, advances the policy underpinning state law by promoting equitable apportionment. We remain aware . . . of the possibility that our holding may tempt lower courts to simply shift property of equivalent value to the spouse not receiving the benefit as an offset. We again caution courts that this practice is unacceptable. A court may not treat social security benefits as the equivalent to marital property. Instead, in arriving at an equitable distribution of the parties' estate, a

court may consider social security benefits generally in determining the economic circumstances of the parties. (358 P.3d at 176).

§ 10–16 SEVERANCE PAY

When an employee resigns or is laid off, the employee may receive a severance package. In a divorce, is severance money marital/community property or separate property? What purpose does the severance serve? If the severance is a reward for past service to the employer, and the employee was married during the period of service, then the severance is marital/community property. On the other hand, if the severance is intended to replace lost future income after a couple separates or divorces, then the severance is the separate property of the employee.

In *Wheat v. Wheat*, 37 So. 3d 632 (Miss. 2010), wife resigned from her employer of more than thirty years. The employer offered wife a severance package of $395,000. Not long after wife resigned, she and husband commenced divorce proceedings. The Mississippi Supreme Court ruled that the severance was marital property.

§ 10–17 VACATION DAYS AND SICK DAYS

In some jobs, employees can accrue unused vacation and sick days. These days can be "cashed in" at retirement or when the employee leaves employment. Are unused vacation and sick days accrued during marriage marital/community property? In *Marriage of Abrell,* 236 Ill. 2d 249, 923

N.E.2d 791, 337 Ill. Dec. 940 (2010), the Illinois Supreme Court described the diversity of opinion on the issue: "Jurisdictions are split on the issue of whether vacation and sick days are marital property. Courts have held that: (1) accrued vacation and sick days are marital property subject to division at the time of dissolution; (2) accrued vacation and sick days are marital property but are subject to distribution when received, not at the time of dissolution; and (3) accrued vacation and sick days are not marital property." The Illinois Supreme Court ruled that for Illinois, accrued vacation and sick days are not marital property. The court noted, however, "that when a party has actually received payment for vacation and/or sick days accrued during marriage prior to a judgment for dissolution, the payment for those days is marital property subject to distribution in the marital estate." (923 N.E.2d at 801). *See also, Andrews v. Andrews,* 2021 WL 5903259 (Ariz. Ct. App. 2021) ("we hold that the accrued vacation pay constituted community property if it was reimbursable (making it a form of deferred compensation). But if the vacation pay was not reimbursable (making it merely a form of replacement wages that could be used during or after the marriage), then it constituted the employee spouse's separate property").

§ 10–18 PROPERTY ACQUIRED ON CREDIT

For expensive purchases, most Americans rely on credit or a loan from the bank or credit union. The general rule is that property acquired during marriage on credit is presumed to be community/ marital property.

§ 10–19 COLLECTIBLES

People collect just about anything you can imagine: cars, china, baseball cards, stamps, dolls, art, jewelry, jukeboxes, clocks, beer cans, barbed wire (yes, barbed wire; *See Barbed Wire Collector Magazine*). You name it; people collect it. Some collections are worth millions (consider former late-night talk show host Jay Leno's car collection), while other collections are of only sentimental value. To the extent acquired during marriage, collections are marital/community property. Valuing a collection may require an expert.

§ 10–20 WEDDING GIFTS

On your wedding day, guests arrive bearing gifts—ten pancake makers, five toasters, six waffle irons, etc. Hopefully, some guests give you cash. But suppose the marriage doesn't last. Are wedding gifts marital/community property? It depends on the intent of the donor. If Aunt Minnie intended the toaster to belong to you and you alone, it is your separate property. Most of the time, however, there is no evidence of donative intent. In *Coppola v. Farina*, 910 A.2d 1011, 1016–1018 (Conn. Superior Court 2006), the Connecticut Superior Court wrote: "Treatises have stated that if the donor's intent is not clear, there are two basic approaches for classifying wedding gifts. Those two approaches are referred to as the New York rule and the English rule. The New

York rule presumes that a wedding gift is intended as a joint gift unless the gift is appropriate for the use of only one spouse or is peculiarly earmarked for one particular spouse. . . . Under the English rule, the donor is presumed to have given the gift to the party to whom he is more closely related."

§ 10-21 ARE PETS PROPERTY?

Sue and Sam are divorcing. For the three years prior to divorce, Sue and Sam enjoyed the companionship of two miniature dachshunds, Bindy and Chibby. Sue and Sam dearly love Bindy and Chibby, and the dogs are very attached to each other. In the divorce, Sue and Sam cannot agree on who should get the dogs. In a divorce case are family pets property subject to division under principles of marital property law? Or are family pets akin to children, allowing the judge to apply a "best interests of the puppy" test? Courts traditionally treated pets as property. (Eric Kotloff (Note) All Dogs Go To Heaven . . . Or Divorce Court: New Jersey Un"Leashes" a Subjective Value Consideration to Resolve Pet Custody Litigation in *Houseman v. Dare*, 55 *Villanova Law Review* 447 (2010)). The California Legislature amended the Family Code to allow "custody" litigation over family pets. (Cal. Family Code § 2605). In *Hament v. Baker*, 97 A.3d 461 (Vt. 2014), a divorcing couple agreed on everything except the dog, and took their fight over rover all the way to the state supreme court. The Vermont Supreme Court wrote, "In contrast to a child, a pet is not subject to a custody award following a determination of its best interests. Because a pet is property, the family [court] must assign it to one party or the other." The Supreme Court was not unsympathetic to animal welfare, writing that trial courts may consider "the welfare of the animal and the emotional connection between the animal and each spouse. These factors underlie our animal welfare laws and our case law, which recognizes the value of the bond between the animal and its owner. Evidence concerning the welfare of the animal includes evidence about its daily routine, comfort, and care. Evidence concerning the emotional connection may include testimony about the role of the animal in the lives of the spouses." The court concluded that a judge may not award "visitation" with a pet. In *Marriage of Niemi*, 496 P.3d 305 (Wash. Ct. App. 2021), the Washington Court of Appeals wrote, "Judicially imposed visitation rights for pets would run contrary to the current statutory directive that marital property distributions should be final."

§ 10–22 TRANSMUTATION AGREEMENTS DURING MARRIAGE

During marriage, spouses may contract with each other to change ownership of property. In some states, these agreements are called transmutations. Other states refer to them as postnuptial agreements. Thus, a couple could transmute separate property to marital/community property, or the opposite. States generally require such contracts to be in writing. In California, for example, transmutations after 1985 must be written, signed by the party whose property interest is adversely affected, and must specify that ownership is changing. (Cal. Family Code § 852). A married couple can contract regarding property in order to plan for the eventuality of death.

The parties can select what state's law governs interpretation of their contract. In *Ritter v. Hussemann*, 847 N.W.2d 219 (Iowa, 2014), wife and husband lived in Florida. They entered into a postnuptial agreement by which each waived the right to an elective share of the other's estate. The agreement specified that Florida law controlled. Years later, they moved to Iowa, where husband died, and wife sought an elective share of his estate. The Iowa Supreme Court ruled that Florida law controlled; the agreement was enforceable, and wife could not claim a share.

§ 10–23 MARITAL SETTLEMENTS AGREEMENTS

An important part of the family law lawyer's job is negotiating settlement of property and other issues in divorce. Matters on which the parties reach agreement are memorialized in a Marital Settlement Agreement (MSA).

§ 10–23[A] MSA IS A CONTRACT

Public policy favors settlement of disputes, including marital disputes. (*Quinn v. Quinn*, 137 A.3d 423 (N.J. 2016)). The Mississippi Supreme Court wrote in *McManus v. Howard*, 569 So. 2d 1213, 1215 (Miss. 1990), "The law favors the settlement of disputes by agreement of the parties and, ordinarily, will enforce the Agreement which the parties have made, absent any fraud, mistake or overreaching." Similarly, the Indiana Supreme Court wrote in *Pohl v. Pohl*, 15 N.E.3d 1006, 1010 (Ind. 2014), "Indiana encourages such settlement agreements to promote the amicable settlements of dissolution-related disputes, on the expectation that freedom of contract will produce mutually acceptable accords, to which parties will voluntarily adhere." In most states, an MSA is effective as a contract when it is signed. In some states, an MSA is not effective until it is approved by a court.

An MSA is a contract, and courts apply normal principles of contract law. (*Herring v. Herring,* 373 P.3d 521 (Alaska 2016); *Feliciano v. Munoz-Feliciano*, 190 So.3d 232 (Fla. Ct. App. 2016)). So long as an MSA is entered into voluntarily, it is enforceable. (*Hall v. Hall*, 171 So. 3d 817 (Fla. Ct. App. 2015); *Sabowitz v. Sabowitz,* 123 A.D.3d 794, 999 N.Y.S.2d 80 (2014)).

Like other contracts, MSAs are subject to the parole evidence rule. If an MSA is clear and complete, resort may not be had to extrinsic or parole evidence to elucidate its terms. When an MSA is ambiguous, extrinsic evidence is allowed to determine its meaning.

§ 10–23[B] DEFENSES AGAINST ENFORCEMENT OF MSA

An MSA may be attacked and defended under normal contract principles. (*Marriage of Labuz,* 2016 IL App. 3d 140990, 54 N.E.3d 886 (2016)). In *Herring v. Herring*, 231 N.C. App. 26, 752 S.E.2d 190 (2013), the North Carolina Court of Appeals observed, "A marital separation agreement is subject to the same rules pertaining to enforcement as any other contract. Thus, like any other contract, a separation agreement may be set aside or reformed based on grounds such as fraud, mutual mistake of fact, or unilateral mistake of fact procured by fraud." The Virginia Court of Appeals, in *MacDougall v. Levick*, 66 Va. App. 50, 782 S.E.2d 182 (2016), wrote, "Property settlement agreements are contracts subject to the same rules of formation, validity, and interpretation as other contracts. . . . If certain facts are assumed by both parties as the basis for a contract, and it subsequently appears that such facts did not exist, the contract is inoperative." (*See Bhongir v. Mantha,* 374 P.3d 33 (Utah Ct. App. 2016) (mistake)).

Regarding defenses against enforcement of marital agreements, *See* Claude D. Rohwer & Anthony M. Skroky, *Contracts in a Nutshell* (7th ed. 2010); Brett R. Turner & Laura W. Morgan, *Attacking and Defending Marital Agreements* (2d ed. 2013).

A spouse may claim an MSA was signed under duress. Duress occurs when one side of a contract makes an unlawful threat that causes the other party to sign against the party's will, and the threat would overcome a reasonable person's will to resist. The Illinois Appellate Court defined duress in *Marriage of Akbani*, 16 N.E.3d 399, 404–405, 384 Ill. Dec. 303, 308–309 (2014) "as including the imposition, oppression, undue influence or the taking of undue advantage of the stress of another whereby one is deprived of the exercise of his free will." Is the stress caused by divorce sufficient to deprive someone of free will? The Illinois court said no: "It is generally accepted that stress is common in dissolution proceedings. Stress alone does not prove duress. Even the stress of possibly losing custody of a child does not demonstrate that one lacked the ability to make a voluntary decision. The person asserting duress has the burden of proving by clear and convincing evidence that he was bereft of the quality of mind essential in making the contract."

An MSA can be set aside based on fraud in which one spouse intentionally made a material misrepresentation of fact and the other spouse reasonably relied on the misrepresentation. An MSA can be challenged on the basis of a material mutual mistake or a unilateral mistake that was caused by the other spouse's conduct. Courts scrutinize MSAs more closely than arm's length commercial contracts because of the marital relationship. (*Ruparella v. Ruparella*, 136 A.D.3d 1266, 26 N.Y.S.3d 394 (2016)).

An MSA that divides property unequally is not necessarily unfair or unconscionable. The California Court of Appeal observed in *Marriage of Woolsey*, 220 Cal. App. 4th 881, 897, 163 Cal. Rptr. 3d 551, 562 (2013), "The parties in a marital dissolution action can agree [in writing] on a lopsided division of community property." In *Lounsbury v. Lounsbury*, 300 A.D.2d 812, 814, 752 N.Y.S.2d 103 (2002), the Appellate Division of the New York Supreme Court wrote, "Indeed, a separation agreement is not per se unconscionable simply because marital assets are divided unequally, because one spouse gave away more than that spouse might have been legally required to do, or because the spouse's decision to approve the agreement might be characterized as unwise." Absent fraud, oppression, duress, overreaching, or incompetence, the parties are free to divide their property as they see fit. However, an MSA that makes a grossly unfair distribution of property may be unconscionable. The Illinois Appellate Court wrote in *Marriage of Akbani*, 16 N.E.3d 399, 405, 384 Ill. Dec. 303, 309 (2014), "In order to rise to the level of being unconscionable, a settlement has to be improvident, totally one-sided or oppressive." In *Eberle v. Eberle*, 766 N.W.2d 477 (N.D. 2009), wife did not have an attorney. She signed an MSA that gave almost everything to her husband. The North Dakota Supreme Court ruled the MSA unconscionable. The court wrote that although MSAs are encouraged, judges must not "blindly accept settlement agreements." (p. 484). The Supreme Court went on to say, "An agreement is unconscionable if it is one no rational, undeluded person would make, and no honest and fair person would accept. . . . Settlement agreements in divorce cases are more susceptible to overreaching and oppressive conduct because of the relationship between the husband and wife, particularly when the negotiations are between the parties rather than through their lawyers. Behavior that may not constitute fraud, duress, mistake, menace, or undue influence in an arm's length context may be sufficient to make an agreement unconscionable when the relationship is used to take advantage of a situation and achieve an oppressive result." (pp. 484–485).

In a case decided shortly after *Eberle, supra,* the North Dakota Supreme Court wrote that although lack of legal representation is a factor in the unconscionability calculation, absence of legal advice does not doom all MSAs. "That fact alone does not conclusively establish the parties' agreement was unconscionable." (*Vann v. Vann,* 767 N.W.2d 855, 861 (N.D. 2009)). In *Vann,* the spouse attacking the MSA signed a document stating that he had the opportunity to seek legal advice. He had the MSA in his possession more than a month before he signed it. "Based on these facts, we conclude the involvement of only one attorney does not establish the agreement was procedurally unconscionable." (p. 862).

§ 10–23[C] INCORPORATION OF MSA INTO JUDGMENT OR DECREE OF DIVORCE

A divorcing couple may ask the court to incorporate the MSA into the court's judgment or decree of divorce, transforming the MSA from a contract into a court order. The MSA becomes part of the judgment/decree, and can be enforced as other court orders are enforced, including, in extreme cases, with proceedings to hold one party in contempt for disobeying the court's order. (For discussion of contempt, *see Sickler v. Sickler,* 293 Neb. 521, 878 N.W.2d 549 (2016)).

In some divorces the court approves the MSA but does not incorporate the MSA into the judgment/ decree of divorce. In such cases the MSA remains a contract and enforcement for breach is under contract law.

As with all other aspects of family law, it is necessary to check the law in your state to determine when and how MSAs are incorporated or approved by the court.

§ 10–23[D] BOILERPLATE AND PROVISIONS UNIQUE TO THIS MARRIAGE

The typical MSA is between ten and thirty single spaced pages. For individuals of great wealth, an MSA can run much longer. Probably seventy-five percent of a typical MSA is boilerplate that is standard in most MSAs, including provisions for the following: (1) Warranty that all assets and debts have been disclosed; (2) Provision describing what happens if assets or debts are discovered that were inadvertently omitted from the MSA; (3) Statement that the parties will sign any documents needed to accomplish the agreed upon division of property; (4) Waiver of rights to inherit on death; (5) Promise to indemnify and hold harmless if creditors impose obligations on one party that should be paid by the other party; (6) Declarations that the MSA is entered into with full knowledge and voluntarily; (7) Provision for modification or revocation of the MSA; (8) Effective date of the MSA; (9) Choice of law, that is, what state's law will govern interpretation of the agreement; (10) Agreement that the MSA will be incorporated into the judgment or decree of divorce, making it a court order, or that the MSA will remain a contract, and not be incorporated into the judgment or decree; (11) Provision that the MSA constitutes the entire agreement; (12) Effect of partial invalidity—severability clause.

With the standardized language out of the way, the MSA describes the agreements that are unique to this family: Child custody and support, spousal support, and division of property.

§ 10–24 PROPERTY TRANSFERS TO AVOID PAYING DEBTS

Sometimes, people with debts transfer money or property to family members or friends for little or no consideration so creditors cannot attach the property to satisfy the debts. (*Porenta v. Porenta*, 416 P.3d 487 (Utah 2017) (Husband's transfer of interest in marital home was voidable)). All states have laws that allow creditors to challenge these and similar transfers. Half the states have adopted the Uniform Fraudulent Transfer Act (UFTA). In 2014, the name was changed to the Uniform Voidable Transactions Act (UVTA). Federal Bankruptcy law allows bankruptcy trustees to challenge such transfers. (*See Horton v. Horton*, 785 S.E.2d 891 (Ga. 2016)).

The UVTA and similar laws recognize two kinds of fraudulent transfers. First, transfers that are intentionally designed to remove property from the reach of creditors—actual fraud. Second, constructive fraud, in which the debtor does not intend to defraud creditors, but instead transfers property for less than adequate consideration under circumstances that render the debtor insolvent.

Spouses sometimes transfer property between themselves or change the character of property in order to remove the property from creditors of one spouse. Such transfers are vulnerable to attack under the UVTA. In *State Board of Equalization v. Woo*, 82 Cal. App. 4th 481, 98 Cal. Rptr. 2d 206 (2000), for example, husband owed state taxes. Under California law, the tax collector—the Board of Equalization—could satisfy husband's tax debt by taking all of the community property. (Cal. Family Code § 910). Husband and wife learned that the Board of Equalization planned to garnish wife's wages to satisfy husband's tax debt. To shield wife's wages (community property) they entered into a transmutation agreement changing wife's wages to separate property. Generally, one spouse's separate property is not liable for the other spouse's debts (Cal. Family Code § 913(b)). The Board of Equalization challenged the transmutation under the UVTA, and won. The transmutation was intended to defraud the creditor.

Divorcing couples sometimes transfer property in an MSA that runs afoul of the UVTA. (*See Mejia v. Reed*, 31 Cal. 4th 657, 74 P.3d 166, 3 Cal. Rptr. 3d 390 (2003) (UVTA can apply to MSA and to property transfers in ongoing marriage); *Canty v. Otto*, 304 Conn. 546, 41 A.3d 280 (2013) (accord); *Estes v. Titus*, 751 N.W.2d 493 (Mich. 2008) (accord); *Citizens State Bank Norwood Young America v. Brown*, 849 N.W.2d 55 (Minn. 2014) (accord)).

In *Sturm v. Moyer*, 32 Cal. App. 5th 299, 243 Cal. Rptr. 3d 556 (2019), the Court of Appeal ruled that the UVTA can apply to a premarital agreement in which a couple arranges their property interests in such a way that the agreement "defrauds" creditors. Robert Sturm had a judgment against Todd Moyer for $600,000. Todd steadfastly refused to pay the judgment. Todd and Jessica Schell signed a prenuptial agreement in which their income remained separate property rather than community property. But for the premarital agreement, Jessica's income during marriage would be community property and would be liable to pay Robert's $600,000 judgment. The Court concluded a premarital agreement can run afoul of the UFTA if there is actual or constructive intent to defraud.

Can one spouse be a creditor for UVTA purposes and challenge the other spouse's transfer of property? Yes. (*See e.g., Buchanan v. Buchanan*, 266, Va. 207, 585 S.E.2d 533 (2003)).

The UVTA is intended primarily as a tool to protect unsecured creditors. If a creditor has a security interest in transferred property, the lien accompanies the transfer and the creditor can foreclose the lien against the property if the debt is not paid.

CHAPTER 11

ANNULMENT

Annulment ends marriage and is an alternative to divorce. Historically, complete divorce (*a vinculo matrimonii*) was unavailable and annulment was the only way to terminate an unhappy marriage. In the relatively recent past (prior to the 1970s), divorce was socially stigmatizing. Eyebrows rose when a woman was a "divorcee." Today, divorce is practically normative. The social reasons to prefer annulment over divorce are disappearing. Some people have religious reasons to prefer annulment. Other people want an annulment because they can say with a straight face that in the eyes of the law the marriage did not exist. In the twenty-first century, annulment is uncommon. The vast majority of unhappy couples divorce.

Annulment is available only if grounds for annulment exist *on the day a couple marries*. That is, from the very outset of the marriage, there was a legal defect in the marriage that rendered it subject to annulment. The person seeking annulment must prove the defect existed at the time of the marriage. Defects arising *after* a couple marries are not grounds for annulment although they may be grounds for divorce.

Marriages subject to annulment are void or voidable. Incestuous and bigamous marriages are void. A void marriage is void from the beginning—void *ab initio*. Void marriages can be annulled during the lifetimes of the spouses and can be attacked after one or both spouses have died. In *MacDougall v. Levick*, 66 Va. App. 50, 782 S.E.2d 182 (2016), the Virginia Court of Appeals wrote, "If such marriages are deemed void ab initio, anyone could challenge the validity of the marriage, at any time. Thus, for example, disgruntled heirs could preclude a mother from inheriting under the intestacy statutes (or receiving her elective share under a will) . . . ."

Because a void marriage was never really a marriage, it is technically not necessary to bring an annulment action—there is nothing to annul. The "marriage" was void *ab initio*. The California Court of Appeal explained in *Marriage of Seaton*, 200 Cal. App. 4th 800, 133 Cal. Rptr. 3d 50 (2011), "In California, a void marriage is invalid for all purposes from the moment of its inception, whether or not it has been so declared in a court of law, and its invalidity may be shown collaterally in any proceeding in which the fact of marriage may be material. . . . There is a fundamental difference between a judgment of dissolution and a judgment of nullity. While a judgment of dissolution terminates a valid marriage, a judgment of nullity declares that the marriage was void from its inception." Yet, void "marriages" often last years, and it is useful to bring an annulment proceeding or a divorce so the court can clarify the parties' marital status and adjudicate issues pertaining to custody of children and property.

A voidable marriage is a valid marriage unless and until it is annulled. (*Marriage of Seaton,* 200 Cal. App. 4th 800, 133 Cal. Rptr. 3d 50 (2011)). A voidable marriage can only be annulled during the lifetime of the parties. (*Ponder v. Graham*, 4 Fla. 23 (1851)). Once one spouse dies, a voidable marriage is immune from attack.

§ 11-1 GROUNDS FOR ANNULMENT

This section describes the grounds for annulment. As stated above, grounds for annulment exist on the wedding day.

§ 11–1[A] INCEST

Incestuous marriages are void. Incestuous marriage is marriage between parents and children, ancestors and descendants, brothers and sisters, and aunts and nephews and uncles and nieces. States vary slightly in their definitions of incest.

§ 11–1[B] BIGAMOUS

Bigamous marriage occurs when a married person marries a second time while the first marriage continues. (Cal. Family Code § 2201; Tex. Family Code § 6.202(a); Wash. Rev. Code Ann. § 26.04.020(1)(a)). As the Texas Court of Appeals explained in *Nguyen v. Nguyen*, 355 S.W.3d 82 (Tex. Ct. App. 2011), "A marriage is void if it is entered into when either party to the marriage has an existing marriage to another person that has not been dissolved by legal action or terminated by the death of the other spouse."

When a person has been married to different people, the law presumes the most recent marriage is valid. In *Mack v. Brown*, 82 A.D.3d 133, 141, 919 N.Y.S.2d 166 (2011), the Appellate Division of the

New York Supreme court wrote, "Where, as here, two competing putative spouses come forward with proof of their respective marriages, there is a presumption that the second marriage is valid and that the prior marriage was dissolved by death, divorce, or annulment." The Texas Court of Appeals explained in *Nguyen v. Nguyen*, 355 S.W.3d 82 (Tex. Ct. App. 2011), "This presumption is one of the strongest known to law; it is, in itself, evidence; and it may even outweigh positive evidence to the contrary. The presumption's strength increases with the lapse of time, acknowledgments by the parties to the marriage, and the birth of children. . . . The party attacking the validity of the subsequent marriage must also introduce sufficient evidence, standing alone, to negate the dissolution of the previous marriage. To rebut the presumption, the proponent of the earlier marriage must prove that (1) the first spouse was alive at the time the husband married the second wife; (2) the husband never secured a divorce or annulment from the first wife; and (3) the first wife never secured a divorce or annulment from the husband."

§ 11–1[C] TOO YOUNG TO MARRY

States establish a minimum age below which a person cannot consent to marriage. Such a marriage is voidable, and the under-age person may annul the marriage.

§ 11–1[D] UNSOUND MIND

Mental illness or developmental disability may deprive a person of the capacity to consent to marriage. Such a marriage is voidable. (*See Marriage of Thrash*, 605 S.W.3d 224 (Tex. Ct. App. 2020) (annulment proper because person lacked capacity to marry)).

§ 11–1[E] FRAUD

If consent to marry was obtained by fraud the marriage is voidable and may be annulled. Not all types of fraud will suffice, however. (*Meadows v. Meadows*, 330 S.W.3d 798 (Mo. Ct. App. 2011); *Travis A. v. Vilma B.*, 197 A.D.3d 1401, 153 N.Y.S.3d 674 (2021)). The California Court of Appeal explained in *In Marriage of Ramirez,*165 Cal. App. 4th 751, 81 Cal. Rptr. 3d 180 (2008), *disapproved on other grounds*, 56 Cal. 4th 113, 302 P.3d 211, 158 Cal. Rptr. 3d 21 (2013), "A [false] promise to be a kind, dutiful and affectionate spouse cannot be made the basis of an annulment. Instead, the particular fraudulent intention must relate to the sexual or procreative aspects of marriage. In the absence of this type of fraud, the longstanding rule is that neither party may question the validity of the marriage upon the ground of express or implied representations of the other with respect to such matters as character, habits, chastity, business or social standing, financial worth or prospects, or matters of a similar nature. Concealment of incontinence, temper, idleness, extravagance, coldness or lack of represented fortune will not justify an annulment." In *Marriage of*

Todorov and Ha, 501 P.3d 1216, 1220–1221 (Wash. Ct. App. 2022), the Washington Court of Appeal wrote, "'[N]o state has determined that misrepresentations about chastity involve the essentials of the marriage. . . . We agree with those jurisdictions that misrepresentations about chastity do not amount to fraud involving the essentials of marriage."

Fraud must be proven by clear and convincing evidence. (*Wisniewski v. Dolecka,* 251 Ariz. 240, 489 P.3d 724, 727 (2021); *Marriage of Todorov and Ha,* 501 P.3d 1216 (Wash. Ct. App. 2022)).

Courts grant annulment upon proof that a person promised to marry a U.S. citizen not out of love but in order to gain entry to the United States. (*Marriage of Ankola,* 53 Cal. App. 5th 369, 267 Cal. Rptr. 3d 569 (2020); *Travis A. v. Vilma B.,* 197 A.D.3d 1401, 153 N.Y.S.3d 674 (2021)).

§ 11–1[F] FORCE

Consent obtained by force or threat of force—so-called "shotgun wedding"—is not valid consent. Such marriages are voidable and may be annulled.

§ 11–1[G] INCAPABLE

A marriage is voidable and may be annulled if one party, at the time of the marriage, was physically incapable of entering into the marriage state.

§ 11-2 DEFENSES TO ANNULMENT

Today, there are no viable defenses to divorce. If one spouse wants a divorce, the other spouse cannot stop it. The divorce-seeking spouse pleads irreconcilable differences or a similar ground for no-fault divorce and the judge will not second guess the grounds. Not so with annulment. To obtain annulment, the moving party must plead and prove that grounds for annulment existed on the wedding day. (*Stuhr v. Oliver*, 363 S.W.3d 316 (Ark. 2010)). Failure to carry the burden of proof means the judge denies the annulment. In this situation, the party may get a divorce but not an annulment.

§ 11-3 CHURCH ANNULMENT NOT BINDING ON SECULAR COURT

An annulment granted by a religious organization is not binding on a secular court. In *Age v. Age*, 340 S.W.3d 88 (Ky. Ct. App. 2011), Janet and Steve were married 33 years when Janet filed for divorce. The divorce was finalized, and Steve was ordered to pay spousal support. A year after the divorce was entered, Steve filed a motion to vacate the divorce decree. Steve had obtained an annulment from his church. The religious tribunal ruled that the marriage was based on fraud perpetrated by Janet. In state court, Steve argued that the judge should vacate the divorce based on the religious tribunal's annulment. With the marriage annulled, Steve argued that his duty to pay spousal support should terminate. The Kentucky Court of Appeal disagreed.

§ 11-4 RELATION-BACK DOCTRINE IN ANNULMENT

The relation-back doctrine is a legal fiction under which a decree of annulment "relates back" to the date of marriage and erases the marriage. As the California Court of Appeal put it in *Marriage of Seaton*, 200 Cal. App. 4th 800, 133 Cal. Rptr. 3d 50 (2011), "A judgment of nullity has been said to relate back and erase the marriage and all its implications from the outset. At the same time, this legal fiction was fashioned by the courts to do substantial justice between the parties to a void or voidable marriage, and is desirable only when used as a device for achieving that purpose. In cases involving the rights of third parties, courts have been especially wary lest the logical appeal of the fiction should obscure fundamental problems and lead to unjust or ill-advised results respecting a third party's rights."

Consider Sue and Bill, who were married fifteen years. They divorced three years ago. In the divorce, Sue was ordered to pay Bill spousal support of $4,000 per month. The divorce decree provided that spousal support would end on Bill's death or remarriage. A year ago, Bill married Beth. Upon Bill's marriage to Beth, Sue stopped paying spousal support. Recently, Bill obtained an annulment of his marriage to Beth. As soon as the annulment was final, Bill returned to family court and filed a motion requesting the judge to order Sue to resume spousal support. Bill relies on the relation-back theory. According to Bill, the annulment relates back and wipes out his marriage to Beth. In other words, Bill did not remarry, and Sue owes him support. In cases like this, courts generally refuse to utilize relation back to reinstitute spousal support. Courts believe the supporting former spouse is entitled to rely on the remarriage and to reallocate their money. (*Sefton v. Sefton,* 45 Cal. 2d 872, 291 P.2d 439 (1955); *Flaxman v. Flaxman,* 57 N.J. 458, 273 A.2d 567 (1971)). One can imagine a case in which an extremely short marriage is annulled so promptly that the supporting spouse did not have time to reallocate funds, and in that case a court might be sympathetic to a former spouse in economic need.

§ 11-5 DIVISION OF PROPERTY ON ANNULMENT

In divorce proceedings, courts divide marital/community property. How does a court divide property when a void or voidable marriage is annulled? In *Liming v. Liming,* 117 Ohio App. 3d 617, 691 N.E.2d 299 (1996), the Ohio Court of Appeals wrote, "Most courts have held that the property rights of litigants in an annulment proceeding are only those that attach to persons in an individual capacity and are not the same rights usually affiliated with a husband and wife in a divorce proceeding. A property division in annulment is not based on a legal status such as marriage but is more of an adjustment of property interests between parties similar to a dissolution of a business partnership. The judgment annulling a marriage should place the parties in the same position that they would have been in had the annulled marriage not taken place." In some states (*e.g.*, California), the court granting an annulment has authority to divide property in a manner very similar to division of property on divorce.

§ 11–6 ESTOPPEL TO DENY VALIDITY OF MARRIAGE

A party to a void or voidable marriage may be estopped from denying the validity of the marriage. In *Spellens v. Spellens*, 49 Cal. 2d 210, 317 P.2d 613, 618–620 (1957), the California Supreme Court wrote:

> The theory is that the marriage is not made valid by reason of the estoppel but that the estopped person may not take a position that the divorce or latter marriage was invalid . . . . We think it may not be stated that the general public policy in this jurisdiction, as judicially interpreted, no longer prevents application in annulment actions of the laches and estoppel doctrines in determining the effect to be given such divorce decrees . . . . Rather it is that defendant by reason of his conduct will not be permitted to question the validity of the divorce; so far as he is concerned, he and plaintiff are husband and wife. . . . It may be noted also that we are not recognizing a common law marriage which does not exist in this state for the theory is that the marriage is not validated; it is merely that defendant cannot contest it.

Accord, Fares v. Fares, 563 S.W.3d 574 (Ark. Ct. App. 2018).

CHAPTER 12

INTIMATE PARTNER VIOLENCE

Intimate partner violence is common in the United States and around the world. Intimate partner violence (IPV) is defined in criminal law and civil law. IPV includes use of physical force in an intimate relationship.

§ 12-1 BRIEF HISTORY OF INTIMATE PARTNER VIOLENCE

Intimate partner violence is as old as humanity. During much of Western history, society not only turned a blind eye toward most IPV, the law actually approved moderate physical chastisement of a woman by her husband. In early Roman law "the husband had the power to chastise, sell or even kill the wife, having the same authority over her as over his child." (William L. Burdick, *The Principles of Roman Law and Their Relation to Modern Law*, p. 225 (1938)). In early English law, a husband had authority to employ "moderate" physical chastisement of his wife. In 1765, William Blackstone wrote in his *Commentaries on the Laws of England* that a "husband also (by the old law) might give his wife moderate correction." Yet, Blackstone noted that as early as the reign of Charles II (1660–1685), "this power of correction began to be doubted: and a wife may now have security of the peace against her husband."

In America, a husband's right of chastisement took shallow root, and soon withered on the vine. In 1824, the Mississippi Supreme Court acknowledged chastisement, but ruled that a husband could be prosecuted for excessive force. (*Bradley v. State*, 2 Miss. 156 (1824)). Although the Mississippi court stated that prosecution was possible, the court felt domestic squabbles should generally not be litigated in public. The court wrote, "Family broils and dissentions cannot be investigated before the tribunals of the country, without casting a shade over the character of those who are unfortunately engaged in the controversy. To screen from public reproach those who may be thus unhappily situated, let the husband be permitted to exercise the right of moderate chastisement, in cases of great emergency, and use salutary restraints in every case of misbehavior, without being subjected to vexatious prosecutions, resulting in the mutual discredit and shame of all parties concerned."

In 1873, the North Carolina Supreme Court ruled that a husband had no right of physical chastisement. (*State v. Oliver*, 70 N.C. 60 (1873)). The Court wrote, "We may assume that the old doctrine, that a husband had a right to whip his wife, provided he used a switch no larger than his thumb, is not the law in North Carolina. Indeed, the Courts have advanced from that barbarism until they have reached the position, that the husband has no right to chastise his wife, under any circumstances." Cases of serious spousal abuse were prosecuted in North Carolina. Like their colleagues in Mississippi, however, the justices of the North Carolina Supreme Court felt it was unseemly for family matters to be aired in public prosecutions. In 1868, the North

Carolina court wrote, "The courts have been loath to take cognizance of trivial complaints arising out of the domestic relations—such as master and apprentice, teacher and pupil, parent and child, husband and wife. Not because those relations are not subject to the law, but because the evil of publicity would be greater than the evil involved in the trifles complained of; and because they ought to be left to family government." (*State v. Rhodes*, 61 N.C. 453, 454 (1868)).

By 1890, the North Carolina court had changed its mind about the propriety of litigating domestic assaults in public. In *State v. Dowell*, 11 S.E. 525 (N.C. 1890), the Court wrote, "It was at one time held in our state that the relation of husband and wife gave the former immunity to the extent that the court would not go behind the domestic curtain, and scrutinize too nicely every family disturbance, even though amounting to an assault. . . . But since *State v. Oliver* [1873] . . . , we have refused 'the blanket of the dark' to these outrages on female weakness and defenselessness. So it is now settled that, technically, a husband cannot commit even a slight assault upon his wife, and that her person is as sacred from his violence as from that of any other person."

Joel Bishop was one of the nineteenth century's leading commentators on the law of domestic relations and criminal law. In 1877, Bishop wrote, "The right of chastisement does not pertain to [husbands] in this country. . . . Therefore, [a husband] may be indicted for assault and battery committed on [his wife]." (Joel P. Bishop,

Commentaries on the Criminal Law pp. 497–498 (6th ed. 1877)). The Connecticut Supreme Court wrote to similar effect in 1914, "It is now as unlawful for him to beat or falsely imprison his wife as for another to do so, and he is amenable to the criminal law for such an offense." (*Brown v. Brown*, 89 A. 890 (Conn. 1914)).

Today there are wide-ranging laws and social policies on IPV. These laws and policies find their roots in the 1960s and 1970s. (Evan Stark & Eve S. Buzawa, *Violence Against Women*, in four volumes (2009)). The women's movement focused national attention on violence against women. (Deborah DeBare, The Evolution of the Shelter Movement. In Evan Stark & Eve S. Buzawa, *Violence Against Women* vol. 1, pp. 15–32, at 16–17 (2009)). Shelters for battered women sprang up around the country. (Sharon Rice Vaughan, The Story of the Shelter, "Women's Advocates." In Evan Stark & Eve S. Buzawa, *Violence Against Women* vol. 1, pp. 1–14 (2009)). Deborah DeBare writes, "The first official battered woman's shelter in the modern period opened in England, the Chiswick Women's Aid in 1971. Very shortly thereafter, battered women's shelters started to develop throughout the United States. Woman House in St. Paul Minnesota, opened in 1974." (Deborah DeBare, The Evolution of the Shelter Movement. In Evan Stark & Eve S. Buzawa, *Violence Against Women,* vol. 1, pp. 15–32, at 17 (2009)). Legislatures passed laws authorizing civil protection orders for battered women. Police departments rethought their approach to IPV. Prosecutors took IPV cases more seriously.

§ 12-2 PREVALENCE OF IPV

IPV is common. One in four women and one in nine men experience severe IPV or stalking. Every day, there are more than 20,000 calls to domestic violence hotlines. Twenty percent of IPV involves a weapon. Fincham and Beach write, "A World Health Organization study across 10 countries also showed that 15%–71% of ever-partnered women had experienced physical or sexual violence, or both, at some point in their lives by a current of former partner." (Frank D. Fincham & Steven R. H. Beach, Marriage in the New Millennium: A Decade in Review, 72 *Journal of Marriage and Family* 630–649, 632 (2010)). Graham-Bermann and her colleagues report, "The annual rate of intimate partner violence in America is conservatively estimated at between 17% and 28% of all married or cohabiting couples." (Sandra A. Graham-Bermann, et al., Community-Based Intervention for Children Exposed to Intimate Partner Violence: An Efficacy Trial, 75 *Journal of Consulting and Clinical Psychology* 199–209, 199 (2007)). Men and woman experience IPV, although four out of five victims are women, and women are much more likely than men to suffer serious injury as a result of IPV. Regarding homicide, nearly 40% of female homicide victims are killed by an intimate partner, while only 3% of male victims are killed by an intimate. Abrahams observes, "Homicide statistics in both the United States and the United Kingdom show that most women are killed by partners or ex-partners and that the danger is greatest at the point of leaving, as he tries to stop her, or just afterward, as he tries to find and punish her for doing so." (Hilary Abrahams, Changing from Victim to Survivor. In Evan Stark & Eve S. Buzawa, *Violence Against Women* vol. 1, pp. 33–54, at 40 (2009)).

§ 12–3 CHILDREN EXPOSED TO IPV

Slightly more than half of women victimized by IPV live in households with children under age twelve. Graham-Bermann and her colleagues write, "Estimates are that 11%–16% of children will be exposed to intimate partner violence each year." (Sandra A. Graham-Bermann, et al., Community-Based Intervention for Children Exposed to Intimate Partner Violence: An Efficacy Trial, 75 *Journal of Consulting and Clinical Psychology* 199–209, 199 (2007)). It is likely that more than three million children are exposed to IPV every year in the United States. Many parents in violent relationships believe their children are unaware of the violence, but this is usually wishful thinking.

A man who beats his wife is apt to beat his child. Studies of the co-occurrence of IPV and child abuse indicate a co-occurrence rate of 30 percent to 60 percent. Children are sometimes injured when they try to protect their mother. *See Shella H. v. Department of Child Safety*, 366 P.3d 106 (Ariz. Ct. App. 2016) (child's wrist broken when he tried to protect his mother). Even when they do not intervene, children are injured accidentally during episodes of IPV.

Witnessing IPV isn't good for anyone. Graham-Bermann writes, "Children can be traumatized by overhearing beatings as well as by viewing them." (Sandra A. Graham-Bermann, Child Abuse in the Context of Domestic Violence. In John E.B. Myers et al. (Eds.), *The APSAC Handbook on Child Maltreatment*. pp. 119–129, 124 (2002)). Exposure during childhood to IPV is a risk factor for depression, low self-esteem, and other trauma-related symptoms. Children exposed to IPV fear for their mother and for themselves. Living in constant apprehension of the next outburst of violence takes a toll. Abusive men often isolate their wife or girlfriend, and the isolation imposed on the woman is visited on the children, cutting off children from sources of positive feedback and constructive adult role models. Children who grow up in violent, socially isolated homes may come to view violence as normal. Some abusive men heap psychological abuse on their children, undermining the children's sense of self-worth. Finally, some chronically abused mothers are so emotionally exhausted and depressed that they do not provide adequate parenting.

Exposing children to IPV can constitute neglect, although it does not do so in all cases. (*See Department of Human Services v. A.W.*, 276 Or. App. 276, 367 P.3d 556 (2016) (evidence not sufficient to justify juvenile court involvement)). In *D.W.G. v. Department of Children and Families*, 833 So. 2d 238 (Fla. Ct. App. 2002), a father appealed a juvenile court order that his two sons were neglected. Father sexually abused one boy, and exposed both children to IPV perpetrated against their mother. On appeal, father argued that the evidence did not prove the children knew of the violence, and that children must actually observe violence to be neglected. The Florida Court of Appeals disagreed, writing, "Children may be affected by domestic violence and may be aware of the violence, even if they do not see it occur with their own eyes. There was ample evidence in this case that the children were in the house when the father was abusing the mother. The mother testified that she heard the children crying when the father took her in the bathroom to abuse her. There also was evidence that the older son walked into the bathroom when the father was sexually abusing the mother. Moreover, the mother fled the home on more than one occasion with the children due to the domestic violence incidents. This evidence supports a finding that the incidents of domestic violence constituted abuse sufficient to support an adjudication of dependency." In *Shella H. v. Department of Child Safety,* 239 Ariz. 47, 366 P.3d 106, 110 (Ct. App. 2016), the Arizona Court of Appeals wrote, "Domestic violence need not be continuous or actively occurring at the time of the adjudication hearing to support a finding of dependency on these grounds; the substantial and unresolved threat is sufficient." The court added that concern about child safety is elevated when the victim of domestic violence lies about it or minimizes its severity in an effort to shield the abuser. *See also, In re M.M.,* 240 Cal. App. 4th 703, 192 Cal. Rptr. 3d 849 (2015) (severe domestic violence in the child's presence; parent lied about it in effort minimize the violence).

In a landmark decision in 2002, Federal District Court Judge Jack Weinstein granted an injunction against New York City's child protection agency

(CPS) for its practice of routinely removing children from mothers who were abused by an intimate partner. CPS accused these mothers of neglect, based on failure to protect. (*Nicholson v. Williams,* 203 F. Supp. 2d 153 (E.D. N.Y. 2002), *aff'd,* 344 F.3d 154 (2d Cir. 2003)). Judge Weinstein ruled that it is unconstitutional for CPS to remove children from a fit parent simply because the parent is a victim of IPV. The Second Circuit Court of Appeals approved the injunction, and certified questions to the New York Court of Appeals, which issued its ruling in 2004. (*Nicholson v. Scoppetta,* 3 N.Y.3d 357, 820 N.E.2d 840, 787 N.Y.S.2d 196 (2004)). Agreeing with the federal courts, the New York Court of Appeals wrote, "Exposing a child to domestic violence is *not* presumptively neglectful. Not every child exposed to domestic violence is at risk of impairment. A fortiori, exposure of a child to violence is not presumptively ground for removal, and in many instances removal may do more harm to the child than good." (emphasis in original). Removal from a mother who has been victimized by IPV is warranted only if the facts establish that the mother was herself in some way was at fault. In deciding whether a mother failed to protect her children, CPS and the juvenile court must consider "risks attendant to leaving, if the batterer has threatened to kill her if she does; risks attendant to staying and suffering continued abuse; risks attendant to seeking assistance through government channels, potentially increasing the danger to herself and her children; risks attendant to criminal prosecution against the abuser; and risks attendant to relocation. Whether a particular mother in these circumstances has actually failed to exercise a minimum degree of care is necessarily dependent on facts such as the severity and frequency of the violence, and the resources and options available to her." When the *sole* allegation against a mother is that she was abused and her child witnessed the IPV, removal from her custody is not warranted. On the other hand, the Court of Appeals wrote, "This does not mean, however, that a child can never be 'neglected' when living in a household plagued by domestic violence. Conceivably, neglect might be found where a record establishes that, for example, the mother acknowledged that the children knew of repeated domestic violence by her paramour and had reason to be afraid of him, yet nonetheless allowed him several times to return to her home, and lacked awareness of any impact of the violence on the children, or where the children were exposed to regular and continuous extremely violent conduct between their parents, several times requiring official intervention, and where caseworkers testified to the fear and distress the children were experiencing as a result of their long exposure to violence." (820 N.E.2d at 846–847).

A man who beats a woman in the presence of her children may be prosecuted for endangering the welfare of the children. The New York Court of Appeals addressed this issue in *People v. Johnson,* 95 N.Y.2d 368, 740 N.E.2d 1075, 718 N.Y.S.2d 1 (2000). Vanessa Parker obtained a civil order of protection against Theodore Johnson. In violation of the order, Johnson approached Parker as she walked down the street with her three daughters, aged twelve, seven, and an infant. Johnson struck Parker in the back of the head, knocking her against a fence and tipping over the baby carriage. The children started crying. Johnson yelled at Parker for having him arrested, grabbed her by the back of the neck, and dragged her to her apartment, where he knocked her head against the door. Once inside, the children escaped to their room and closed the door. Over a period of ten hours, Johnson beat Parker with his hands, his feet, and with a metal pipe. He cursed her and threatened to kill her. Johnson threw plates and glassware against walls. The children heard all this, including their mother's screams, from their room. Finally, Parker managed to call the police, and Johnson was arrested.

Johnson was convicted of endangering the welfare of a child under a statute stating that a person endangers a child when "he knowingly acts in a manner likely to be injurious to the physical, mental or moral welfare of a child less than seventeen years old." On appeal, the Court of Appeals was "asked to determine whether the evidence was legally sufficient to support defendant's conviction for endangering the welfare of a child when his actions were not specifically directed at the children." Answering in the affirmative, the court stated that exposure to IPV harms children. The court noted, "Nothing in the statute restricts its application solely to harmful conduct directed at children. The statute is broadly written and imposes a criminal sanction for the mere 'likelihood' of harm. Moreover, the language provides that defendant 'knowingly' act in such a manner, further suggesting that the statute does not require that the conduct be specifically directed at a child; rather, a defendant must simply be *aware* that the conduct may likely result in harm to a child, whether directed at the child or not." The evidence was more than sufficient to prove "that defendant's assaultive conduct in this case created a likelihood of harm to the children of which he was aware."

§ 12–4 IPV AS A FACTOR IN CHILD CUSTODY AND VISITATION

Child custody and visitation are addressed in Chapter 6. Suffice to say that when IPV is present, it is an important factor in determining a child's best interests. (*See Caroline J. v. Theodore J.*, 354 P.3d 1085 (Alaska 2015) (because father had history of IPV "there was a rebuttable presumption that he could not be awarded joint physical or legal custody of the children."); *Fountain v. Fountain*, 12 N.Y.S.3d 641, 130 A.D.3d 1107 (2015) (IPV is a factor in best interest analysis); *Schurmann v. Schurmann*, 877 N.W.2d 20 (N.D. 2016) (IPV can be relevant to changed circumstances)).

§ 12–5 PARENTING BY BATTERED WOMEN

Most victims of IPV provide competent parenting. Yet, battering takes a psychological and physical toll that can interfere with the ability to nurture children. Carter and her colleagues write, "Battered mothers may be less emotionally available to their children because they are preoccupied with the violence and trying to stay safe, and/or because they are experiencing depression." (Lucy Salcido Carter, Lois A. Weithorn & Richard E. Behrman, Domestic Violence and Children: Analysis and Recommendations, 9 *The Future of Children* 4–20, at 6 (1999)). Fantuzzo and Mohr add that battered parents "may be numbed, frightened, and depressed, unable to deal with their own trauma and/or grief, and emotionally unavailable for their children." (John W. Fantuzzo & Wanda K. Mohr, Prevalence and Effects of Child Exposure to Domestic Violence, 9 *The Future of Children* 21–42, at 40 (1999)).

§ 12-6 CRIMINAL AND CIVIL LAWS ON IPV

Every state has an array of laws to respond to IPV. Thus, victims of IPV can obtain protective orders to restrain IPV. In child custody litigation, a parent with a history of IPV has an uphill battle to convince a judge it is in a child's best interest to be placed with the batterer. IPV is a crime. A batterer can be prosecuted under traditional crimes such as battery, mayhem, and murder. As well, many states have specialized IPV crimes.

§ 12-7 IPV PROTECTIVE ORDERS

Statutory law on protective orders, also called restraining orders, varies from state to state. Although the wording of statutes varies, the basic procedures and protections are similar across the country.

§ 12–7[A] DEFINING IPV

For purposes of protective orders, states define domestic violence broadly to include actual or attempted striking or assaulting, sexual abuse, and stalking. Pointing or firing a gun is included. Threats to harm or kill constitute IPV. *See Shirley v. Shirley*, 107 So. 3d 99 (La. Ct. App. 2012) (victim's husband threatened to burn down the house with her and the child in it; and to have a "crack whore" kill her); *In re T.W.J. & I.B.J.*, 367 P.3d 607 (Wash. Ct. App. 2016) (man told his family law attorney he would kill the mother of his children if custody case went against him; man then fired his attorney; fired attorney emailed mother's attorney to warn her of the threat; this was sufficient evidence to support a restraining order)). The Kentucky Court of Appeals ruled that a threat to commit suicide in front of the couple's children constituted domestic violence. (*Crabtree v. Crabtree*, 484 S.W.3d 316 (Ky. Ct. App. 2016)). An occasional abuser who thinks he has talent sets his threats to music. (*See Holcomb v. Commonwealth*, 58 Va. App. 339, 709 S.E.2d 711 (2011)). Many definitions of IPV include false imprisonment or kidnapping, harassment (including electronic harassment), arson of the family home, and other destruction of property, preventing the victim from reporting IPV, and violation of a protective order. A few states include controlling property in such a way that the victim is forced to return to the abuser out of fear of inability to meet basic needs. Some states add harming or killing an animal in order to terrorize or control the human victim. (*See Pettingill v. Pettingill*, 480 S.W.3d 920 (Ky. 2016) (among other types of abuse and intimidation, victim's husband abused the family pet)). In California, IPV includes disturbing the peace of the victim. Disturbing the peace refers "to conduct that, based on the totality of the circumstances, destroys the mental or emotional calm of the other party. This conduct may be committed directly or indirectly, including through the use of a third party, and by any method or through any means, including but not limited to, telephone, online accounts, text messages, internet-connected devices, or other electronic technologies. This conduct, includes, but is not limited to, coercive control, which is a pattern of behavior that in purpose or effect unreasonably interferes with a person's free will and personal liberty. (Cal. Family Code § 6320(c)).

§ 12–7[B] WHO MAY OBTAIN AN IPV PROTECTIVE ORDER

An IPV protective order may be obtained by past and present spouses, domestic partners, household members, and parties to a present or past dating relationship. Same sex partners are entitled to protection.

§ 12–7[C] RELIEF AVAILABLE

A court may enter a range of orders, including: (1) The perpetrator shall not commit or threaten violence against the victim or other people (*e.g.*, children) protected by the protective order; (2) Orders against harassment, threats, stalking, and other types of abuse; (3) A "kick-out" order, requiring the perpetrator to leave the home; (4) The court may order the perpetrator to stay a specified distance (*e.g.*, 100 yards) away of the victim; (5) The court may make orders regarding child custody and visitation; (6) Some states authorize the court to make orders regarding child support; and (7) A person subject to an IPV protective order cannot possess firearms.

§ 12–7[D] PROCEDURE TO OBTAIN IPV PROTECTIVE ORDER

The person seeking an IPV protective order fills out preprinted forms. The first step is usually to apply for an ex parte temporary IPV restraining order (IPV-TRO). On the application, the victim provides demographic information about the victim (protected person), the alleged abuser (restrained person), children, and other persons living in the home. The protected person then provides a written description of the IPV. Pictures of injuries and police or medical reports may be attached to the application. In most communities, a ruling is made to grant or deny the application for an IPV-TRO the same day it is filed or the day following. Typically, there is no filing fee.

The court sets a date for an evidentiary hearing, often two weeks later. The IPV-TRO paperwork must be served on the restrained person. At the evidentiary hearing, the court can only grant a permanent IPV protective order (IPV-PO) if the restrained person was served with the papers, and a "Proof of Service" is in the court file. If the restrained person was properly served, but fails to appear at the hearing, the judge typically grants an IPV-PO. If the protected person is unable to serve the restrained person, the judge usually extends the TRO to allow more time for service. Once served with the IPV-TRO, the restrained person can file a response giving his side of the story. If the restrained person contests the application the court conducts a trial. The protected person has the burden of proof by a preponderance of the evidence. (*King v. W.T.F.*, 276 Or. App. 533, 369 P.3d 1181 (2016)).

The party restrained may petition the court to end or modify a restraining order. *See Ashby v. Ashby*, 68 Cal. App. 5th 491, 283 Cal. Rptr. 3d 784 (2021).

§ 12–7[E] LENGTH OF IPV-PO

States vary in the length of IPV-POs, ranging from six months to permanent. In most states, the judge has discretion to select the appropriate duration for the order. States have procedures allowing protected persons to return to court to seek extension or renewal of an IPV-PO.

§ 12–7[F] ARREST FOR VIOLATION OF IPV-PO

More than half the states mandate arrest for violation of an IPV-PO.

The protected person should carry the protective order with them at all times. A police officer is more likely to feel comfortable arresting a restrained person who violates a protective order when the officer is provided a copy of the order. In most states, temporary and permanent protective orders are entered in a law enforcement data base, and a police officer can log onto the computer in the patrol car to verify the existence and terms of an order. In many states, a police officer can request an emergency temporary protective order by calling a judge any time of the day or night.

§ 12–7[G] MUTUAL RESTRAINING ORDERS

A mutual restraining order restrains both persons based on evidence that each inflicted IPV. Mutual restraining orders are sometimes appropriate, but they are subject to abuse. Too often, there is only one perpetrator, but when the victim seeks protection the perpetrator manufactures or exaggerates evidence that he was the victim or that there was mutual violence. The perpetrator seeks an advantage over the victim by portraying her as the villain. Most states deal with this issue by providing that a person who seeks protection must file their own application and must carry the burden of proof.

§ 12–7[H] PROCEEDINGS WHERE IPV PROTECTIVE ORDERS ARE AVAILABLE

IPV protective orders are available not only in civil proceedings focused exclusively on IPV. Protective orders can be granted in criminal law proceedings, family court cases, and juvenile court matters.

§ 12–7[I] ADDITIONAL TYPES OF RESTRAINING ORDERS

In addition to IPV-POs to protect victims in intimate relationships, states have laws to restrain stalking, harassment, and sexual assault. These laws do not require a close, intimate relationship. For example, a victim may be stalked by a stranger. A neighbor across the street may engage in harassment.

§ 12–7[J] NOT A PANACEA

Protective orders are extremely valuable, but they are not a panacea. After all, a protective order is "a piece of paper." Some batterers are not deterred by a protective order and continue harassing or battering. Tragically, cases arise in which a protected person is killed despite a protective order. (*See State v. Supanchick,* 354 Or. 737, 323 P.3d 231 (2014)).

Taylor, Stoilkov, and Greco discuss another concern with protective orders, particularly ex parte orders. They write, "As the doors of the courthouse have been opened to actual victims of domestic violence, they also have inadvertently been opened to persons who are not victims of domestic violence. In fact, they have been opened to the actual abuser who seeks relief for improper motives, such as trying to gain a tactical advantage in an anticipated domestic violence proceeding or divorce action." (David H. Taylor, Maria V. Stoilkov & Daniel J. Greco, Ex parte Domestic Violence Orders of Protection: How Easing Access to Judicial Process has Eased the Possibility for Abuse of the Process, 18 *Kansas Journal of Law and Public Policy* 83, 85–86 (2008)).

§ 12-8 ADDITIONAL REMEDIES

In addition to IPV protective orders, states provide other remedies for victims. States allow victims to register for a confidential address to make it difficult for the perpetrator to track the victim. States allow victims to terminate a lease early by giving the landlord notice of the abuse. As well, many states prohibit landlords from evicting tenants simply because a tenant was victimized by IPV. Most states authorize tenants to change apartment locks. A landlord may not restrict a tenant's right to call 911 for help. A few states provide relocation assistance for victims. Most states authorize courts to order perpetrators to pay for the victim's housing.

§ 12-9 ARREST FOR IPV

Every year, police respond to hundreds of thousands of domestic disputes. Often there is no violence. When there is, however, police decide whether to make one or more arrests. In bygone days, the accepted police practice in most cases was to separate the parties, talk to them, and try to cool things down without arresting anyone. Arrest was reserved for the most serious cases. Times have changed. Today, roughly half the states require arrest when police have probable cause to believe IPV occurred. A number of statutes provide that when both parties engaged in violence, the police can arrest the "principal physical aggressor," without arresting the other party. Hafemeister observes, "Mandatory-arrest laws have been extremely controversial. Supporters of mandatory-arrest laws contend that such laws force police officers to take IPV seriously and undercut the stereotypical views that otherwise downplay the gravity of IPV. . . . [C]ritics of mandatory-arrest laws say that they disempower victims of IPV by taking away their ability decide whether the batterer should be removed or punished. . . . Critics also argue that mandatory-arrest policies harm victims in other ways. For example, they have resulted in a dramatic increase in the number of women arrested." (Thomas L. Hafemeister, If All You Have Is a Hammer: Society's Ineffective Response to Intimate Partner Violence, 60 *Catholic University Law Review* 919, 989–990 (2011)).

States have felony and misdemeanor IPV laws. The law of arrest provides that a police officer who has probable cause can make a warrantless arrest for a felony whether or not the felony was committed in the presence of the officer. By contrast, an officer can arrest for a misdemeanor only if the offense was committed in the officer's presence. Quite a few states provide that an officer can arrest for misdemeanor IPV even if the officer did not observe the violence.

§ 12–10 PROSECUTION OF IPV

One of the greatest impediments to prosecuting IPV is that quite a few victims are uncooperative. Many victims are initially cooperative—describing abuse to police, nurses, or doctors—but later refuse to cooperate or testify. Victims change their minds for many reasons. Some batterers threaten victims to change the story. Many batters use psychological pressure to bring about change. Many victims love the batterer and don't want him sent to jail. In a fascinating study of recorded telephone calls between jailed batterers awaiting trial and their victims, Monomi and her colleagues describe the process by which batterers use psychological pressure to ware down the resolve of victims to cooperate with prosecution. (Amy E. Bonomi, Rashmi Gangamma, Chris R. Locke, Heather Katafiasz & David Martin, "Meet me at the hill where we used to park": Interpersonal Processes Associated with Victim Recantation, 73 *Social Science and Medicine* 1054 (2011)).

One way to reduce the number of uncooperative victims is to provide a robust network of social, safety, psychological, financial, and legal services for IPV victims. When victims believe the system will protect them and their children, victims are more likely to proceed with prosecution.

Many jurisdictions have so-called "no drop prosecution" policies. Prosecutors do not drop—decline to pursue—IPV cases when victims refuse to cooperate. A hard no drop policy requires prosecution whether or not the victim cooperates. If the victim won't testify voluntarily, she may be subpoenaed. Soft no drop policies afford prosecutors flexibility in deciding which cases to pursue. Critics of "no drop" prosecution, like critics of mandatory arrest, are concerned about the impact on victims. Mills argues, "Such policies as mandatory arrest, prosecution, and reporting [of IPV], which have become standard legal fare in the fight against domestic violence and which categorically ignore the battered woman's perspective, can themselves be forms of abuse." (Linda G. Mills, Killing Her Softly: Intimate Abuse and the Violence of State Intervention, 113 *Harvard Law Review* 550 (1999)).

§ 12–11 THREATENING PHONE CALLS

In many domestic violence cases the most powerful evidence of verbal abuse is the angry telephone call or the heated face-to-face confrontation where the abuser thinks the only one listening is the victim. It is in these circumstances that the full extent of the abuser's fury is on display.

In court, the victim is free to repeat what the abuser said, but if the abuser denies it—he will—it is her word against his. May a victim surreptitiously record telephone calls or face-to-face encounters to preserve evidence? The answer depends on the state's eavesdropping law. Attorneys must be familiar with their state's eavesdropping law and advise clients accordingly. In some states, it is a crime to surreptitiously record confidential communications without the consent of both parties to the communication.

Congress has passed laws dealing with wiretapping and eavesdropping. (Clifford S. Fishman & Anne T. McKenna, *Wiretapping and Eavesdropping: Surveillance in the Internet Age* (3d ed. 2012)). Most federal laws concern conduct by law enforcement and national security officials. One provision, however, 18 U.S.C. § 2511, forbids eavesdropping by private citizens. Under the federal eavesdropping law, an individual who is not acting under color of law, *i.e.*, a private individual, who is a party to a communication, may record the communication without consent of the other party. Section 2511(2)(d) specifies that it is not a violation of the federal eavesdropping statute for one side of a communication record the communication. Thus, the federal eavesdropping statute is a one-party consent statute: Only one party need consent to recordation.

Like federal law, the majority of states have one-party consent laws. As the California Supreme Court put it in *Kearney v. Salomon Smith Barney, Inc.*, 39 Cal. 4th 95, 137 P.3d 914, 932, n. 14, 45 Cal. Rptr. 3d 730 (2006), "Privacy statutes in a majority of states (as well as the comparable federal provision) . . . prohibit the recording of private conversations except with the consent of one party to the conversation." Rasmussen and her colleagues write, "Thirty-eight states and the District of Columbia permit individuals to record conversations to which they are a party without informing the other parties that they are doing so." (*See* Kristen Rassmussen, Jack Komperda & Raymond Baldino, Committee for Freedom of the Press, *Reporter's Recording Guide: A State-by-State Guide to Taping Phone Calls and In-Person Conversations* (2012)).

In some states, both parties must consent to recording of a confidential telephone call or in-person interaction. Rassmussen and her colleagues, *supra*, write, "Twelve states require, under most circumstances, the consent of all parties to a conversation. Those jurisdictions are California, Connecticut, Florida, Illinois, Maryland, Massachusetts, Michigan, Montana, Nevada, New Hampshire, Pennsylvania and Washington." In two-party consent states, both sides of the communication must consent to recording. The California statute provides in part, "A person who, intentionally and without the consent of all parties to a confidential communication, uses an electronic . . . device to eavesdrop upon or record the confidential communication" is guilty of a misdemeanor. (Penal Code § 632(a)). This law made it potentially illegal for victims of domestic violence to record threatening telephone calls. The California Legislature remedied the problem in 2017 with a provision that provides that Penal Code § 632 does "not prohibit one party to a confidential communication from recording the communication for the purpose of obtaining evidence reasonably believed to related to the commission by another party to the communication of the crime of . . . . domestic violence . . . ."

§ 12-12 STALKING

The seriousness of stalking cannot be overstated. The U.S. Department of Justice reports that every year more than 3 million adults are stalked. (Shannan Catalano, *Stalking Victims in the United States—Revised* (Sept. 2012) (Bureau of Justice Statistics; U.S. Department of Justice)). Stalking includes unwanted phone calls, emails, texts; following or spying on the victim; appearing at places for no apparent reason; and leaving unwanted gifts.

Anti-stalking statutes prohibit a variety of acts that annoy, threaten, and frighten victims. Physical contact with the victim is not required for stalking. A threat may be made to a third person who is likely to convey the threat to the victim.

Criminal stalking statutes generally require defendant's conduct to be intentional, purposeful, knowing, malicious, or willful. Proof of intent is usually a combination of circumstantial evidence and defendant's words and acts.

In many stalking prosecutions, the defendant's conduct is so outrageous that it virtually screams intent. (*See Austin v. State,* 335 Ga. App. 521, 782 S.E.2d 308 (2016); *State v. Whittaker*, 192 Wash. App. 395, 367 P.3d 1092 (2016)). Consider, for example, *State v. Higginbotham,* 790 So. 2d 648 (La. Ct. App. 2001), in which the defendant dated victim's daughter. While he dated the daughter, defendant lived in victim's home. Trouble started when the defendant became violent and the victim called police. After the defendant moved out, he started calling the victim several times a day, at all hours, cursing her when she picked up the phone. During one call, the defendant said, "I'm going to fuck you in the rectum 'till you die.'" In another call, he threatened to kill the victim. On several occasions, the defendant appeared near the victim's home, stared at her, shook his fist at her, and gave her "the finger." When the victim obtained a restraining order, the defendant said it wouldn't do any good. The *Higginbotham* court held these facts clearly demonstrated that defendant harassed the victim with intent to inflict emotional distress.

Following the victim is a common mode of stalking. The stalker may keep the victim under surveillance. In *People v. Sullivan*, 53 P.3d 1181 (Colo. Ct. App. 2002), the victim commenced divorce proceedings against her husband. When the victim refused to dismiss the divorce, as her husband requested, he burned her clothes in the backyard. The victim obtained a restraining order but the defendant continued contacting her. The defendant installed a GPS device on the victim's car so he could track her. The defendant's conviction for stalking was affirmed.

Stalking generally requires repeated acts. The compulsive repetition of some stalkers is truly frightening. Sometimes the stalker makes no attempt to hide his identity and it is easy to attribute repeated acts to the defendant. In other cases, the annoying or frightening acts are anonymous, and it is difficult to prove that the defendant was responsible.

Some stalking statutes require two elements. First, the defendant must intentionally and repeatedly follow or harass the victim. Second, the defendant must make a "credible threat." Colorado's stalking statute, for example, provides, "A person commits stalking if the person knowingly makes a credible threat to another person and, in connection with the threat, repeatedly follows, approaches, contacts, or places under surveillance that person." (Colorado Rev. Stat. § 18-3-602).

To constitute a "credible threat," a prosecutor does not have to prove the stalker actually intended to carry through on the threat. (*See Hayes v. State*, 717 So. 2d 30 (Ala. Crim. App. 1997); *People v. Falck*, 52 Cal. App. 4th 287, 60 Cal. Rptr. 2d 624 (1997); *People v. Sucic*, 401 Ill. App. 3d 492, 928 N.E.2d 1231 (2010)). The Alabama Court of Criminal Appeals ruled in *Hayes v. State*, 717 So. 2d 30 (Ala. Crim. App. 1997), "The State need only show that the accused intended to cause the victim to fear for his safety or the safety of his family." In *State v. McCauley*, 317 S.W.3d 132 (Mo. Ct. App. 2010), the Missouri Court of Appeals ruled that the Missouri stalking statute does not require proof that the defendant was actually capable of carrying out threats.

A threat does not have to be verbal. In *People v. Cross*, 114 P.3d 1 (Colo. Ct. App. 2004), *rev'd on other grounds*, 127 P.3d 71 (Colo. 2006), the Colorado Court of Appeals ruled there was sufficient evidence that defendant committed a credible threat. The victim worked at a kiosk in a shopping center. For nearly two months, defendant went to the shopping center almost daily when the victim was working. He would spend several hours a day sitting on benches near victim's kiosk, staring at her. Occasionally he would circle the kiosk. Once, he approached the kiosk, tapped on it, smiled at victim, and returned to the bench where he watched her for two-and-a-half hours until she got off work. One day, victim went to church only to see defendant watching her. Defendant's behavior frightened the victim. The Court of Appeals ruled that threats do not have to be verbal to violate the stalking statute.

There are innumerable ways to threaten victims. In *Moses v. State*, 72 Ark. App. 357, 39 S.W.3d 459 (2001), the defendant repeatedly called his estranged wife. Eventually, victim refused to talk to him. Over the phone, the defendant said, "Call me before it's too late." This threat, in conjunction with the defendant's other conduct, amounted to a terroristic threat supporting a stalking conviction. In *Lowry v. State*, 90 Ark. App. 333, 205 S.W.3d 830 (2005), the defendant threatened to burn the victim. In *McComas v. Kirn*, 105 P.3d 1130 (Alaska 2005), the Alaska Supreme Court ruled that threatening mail can constitute stalking.

Some stalking statutes require proof that the victim suffered emotional distress. In *People v. Cross*, discussed above—the shopping center case—the Colorado Court of Appeals found sufficient evidence of distress. "The victim testified that defendant's behavior caused her to change her work schedule, take days off from work, and feel unsafe; she was nervous and had trouble sleeping; and she felt she was constantly being watched by defendant. The statute is clear that serious emotional distress need not be such as would compel professional treatment or a breakdown." In *People v. Strawbridge*, 404 Ill. App. 3d 460, 935 N.E.2d 1104, 343 Ill. Dec. 876 (2010), the Illinois Appellate Court wrote, "Any history between a defendant and a victim may be relevant to assessing whether a reasonable person in the victim's position would be in apprehension of future confinement or restraining."

§ 12–13 FEDERAL VIOLENCE AGAINST WOMEN ACT (VAWA)

In 1994, Congress enacted the Violence Against Women Act (VAWA) to combat interstate IPV and interstate violation of IPV protection orders. (18 U.S.C. § 2261(a)). VAWA provides money to states for IPV prevention and prosecution. As well, VAWA provides that a "person who travels in interstate or foreign commerce . . . with the intent to kill, injure, harass, or intimidate a spouse, intimate partner, or dating partner, and who, in the course of or as a result of such travel, commits or attempts to commit a crime of violence against that spouse, intimate partner, or dating partner, shall be punished." VAWA also criminalizes interstate stalking: "Whoever travels in interstate or foreign commerce . . . with the intent to kill, injure, harass, or place under surveillance with intent to kill, injure, harass, or intimidate another person, and in the course of, or as a result of, such travel places that person in reasonable fear of death, or serious bodily injury to, or causes substantial emotional distress to that person, a member of the immediate family of that person, or the spouse or intimate partner of that person" shall be punished (18 U.S.C. § 2261A).

CHAPTER 13

ASSISTED REPRODUCTION

Thousands of people who would love to have a child are unable to do so due to infertility or another medical condition. Some people who are biologically capable of "normal" reproduction eschew traditional reproduction to avoid passing to their offspring an inheritable disease or condition. To have the family they crave, some lesbian and gay individuals pursue reproductive alternatives.

Virginia's statute on "assisted conception" provides insight into this complicated and evolving area of law and medicine. Virginia defines assisted conception as "a pregnancy resulting from any intervening medical technology, whether in vivo or in vitro, which completely or partially replaces sexual intercourse as the means of conception. Such intervening medical technology includes, but is not limited to, conventional medical and surgical treatment as well as noncoital reproductive technology such as artificial insemination by donor, cryopreservation of gametes and embryos, in vitro fertilization, uterine embryo lavage, embryo transfer, gamete intrafallopian tube transfer, and low tubal ovum transfer." (Va. Code Ann. § 20–156).

State legislatures are enacting comprehensive statutes on alternative means of reproduction. New York's Child-Parent Security Act, for example, went into effect in 2021. (Family Court Act Article 5). Judges generally believe the legislative branch should tackle the issue. In *Marriage of Buzzanca*, 61

Cal. App. 4th 1410, 1428 (1998), the California Court of Appeal implored the legislature "to sort out the parental rights and responsibilities of those involved in artificial reproduction." The Legislature responded with amendments to the Family Code (*See* Cal. Family Code § 7960). Similarly, the Connecticut Supreme Court observed in *Raftopol v. Ramey*, 299 Conn. 681, 12 A.3d 783 (2011), "The broad public policy issues raised by modern reproductive technology . . . more appropriately would be addressed by the legislature."

§ 13-1 INTRAUTERINE INSEMINATION

Intrauterine insemination, often called, artificial insemination (AI), is a process by which sperm is placed in a woman's reproductive track to induce pregnancy. (*See Matter of W.L. and G.L.*, 312 Kan. 367, 475 P.3d 338 (2020)). The sperm donor may be the woman's partner or a donor. A non-partner sperm donor may be used if there is no partner or if the partner is sterile or has a low sperm count. A non-partner sperm donor may be used so the partner does pass along a genetic condition to the baby. In *People v. Sorensen*, 68 Cal. 2d 280, 437 P.2d 495, 66 Cal. Rptr. 7 (1968), the California Supreme Court ruled that when an infertile husband consents to the artificial insemination of his wife, the husband is the "lawful father" of the resulting baby because he consents to creation of the child. Similarly Arkansas law provides, "Any child born to a married woman by means of artificial insemination shall be deemed the legitimate natural child of the woman and the woman's husband if the husband consents in writing to the artificial insemination." (Ark. Code Ann. § 9–10–201(a)). In *Adoption of a Minor,* 471 Mass. 373, 29 N.E.3d 830 (2015), a same sex married couple produced a child through AI with sperm from a known donor. Later, the non-genetically related parent decided to adopt the child and the question arose: Is it necessary in the adoption proceeding to give notice to the sperm donor? The Massachusetts Supreme Judicial court said no. (*See also, Foust v. Montez-Torres*, 456 S.W.3d 736 (Ark. 2015); *Gatsby v. Gatsby,* 169 Idaho 308, 495 P.3d 996 (2021); *Stankevich v. Milliron*, 882 N.W.2d 194 (Mich. Ct. App. 2015)).

§ 13–2 IN VITRO FERTILIZATION

In vitro fertilization (IVF) is a well-established medical "procedure in which an ovum is surgically removed from a genetic mother's ovary and fertilized with the sperm of the genetic father in a laboratory procedure, with the resulting embryo implanted in the uterus of a birth mother." (D.C. Stat. § 16–401(3); *Jocelyn P. v. Joshua P.*, 250 Md. App. 435, 250 A.3d 373 (2021); *Matter of Schnitzer*, 312 Or. App. 71, 493 P.3d 1071 (2021)). The New Jersey Supreme Court explained in *J.B. v. M.B.*, 170 N.J. 9, 783 A.2d 707, 709 (2001), "The in vitro fertilization procedure requires a woman to undergo a series of hormonal injections to stimulate the production of mature oocytes (egg cells or ova). The medication causes the ovaries to release multiple egg cells during a menstrual cycle rather than the single egg normally produced. The eggs are retrieved from the woman's body and examined by a physician who evaluates their quality for fertilization. Egg cells ready for insemination are then combined with the sperm sample and allowed to incubate for approximately twelve to eighteen hours. Successful fertilization results in a zygote that develops into a four- to eight-cell preembryo. At that stage, the preembryos are either returned to the woman's uterus for implantation or cryopreserved at a temperature of −196C and stored for possible future use." Kindregan and McBrien write, "For the most part, there is no state statutory regulation of in vitro fertilization that restricts or controls choices made by medical personnel, patients, or donors." (Charles P. Kindregan, Jr. & Maureen McBrien, *Assisted Reproductive Technology* p. 96 (2011)).

Medical science moves steadily onward. For example, with Intracytoplasmic Sperm Injection (ICSI), a doctor injects a single sperm into an egg, using an extremely small needle. The procedure helps some men with a low sperm count.

As science invents new techniques, novel legal issues arise. In *Sieglein v. Schmidt*, 224 Md. App. 222, 120 A.3d 790 (2015), for example, a married couple signed a contract for IVF. The wife gave birth to a baby that was conceived with donated eggs and sperm. Shortly after the child was born the couple divorced and husband argued that under Maryland law he was not the father because he was not genetically related to the child. The Court of Special Appeals was not sympathetic to father's argument.

Typically with IVF more than one egg is removed and fertilized. The "extra" embryos—sometimes called pre-embryos—are frozen for later use in case the initial effort at pregnancy fails. What should be done with unused embryos if a couple decides not to have children, divorces, separates, or dies? (*Marriage of Brooks*, 429 P.3d 579 (Colo. 2018)(excellent analysis of the issue); *Jessee v. Jessee*, 866 S.E.2d 46 (Va. Ct. App. 2021) (court describes balance of interests when the parties do not have an express agreement)). One of the first decisions grappling with this question was *Davis v. Davis*, 842 S.W.2d 588 (Tenn. 1992), handed down in 1992 by the Tennessee Supreme Court. Wife and husband divorced and agreed on everything except who was to have "custody" of seven unused frozen embryos. When the couple enrolled in IVF they did not sign a document providing for disposition of unused embryos. The trial judge concluded the embryos were human beings and awarded custody to wife so she could "bring these children to term through implantation" if she so desired. The intermediate court of appeal reversed, concluding that husband had a constitutional right *not* to have children. As the case was pending before the Tennessee Supreme Court, wife changed her position and sought to donate the embryos to a couple desiring a child. Husband sought destruction of the embryos.

One issue confronting the Tennessee Supreme Court was whether the embryos were "persons" or "property." The court observed: "Three major ethical positions have been articulated in the debate over preembryo status. At one extreme is the view of the preembryo as a human subject after fertilization, which requires that it be accorded the rights of a person. . . . At the opposite extreme is the view that the preembryo has a status no different from any other human tissue. . . . A third view—one that is most widely held—takes an intermediate position between the other two. It holds that the preembryo deserves respect greater than accorded to human tissue but not the respect accorded to actual persons." The Tennessee court concluded, "preembryos are not, strictly speaking, either 'persons' or 'property,' but occupy an interim category that entitled them to special respect because of their potential for human life."

The court concluded that disputes regarding the disposition of unused frozen embryos should be governed by the preference of the parties. If the parties disagree, a prior agreement concerning disposition should be enforced. If no prior agreement exists, the trial judge balances the interests of the parties in using and not using the embryos. Typically, the wishes of the party who does not want a child should control, provided the other party has some other reasonable means of becoming a parent. If no other means exists, then the court considers the argument in favor of using the embryos to achieve pregnancy. However, if the party seeking to preserve the embryos intends to donate them to someone else, the wishes of the other party should prevail. Since wife intended to donate the embryos, husband's wish to have the embryos destroyed should control. The court concluded that the fertility clinic was free to follows its normal procedure for dealing with unused embryos.

In *Kass v. Kass*, 91 N.Y.2d 554, 696 N.E.2d 174, 673 N.Y.S.2d 350 (1998), the parties signed an unambiguous contract describing what should be done with unused embryos. The New York Court of Appeal determined "that the parties' agreement providing for donation to the IVF program controls."

In *J.B. v. M.B.* 170 N.J. 9, 783 A.2d 707 (2001), the parties' agreement was not dispositive regarding disposition and the matter was left to the courts. The New Jersey Supreme Court wrote: "In this area, however, there are few guideposts for decision-making. Advances in medical technology have far outstripped the development of legal principles to resolve the inevitable disputes arising out of the new reproductive opportunities now available. . . . We agree with the Tennessee Supreme Court [in *Davis v. Davis*, 842 S.W.2d 588 (Tenn. 1992)] that ordinarily, the party wishing to avoid procreation should prevail. . . . In the present case, the wife's right not to become a parent seemingly conflicts with the husband's right to procreate. . . . We believe that the better rule, and the one we adopt, is to enforce agreements entered into at the time in vitro fertilization is begun, subject to the right of either party to change his or her mind about disposition up to the point of use or destruction of any stored preembryos. . . . Only when a party notifies a clinic in writing of a change in intention should the disposition issue be reopened."

The Louisiana Legislature tackled the question, "Is a fertilized ovum a person?" Louisiana law states, "An in vitro fertilized ovum is a juridical person which cannot be owned by the in vitro fertilization parents who owe it a high duty of care and prudent administration. If the in vitro parents renounce, by notarial act, their parental rights for in utero implantation, then the in vitro fertilized human ovum shall be available for adoptive implantation in accordance with written procedures of the facility where it is housed or stored." (La. Stat. Ann. Tit. 9, § 130).

When an individual or couple decides to donate unused frozen embryos to others who desire a child, who is the parent of a resulting baby? Ohio law provides, "A woman who gives birth to a child as a result of embryo donation shall be treated in law and regarded as the natural mother of the child." (Ohio Rev. Code tit. 31, § 3111.97(A)).

Should embryo donation be treated as an adoption and governed by adoption law? If an embryo is a "person," adoption law applies. In 1997, an organization called Nightlight Christian Adoptions, pioneered "embryo adoption" with its Snowflakes Frozen Embryo Adoption Program. Several other adoption agencies offer embryo adoption services.

The American Society for Reproductive Medicine takes the position that embryo donation should not be considered adoption. (American Society for Reproductive Medicine, Ethics Committee, American Society for Reproductive Medicine: Defining Embryo Donation, 92 *Fertility and Sterility* 1818 (2009)). The Society's Ethics Committee writes: "Donation of embryos to support the family-building efforts of others is an important option for patients considering the disposition of cryopreserved embryos in excess of those needed to meet the patients' own fertility goals. . . . Application of the term 'adoption' to embryos is inaccurate, misleading, and could place burdens that are not appropriate for embryos that have been donated upon infertile recipients. . . . The use of donated embryos for family building is an established successful option for the infertile. Like gamete donation, it has resulted in the birth of many children in the more than 25 years the procedure has been in use. . . . Requiring infertile patients who need donor gametes or patients who need donor embryos to suffer the imposition of unnecessary administrative and legal trappings of adoption and the costs that accompany them is not ethically justifiable. . . . The donation of embryos for reproductive purposes is fundamentally a medical procedure intended to result in pregnancy and should be treated as such."

In a 2011 article in the *International Journal of Law, Policy and the Family,* Blyth and colleagues challenged many of the assumptions supporting the Society's position. (Eric Blyth, Lucy Frith, Marilyn S. Paul & Roni Berger, Embryo Relinquishment for Family Building: How Should It Be Conceptualized?, 25 International *Journal of Law, Policy and the Family* 260 (2011)).

§ 13-3 SURROGACY

Parents desiring a baby may consider entering a surrogacy contract with a woman willing to carry the baby to term and turn the infant over to the parents.

The 2017 Uniform Parentage Act deals in detail with what it calls "Gestation Agreements." (Article 8). The 2017 UPA replaces the term "surrogate mother" with "gestational mother."

The 2017 UPA recommends that states recognize and enforce gestational agreements. Section 801 of the Act provides:

> (a) A prospective gestational mother, her husband if she is married, a donor or the donors, and the intended parents may enter into a written agreement providing that:
>
> (1) the prospective gestational mother agrees to pregnancy by means of assisted reproduction;
>
> (2) the prospective gestational mother, her husband if she is married, and the donors relinquish all rights and duties as the parents of a child conceived through assisted reproduction; and
>
> (3) the intended parents become the parents of the child.
>
> (b) The man and the woman who are the intended parents must both be parties to the gestational agreement.
>
> (c) A gestational agreement is enforceable only if validated as provided in Section 803 [by a court order].

(d) A gestational agreement does not apply to the birth of a child conceived by means of sexual intercourse.

(e) A gestational agreement may provide for payment of consideration.

(f) A gestational agreement may not limit the right of the gestational mother to make decisions to safeguard her health or that of the embryos or fetus.

When the baby is born, Section 807 of the UPA provides that the "intended parents" must file notice with the court. The court issues an order confirming the "intended parents" as *the* parents.

The New York Legislature enacted comprehensive surrogacy legislation that went into effect in 2021. New York now allows gestational surrogacy in which the surrogate does not contribute genetic material.

§ 13–3[A] GESTATIONAL SURROGACY

With gestational surrogacy, an egg is removed from the woman who intends to be the mother. The egg is fertilized in a laboratory with sperm from the father. The fertilized egg is implanted in a surrogate. In this case, the surrogate contributes no genetic material to the baby. All of the baby's genetic material comes from the couple intending to be parents. In *Johnson v. Calvert*, 5 Cal. 4th 84, 851 P.2d 776, 19 Cal. Rptr. 2d 494 (1993), the California Supreme Court approved gestational surrogacy. The surrogate mother argued that the surrogacy contract she signed violated public policy as well as her constitutional rights of privacy and procreative freedom. The California Supreme Court ruled that gestational surrogacy is not against public policy. The court concluded that the husband who donated the sperm, and his wife, who donated the egg, were the child's natural parents. The Court ruled that the surrogate was not a parent; therefore, she did not enjoy the constitutional rights of a parent. In *Raftopol v. Ramey*, 299 Conn. 681, 12 A.3d 783 (2011), a surrogate mother who had no biological relationship to the child had no parental rights.

§ 13–3[B] TRADITIONAL SURROGACY

In a second type of surrogacy—traditional surrogacy—the surrogate provides the egg, and the surrogate is artificially inseminated with sperm from the intended father. The difference between the first and second forms of surrogacy, of course, is that in the second form, the surrogate provides half the baby's genetic material and is the child's biological as well as birth mother.

The most famous surrogacy case concerned traditional surrogacy. In 1988, the New Jersey Supreme Court decided *Matter of Baby M.*, 109 N.J. 396, 537 A.2d 1227 (1988). The court wrote:

> In this matter the Court is asked to determine the validity of a contract that purports to provide a new way of bringing children into a family. For a fee of $10,000, a woman agrees to be artificially inseminated with the semen of another woman's husband; she is to conceive a child, carry it to term, and after its birth surrender it to the

natural father and his wife. The intent of the contract is that the child's natural mother will thereafter be forever separated from her child. The wife is to adopt the child, and she and the natural father are to be regarded as its parents for all purposes. The contract providing for this is called a "surrogacy contract," the natural mother inappropriately called the "surrogate mother."

We invalidate the surrogacy contract because it conflicts with the law and public policy of this State. While we recognize the depth of the yearning of infertile couples to have their own children, we find the payment of money to a "surrogate" mother illegal, perhaps criminal, and potentially degrading to women.

We find no offense to our present laws where a woman voluntarily and without payment agrees to act as a "surrogate" mother, provided that she is not subject to a binding agreement to surrender her child.

§ 13-3[C] GENETIC STRANGER SURROGACY

In a third form of surrogacy—genetic stranger surrogacy—the intended parents *as well as* the surrogate have no genetic relationship to the baby. An embryo that is genetically unrelated to the surrogate and to the intended parents is implanted in the surrogate. In *Marriage of Buzzanca*, 61 Cal. App. 4th 1410, 72 Cal. Rptr. 2d 280 (1998), the California Court of Appeal ruled that in such a case the wife and husband are the "lawful parents" of the baby because their consent to the process that brought the child into existence.

§ 13–3[D] VARIABILITY OF STATE LAW

Many states do not have comprehensive statutes addressing surrogacy. (Anne R. Dana (Note), The State of Surrogacy Laws: Determining Legal Parentage for Gay Fathers, 18 *Duke Journal of Gender Law and Policy* 353 (2011); Charles P. Kindregan, Jr. & Maureen McBrien, *Assisted Reproductive Technology* p. 157 (2011)). A number of states forbid some or all surrogacy contracts. (*See* D.C. Stat. § 16–402; Ind. Code § 31–20–1–2; Ky. Rev. Stat. § 199.590(4); La. Rev. Stat. § 2713; Neb. Stat. § 25–21,200(1); N.Y. Family Court Act, Article 5; the New York law allows surrogacy but not surrogacy in which the surrogate provide genetic material). Arizona law states, "No person may enter into, induce, arrange, procure or otherwise assist in the formation of a surrogate parentage contract." (Ariz. Stat. Ann. § 25–218(A)). In Arizona, the surrogate "is the legal mother . . . and is entitled to custody. . . ." (Ariz. Stat. Ann. § 25–218(B)). Michigan law states, "A surrogate parentage contract is void and unenforceable as contrary to public policy." (Mich. Laws Ann. § 722.855(5)).

Several states approve surrogacy contracts. Nevada and Washington allow surrogacy so long as the surrogate is not paid anything in addition to medical expenses. (Nev. Rev. Stat. § 126.045(3); Wash. Code Ann. § 26.26.210). Illinois, Nevada, and

Utah authorize gestational surrogacy. (Ill. Stat. 750, 45/5; Nev. Rev. Stat. § 126.045(4)(a); Utah Code Ann. § 78B–15–801). Utah adopted a modified version of the 2017 UPA. Utah allows the gestational mother and intended parents to file a petition in court to validate a gestational agreement. A gestational agreement that is not court approved is not enforceable. When the baby is born, the intended parents notify the court, and the court makes an order confirming the intended parents as the legal parents. The gestational mother in Utah may receive reasonable compensation. The UPA does not require the intended parents to be married. Utah does require the intended parents to be married.

New Hampshire allows gestational and traditional surrogacy agreements that are judicially approved. (N.H. Rev. Stat. § 168–B:16(I)(b)). New Hampshire requires the parties to a surrogacy agreement to be evaluated by a mental health professional to ensure "the ability and disposition of the person being evaluated to give a child love, affection and guidance," and to "adjust to and assume the inherent risks of the contract." (N.H. Rev. Stat. § 168–B:18).

§ 13–3[E] INTERNATIONAL SURROGACY

Infertile couples from developed countries sometimes contract for surrogacy services from women, often in developing countries. International surrogacy is largely unregulated. Critics focus on the exploitation of poor women. Supporters acknowledge this concern but point out the benefits of producing wanted children. *See* Xinran Tang, Setting Norms:

Protections for Surrogates in International Commercial Surrogacy, 25 *Minnesota Journal of International Law* 193 (2016).

§ 13–3[F] ABORTION CLAUSES IN SURROGACY CONTRACTS

What if a surrogate decides to terminate the pregnancy? Can the intended parents prevent her from aborting the child? Alternatively, could intended parents force a surrogate to terminate a pregnancy if they changed their minds about being parents? Obviously, these questions raise profound issues of privacy and constitutional rights. Deborah Froman wrote an interesting article on the subject, and stated, "Surrogacy contracts typically include some kind of provision addressing the issue. Most commonly, these provisions anticipate two potential scenarios: a fetus suffering from serious birth defects or a multiple pregnancy, where fetal reduction may be recommended to improve the outcome for the remaining fetus(es). Often the contracts provide that the intended parents have the right to make all termination decisions. . . . Surrogacy agreements usually contain a related clause that restricts the surrogate's ability to terminate the pregnancy without the intended parents' consent, unless she faces substantial harm from continuing the pregnancy. . . . Practitioners routinely describe these as unenforceable. . . . [There is] consensus that specific performance of such provisions would never occur but disagreement about whether a surrogate could be liable in damages for breach of contract." (Deborah L. Forman, Abortion Clauses in Surrogacy

Contracts: Insights from a Case Study, 49 *Family Law Quarterly* 29, 33–35 (2015)).

§ 13–4 EMERGING ISSUES

The science of reproductive technology advances apace. On the horizon is a technique called mitochondrial manipulation. Daar writes, "Can a child have more than two genetic parents? Scientifically unthinkable until the dawn of the twenty-first century, researchers and infertility specialists have been tinkering with the building blocks of human reproduction to improve fertility treatment outcomes for patients and their offspring. The most recent advances focus on the genetic content of the female egg which, if abnormal, is linked to both infertility and disease. Ongoing experiments involve a kind of deconstruction of an unhealthy oocyte and then reassembling it using materials donated from a healthy female volunteer. The result is a germ cell containing the genetic material from two women that, when fertilized by a single sperm, will yield an embryo housing the DNA of three people rather than the traditional two." (Judith Daar, Multi-Party Parenting in Genetics and Law: A View from Succession, 49 *Family Law Quarterly* 71 (2015)). On September 28, 2016, *The New York Times* reported the first baby born with this technique.

§ 13-5 ASSISTED REPRODUCTION FOR LESBIAN, GAY, AND UNMARRIED PERSONS

Unmarried individuals and couples and lesbian and gay individuals and couples (married, unmarried, and domestic partners) have the same desire for children as other adults. The Ethics Committee of the American Society for Reproductive Medicine wrote in 2009:

> Fertility programs often receive requests for treatment from single persons, unmarried heterosexual couples, and lesbian and gay couples, but programs vary in their willingness to accept such patients. For some programs, it is never acceptable to treat unmarried persons, whether heterosexual or gay or lesbian. Other programs that do treat single women and lesbian couples, however, make it a policy not to treat single men or gay male couples seeking to have children.
>
> Single individuals, unmarried heterosexual couples, and gay and lesbian couples have interests in having and rearing children. There is no persuasive evidence that children are harmed or disadvantaged solely by being raised by single parents, unmarried parents, or gay and lesbian parents. Data do not support restricting access to assisted reproductive technologies on the basis of a prospective parents' marital status or sexual orientation.

(American Society for Reproductive Medicine, Ethics Committee, Access to Fertility Treatment By

Gays, Lesbians, and Unmarried Persons, 92 *Fertility and Sterility* 1190 (2009)).

CHAPTER 14

ADOPTION

Adoption creates a new parent-child relationship. Adopting parents have all the rights and responsibilities of genetic parents. (Del. Code Ann. Title 13, § 919(a)). Minnesota adoption law is typical, providing: "Upon adoption, the adopted person shall become the legal child of the adopting persons and they shall become the legal parents of the child with all the rights and duties between them of birth parents and legitimate children." (Minn. Stat. Ann. § 259.59(1)).

An adopted child inherits from the adopting parents and is "issue" for purposes of inheritance. The traditional view is that adopted children do not inherit from the genetic parents, and this remains the law in some states. (Del. Code Ann. Title 13, § 920). In other states, an adopted child may inherit from both sets of parents.

§ 14–1 TYPES OF ADOPTION

The law recognizes seven types of adoption: (1) Independent (private) adoption in which the child is placed in an adoptive home by the child's natural parent or parents; (2) Agency adoption in which the child is relinquished to an adoption agency. The agency selects adoptive parents and places the child with the parents; (3) Stepparent adoption in which the spouse of a child's genetic parent adopts the child; (4) Relative or guardian adoption; (5) International adoption; (6) Adoption of adults for purposes of inheritance; (7) A small number of states have tribal customary adoption for Native American children. (*See In re N.S.*, 55 Cal. App. 5th 816, 269 Cal. Rptr. 3d732 (2020); *Boseman v. Jarrell*, 364 N.C. 537, 704 S.E.2d 494 (2010)).

§ 14–2 CHILD'S OPINION

Many states provide that children of a certain age (*e.g.*, 12) must consent to adoption. Massachusetts law is typical, providing, "A decree of adoption shall not be made, except as provided in this chapter, without the written consent of the child to be adopted, if above the age of twelve." (Mass. Gen. Laws. Ann. Ch. 210, § 2).

§ 14–3 SELLING A CHILD IS A CRIME

It is a crime to pay for or sell a child for adoption or, to put it bluntly, to buy a baby. (Ky. Rev. Stat. § 199.590(2)). Florida law, for example, states, "It is unlawful for any person to sell or surrender, or to arrange for the sale or surrender of, a minor to another person for money or anything of value or to receive such minor child for such payment or thing of value." The Oklahoma Supreme Court emphasized the policy against baby buying in *Adoption of Baby Boy*, 236 P.3d 116 (Okla. 2010), "Oklahoma has a strong public policy against buying or selling children for adoption. The anti-trafficking in children statutes . . . make it a crime to accept, solicit, offer, pay, or transfer anything of value in connection with an adoption except as allowed" by statute.

The prohibition against buying and selling children does not outlaw payment of fees to an adoption agency or an attorney providing adoption-related services. In most states, with independent adoptions, adoptive parents may pay the birth mother's living expenses while she is pregnant as well as maternity-related medical expenses so long as such payments are not contingent on placement of the child for adoption. When payment of expenses is allowed, adopting parents keep detailed records of adoption-related expenses and submit the expenses to the court for approval. In California it is a misdemeanor for a mother to accept payment if she secretly plans not to go through with the adoption. (Cal. Penal Code § 273).

§ 14-4 TERMINATING THE BIOLOGICAL PARENT-CHILD RELATIONSHIP

Before an adoption can take place the biological parent(s) must consent to the adoption or, if the parents do not consent, the parent-child relationship must be terminated or deemed not worthy of recognition. (*J.S.B. v. S.R.V.*, 630 S.W.3d 693 (2021)). Birth parents can voluntarily relinquish a child for adoption. For this purpose it is usually a simple matter to determine who the mother is, and her consent is sought. If the parents are married, fatherhood is usually clear (although not always). When the parents are not married, paternity needs to be established, a subject discussed in Chapter 6. Some biological fathers have such a tenuous relationship to their child that their consent to adoption is not required. (*See* Chapters 2 and 6).

In the case of stepparent adoption, only one genetic parent's rights are terminated. That parent can voluntarily give up parental rights, allowing the stepparent to adopt. If the genetic parent is unwilling to give up parental rights, a legal proceeding is commenced to terminate parental rights. In such proceedings the most frequent ground for termination is abandonment.

Care must be taken to ensure that birth parents are properly served with notice of proceedings to terminate parental rights and adopt their child. *In re J.P.*, 173 N.H. 453, 242 A.3d 823 (2020) was a stepparent adoption case. Notice was intentionally *not* given to the biological father. The New Hampshire Supreme Court ruled the adoption had to be set aside.

It is useful to read the Pennsylvania Supreme Court's thoughtful decision in *Adoption of C.M.*, 255 A.3d 343 (Pa. 2021). The Supreme Court explains differences in termination of parental rights in the child welfare system and in private adoption cases.

§ 14–5 INDEPENDENT (PRIVATE) ADOPTION

Independent adoption is also called private adoption or direct placement. Most states allow independent adoption. Delaware and Massachusetts do not. (Del. Code Ann. Title 13 § 901(14); Mass. Gen. Laws, ch. 210 § 2A). The primary distinction between agency adoption and independent adoption is that with independent adoption placement of the child in the adoptive home is made by the birth parents—

usually the birth mother—rather than by an adoption agency. The birth mother personally selects the adoptive parents. Michigan law is typical, providing, "A parent or guardian shall personally select a prospective adoptive parent in a direct placement. The selection shall not be delegated." (Mich. Comp. Laws Ann. § 710.23a(2)). A direct connection exists between the birth mother and the adopting parents. The adopting parents are often present at the child's birth and take custody of the baby at the hospital. A petition for adoption is filed following birth.

Generally, an adoption agency plays a role in independent adoption. In many states a social worker from an adoption agency counsels the birth parents about giving up the child for adoption. An adoption agency investigates the adoptive parents and files a report with the court.

As mentioned, in an independent adoption the mother personally places the baby with the adoptive parents. But how does a young pregnant woman find a couple to adopt her baby? eBay? Twitter? Facebook? Amazon? Let's hope not. In some cases, the child is placed with family. In other cases a professional assists the mother. Professionals specializing in independent adoptions—often attorneys—maintain files of prospective adoptive parents and provide names and background information to birth parents considering adoption. In some states, limited advertising is allowed.

Can an attorney ethically represent both the birth parents and the adoptive parents in an independent adoption? The law in nearly all states says no, and experienced adoption attorneys agree. (Jennifer Fairfax, *The Adoption Law Handbook* pp. 93–94 (2011)). In California the answer is yes, but subject to limitations. California law provides: "The Legislature declares that in an independent adoption proceeding, whether or not written consent is obtained, multiple representation by an attorney should be avoided whenever a birth parent displays the slightest reason for the attorney to believe any controversy might arise." (Cal. Fam. Code § 8800(c)).

When birth parents and adoptive parents live in different states, the laws of both jurisdictions must be satisfied. As well, compliance with the Interstate Compact on the Placement of Children (ICPC) is required. The ICPC is discussed in Chapter 15. The ICPC does not apply to stepparent adoptions and familial adoptions.

§ 14–6 AGENCY ADOPTION

Adoption agencies are either government or private. With agency adoption, the biological parents who are thinking about "giving up" their child for adoption are counseled by an employee of the agency. If the parents decide adoption is the way to go, they give custody to the agency and sign relinquishment forms. The agency then locates prospective adoptive parents and places the child in their home.

The primary difference between agency adoption and independent adoption is that in independent adoption the birth mother herself places the child with the adoptive parents. In an agency adoption the birth parents relinquish the child to an adoption agency. The agency places the child in the adoptive home. In many agency adoptions the birth parents have no idea who the adoptive parents are.

When a juvenile court terminates the parental rights of abusive parents, the child is placed in the care of the state. If the child is adoptable, an adoption agency works to place the child for adoption. For some children adoption is unlikely, and long-term foster care or guardianship is arranged.

§ 14-7 INTERRACIAL ADOPTION

Before the civil rights movement of the 1960s, interracial adoption was uncommon. Several states, Louisiana and Texas, for example, banned interracial adoption. Most social workers believed it was important to place children with adoptive parents of the same ethnic background. During the 1960s, courts struck down laws against interracial adoption, and increasing numbers of mixed race adoptions occurred—mostly white parents adopting children of color. During the 1970s, critics of interracial adoption campaigned against the practice, led by the National Association of Black Social Workers. In 1972, the Association issued a position paper based on the premise that America is racist. The paper stated in part: "Black children should be placed only with Black families in foster care of for adoption. Black children belong, physically, psychologically and culturally in Black families in order that they receive the total sense of themselves and develop a sound projection of their future. Human beings are products of their environment and develop their sense of values, attitudes and self-concept within their family structures. Black children in white homes are cut off from the healthy development of themselves as Black people."

Opposition to interracial adoption was effective. Unfortunately, children of color are overrepresented in foster care, and these children tend to wait longer for adoption than white children. During the 1980s and 1990s, pressure mounted to lower racial barriers to adoption, and in 1994 Congress passed the Multiethnic Placement Act or MEPA. Congress replaced MEPA with the Removal of Barriers to Interethnic Adoption Act, which mandates that agencies receiving federal funds that are involved in foster care or adoption are prohibited from denying to any person the opportunity to become an adoptive or a foster parent on the basis of the race, color, or national origin of the person or the child.

§ 14–8 STEPPARENT ADOPTION

Stepparent adoption typically arises when mom and dad divorce, mom gets custody, mom remarries, stepdad forms a great relationship with his stepkids, bio dad is not close to the kids, and mom and stepdad decide stepdad will adopt the kids. The primary issue in such cases is whether the biological father will consent to the adoption. If he will—and consenting ends his child support obligation—then, no problem. If he refuses to consent, then the stepparent adoption can go forward only if the biological father's parental rights are terminated against his will. As mentioned earlier, in stepparent adoption, the most common basis for terminating the rights of the non-consenting biological parents is abandonment. (*See Adoption of LZ,* 616 S.W.3d 695 (Ark. Ct. App. 2021); *Adoption of I.B.,* 163 N.E.3d 270 (Ind. 2021)).

§ 14-9 INTERNATIONAL (INTERCOUNTRY) ADOPTION

Intercountry adoption is complicated, time consuming, and expensive for adoptive parents, who must comply with four sets of laws: (1) Law of the country of the child's birth; (2) Law of the U.S. state where the adoptive parents live; (3) Immigration law; and (4) The Hague Convention on Protection of Children and Co-Operation in Respect of Intercountry Adoption.

Nearly 100 countries, including the U.S., are signatories to the Hague Convention. Congress implemented the Convention with the Intercountry Adoption Act of 2000 (42 U.S.C. §§ 14901 et seq.). Federal regulations clarify the Act (22 C.F.R., Part 96, §§ 96.1 et seq.). The U.S. Department of State is the Central Authority for administration of the Convention.

The Hague Convention is designed to safeguard children's best interests and ensure against "the abduction, the sale of, or traffic in children." (Article 1(b)). The Convention recognizes that children "should grow up in a family environment, in an atmosphere of happiness, love and understanding." (Preamble). Under the Convention, authorities in the child's "state of origin" determine: (1) the child is adoptable; (2) adoption in the state of origin is unlikely; (3) proper consents to adoption are obtained (the mother's consent can only be given after the baby is born); (4) the child's wishes are considered; and (5) adoption is in the child's best interests. (Article 4). Authorities in the "receiving state" determine: (1) the adoptive parents are fit and eligible to adopt; (2) the adoptive parents have received proper counseling; and (3) the child is eligible to enter the receiving country.

When Americans think of international adoption they usually think of foreign born children coming to these shores. So-called incoming adoptions are by far the most common. Yet, there is small outflow of U.S. children to adoptive homes abroad. (*See* Cynthia R. Mabry-King, Outgoing-Adoptions: What Should Happen When Things Go Wrong?, 44 *Capital University Law Review* 1 (2016)).

Some nations require adopting parents to formally adopt the child in the child's birth country. In other cases the adoption is finalized in the child's new home country. Once a child is brought to America, many experts recommend re-adopting the child in this country.

Under the U.S. Child Citizenship Act of 2000, a child adopted from abroad can acquire U.S. citizenship. All that is required is that one or both adoptive parents are U.S. citizens, the child is under age 18, the child is lawfully admitted to the U.S., and the adoption is final.

§ 14-10 OPEN ADOPTION, POST-ADOPTION CONTACT AGREEMENTS, ACCESS TO ADOPTION RECORDS

Traditionally, adoption built a wall between the child's past and future. With adoption, the child's life began anew. The child's previous life, including the "old" parents and extended family, were cast away to be forgotten. Generations of adoptive parents did not disclose the fact of adoption. Yet, adopted children often knew or suspected the truth and were curious about their genetic parents. They wondered, "Where did I come from?" and "Didn't my birth parents want me?" These profoundly personal and important questions led to changes in policy and law. Today, states have procedures allowing adopted children to learn about their past.

With open adoption the adoptive and birth parents agree to some form of contact after the adoption is final. Gaddie describes open adoption:

> Open adoption is a general term that encompasses a multitude of circumstances. An adoption may be considered open solely based on the fact that the birth mother is involved in the process of selecting the adoptive family, regardless of whether she has any further contact with them or the child. The birth mother may receive annual updates on the child's well-being, including pictures or phone calls, or even occasionally visit the child. Essentially, the specific terms of an open adoption will fall somewhere on a spectrum, depending how much contact and involvement the birth family is to

have with the child after the adoption has been finalized.

(Leigh Gaddie (Comment) Open Adoption, 22 *Journal of the American Academy of Matrimonial Lawyers* 499 (2009)).

Parties can enter a post-adoption contact agreement that defines post-adoption contact between birth parents and the adopted child. In *Birth Mother v. Adoptive Parents,* 59 P.3d 1233 (Nev. 2002), the Nevada Supreme Court refused to enforce a post-adoption contact agreement. In *Michaud v. Wawuck,* 209 Conn. 407, 551 A.2d 738 (1988), the Connecticut Supreme Court ruled that post-adoption contact agreements are not against public policy.

When a juvenile court terminates the parental rights of maltreating parents, some states authorize the judge to order visitation with the biological parents. *In re Adoption of Vito,* 431 Mass. 550, 728 N.E.2d 292, 299 (2000) ("judges may effect or require postadoption visitation as an outcome of termination proceedings.").

§ 14–11 EQUITABLE AND VIRTUAL ADOPTION

Courts employ "equitable adoption" to avoid injustice to a child that everyone thought was adopted. (*Shearin v. Brown,* 276 N.C. App. 8, 854 S.E.2d 443 (2021)). Consider the following case: Harry and Mary are married. They have two children. Their baby nephew is orphaned when his parents are killed in a car crash. Harry and Mary take the nephew into their home and treat him as one of their children. Harry and Mary decide to formally adopt the nephew.

Unfortunately, unbeknownst to Harry and Mary, there is a defect in the adoption. The adoption is not legal. Harry and Mary treat the nephew as a member of the family. Mary dies. Harry dies intestate a few years later, leaving a large estate. Harry and Mary's two biological children learn of the defect in the adoption and seek to exclude the nephew from inheriting. Equitable adoption allows a person like nephew, who was treated as an adopted child, to share in inheriting property from the person's "equitable" parent. There must be evidence of: (1) an agreement to adopt; (2) evidence the decedent intended to adopt (*e.g.*, an invalid attempt to adopt); and (3) conduct by the parties indicating their recognition of a parent-child relationship. (*See Estate of Ford,* 32 Cal. 4th 160, 82 P.3d 747, 8 Cal. Rptr. 3d 541 (2004); *In re Scarlett Z.-D.*, 28 N.E.3d 776, 390 Ill. Dec. 123 (2015); *Estate of Scherer,* 336 P.3d 129 (Wyo. 2014); David J. Strachman, Equitable Adoption Doctrine, 64 *Rhode Island Bar Journal* 5 (2016)). Not all states recognize equitable adoption.

The North Carolina Supreme Court discussed equitable adoption in *Lankford v. Wright,* 347 N.C. 115, 489 S.E.2d 604, 606 (1997), "By its own terms, equitable adoption applies only in limited circumstances, and the doctrine is not intended to replace statutory requirements or to create the parent-child relationship; it simply recognizes the foster child's right to inherit from the person or persons who contracted to adopt the child and who honored that contract in all respects except through formal statutory procedures."

Georgia recognizes "virtual adoption," described by the Supreme Court "an equitable remedy utilized when the conduct of the parties creates an implied adoption without a court order." (*Morgan v. Howard*, 285 Ga. 512, 678 S.E.2d 882, 883 (2009)). In Georgia, virtual adoption is available after the death of the person who agreed to adopt in order to allowing the "adopted" person to inherit. In *Johnson v. Rogers*, 297 Ga. 413, 774 S.E.2d 647, 649 (2015), the Georgia Supreme Court wrote, "To establish virtual adoption, Georgia has long required at least some showing of an agreement between the natural and adoptive parents, a severance of the actual relationship of parent and child as between the child and the natural parents, the establishment of such a relationship between the child and the adoptive parents, and the intestacy of the adoptive parent." Virtual adoption does not apply if the deceased had a will and left all property to persons other than the "adopted" child.

§ 14–12 ADOPTION OF ADULTS

One adult may adopt another, usually for purposes of inheritance. (*Matter of Marian T.,* 36 N.Y.3d 44, 161 N.E.3d 460, 137 N.Y.S.3d 272 (2020)).

§ 14–13 ICWA AND TRIBAL CUSTOMARY ADOPTION

In the typical adoption, a court terminates the parental rights of the biological parents. Native

American children can be adopted this way so long as the Indian Child Welfare Act (ICWA) is satisfied (25 U.S.C. §§ 1901 et seq. ICWA is discussed in § 15–15). ICWA provides, "In any adoptive placement of an Indian child under State law, a preference shall be given, in the absence of good cause to the contrary, to a placement with (1) a member of the child's extended family; (2) other members of the Indian child's tribe; or (3) other Indian families." (25 U.S.C. § 1915(a)).

A few states have a form of adoption for Native American children called Tribal Customary Adoption. This adoption allows a child to be adopted by Native American adoptive parents *without* terminating the parental rights of the biological parents. In California, the statute provides: "Tribal customary adoption means adoption by and through the tribal custom, traditions, or law of an Indian child's tribe. Termination of parental rights is not required to effect the tribal customary adoption." (Cal. Welfare & Institutions Code § 366.24(a)).

§ 14–14 ADOPTION FAILURE

Despite the best efforts of social workers to ensure a good "fit" between a child and adoptive parents, some adoptions do not work. Perhaps the child and the adoptive parents do not bond. Tragically, some abused and neglected children are so damaged that adoptive parents cannot nurture and control the child.

If an agency adoption "fails" before it is legally finalized, the child can be returned to the agency in what is sometimes called "disrupted adoption." The national rate of disruption is 10 to 20%.

When an agency adoption breaks down after the adoption is final, the law in most states allows the adoption to be dissolved by a judge, and here too the child is returned to the agency. Nationally, 1 to 10% of final adoptions dissolve. Some states impose a time limit after which an adoption cannot be challenged.

May parents who adopt a child from abroad set the adoption aside? The California Court of Appeal grappled with this question in *Adoption of M.S.*, 181 Cal. App. 4th 50, 103 Cal. Rptr. 3d 715 (2010). Adoptive parents adopted a three-year-old Ukrainian child. The parents thought the child was healthy. After bringing the child to America, however, evaluation revealed cerebral palsy, reactive attachment disorder, developmental delay, fetal alcohol syndrome, microcephaly, and post-traumatic stress disorder. The parents sought to set the adoption aside, but the trial and appellate courts ruled that the child could not returned to the Ukraine and California law did not allow set aside. As the Court of Appeal put it, "This is a tragic case in which there can be no good ending for anyone." The U.S. State Department's 2015 report on intercountry adoption found fifty-eight cases of disrupted international adoption in the U.S. in which children were taken into the custody of the state.

§ 14–15 RE-HOMING

Re-homing is a euphemism for the practice by which adoptive parents get rid of an adoptive child by placing the child elsewhere. Testerman writes, "A deplorable practice has emerged in the world of adoption. Adoptive families are now using the Internet to give their unwanted adopted children over to complete strangers, some of whom are traffickers, pedophiles, child pornographers, or worse. This practice is known as private re-homing." (S. Megan Testerman (Note) A World Wide Web of Unwanted Children: The Practice, The Problem, and the Solution to Private Re-Homing, 67 *Florida Law Review* 2103 (2015)). In 2014, a New York trial judge lamented, "Adopted Russian children throughout the United States are currently being exchanged on the Internet through a process called Re-Homing without the benefit of any court or governmental supervision." (*Adoption of Child A and Child C,* 46 Misc. 3d 1033, 997 N.Y.S.2d 312 (2014)). In 2014, Louisiana made re-homing a crime (La. Rev. Stat. § 14:46.4). Wisconsin law gets at re-homing by outlawing "Advertising for the purpose of finding a child to adopt or to otherwise take into permanent physical custody." (Wis. Stat. § 48.825(2)(a)). Florida attacks the problem as follows: "It is unlawful for any person to place or attempt to place a minor for adoption with a person who primarily lives and works outside this state unless all of the requirements of the Interstate Compact for the Placement of Children, when applicable, have been met." It is equally unlawful in Florida for any person "except an adoption agency, to place or attempt to place within the state a minor for adoption unless the minor is placed with a relative or with a stepparent." (Fla. Stat. § 63.212).

§ 14–16 WRONGFUL ADOPTION

In a small number of cases, adoptive parents sue adoption agencies, claiming that social workers did not inform them of their child's medical or psychiatric history. The adoptive parents seek monetary damages against the agency to help pay the child's medical or psychiatric bills. In so-called "wrongful adoption" cases the adoptive parents do not seek to end the adoption.

The first wrongful adoption case, *Burr v. Board of County Commissioners*, 23 Ohio St. 3d 69, 491 N.E.2d 1101 (1986), was decided in 1986 by the Ohio Supreme Court. Russell and Betty Burr contacted the county adoption agency, expressing their desire to adopt. An adoption worker phoned the Burrs and told them a seventeen-month-old boy was available for adoption. The caseworker told the Burrs the child was born to an eighteen-year-old single mother who relinquished the child to the agency. The caseworker told the Burrs the child was "a nice big, healthy, baby boy." The Burrs adopted the child. As the years passed, the child developed numerous medical and psychiatric problems, including twitching, a speech impediment, and learning problems. In high school the child developed hallucinations. Eventually, the child was diagnosed with Huntington's Disease, a genetically inherited disease that damages the nervous system.

In 1982, the Burrs got a court order opening the sealed records of their son's medical history prior to adoption. For the first time they learned that the things the adoption worker told them were false. The records disclosed that the child's mother was not a healthy eighteen-year-old, but a thirty-one-year-old mental patient at a psychiatric hospital. The identity of the genetic father was unknown, but he was presumed to be a mental patient. The mother was psychotic and mildly intellectually disabled. The adoption agency knew this information but did not tell the Burrs. As well, the agency knew the child had a fever at birth and was developing slowly. This information too was withheld from the Burrs. Apparently, the adoption worker fabricated the story of the birth mother.

To recoup the more than $80,000 they spent on their son's medical care, the Burrs sued the county, the adoption agency, and the caseworker. The jury concluded the adoption agency committed fraud against the Burrs and awarded them $125,000. The Ohio Supreme Court approved the jury's award.

Burr established that an adoption agency cannot deliberately lie about a child's history. But what about a scenario in which an adoption agency does not intentionally lie, but mistakenly fails to tell adoptive parents some detail of a child's medical history? Judges have difficulty deciding whether adoptive parents should be able to sue adoption agencies that try to act responsibly but that make mistakes or act negligently.

§ 14-17 ADOPTION BY GAY AND LESBIAN INDIVIDUALS

In the past, apart from stepparent adoption, adopting parents were heterosexual married couples.

Lesbian and gay individuals were not allowed to adopt. In 1995, the New York Court of Appeals ruled in *Matter of Jacob,* 86 N.Y.2d 651, 660 N.E.2d 387, 636 N.Y.S.2d 716 (1995) that unmarried couples—gay and straight—can adopt. The New York court's decision helped change the law around the country. In *Adoption of X.X.G.,* 45 So. 3d 79 (Fla. Ct. App. 2010), the Florida Court of Appeal ruled that a statute that prohibited gay or lesbian people from adopting served no rational purpose and was unconstitutional. Joslin and Minter report, "As of January 2011, no state bars all lesbian and gay individuals from adopting children. There are, however, a small number of states that limit the ability of lesbian and gay people to adopt or become foster parents. Most commonly these states prohibit people living in nonmarital relationships from adopting and/or serving as foster parents." (Courtney G. Joslin & Shannon P. Minter, *Lesbian, Gay, Bisexual and Transgender Family Law* § 2:10, p. 97 (2011)). With same sex marriage legal, remaining barriers should fall.

CHAPTER 15

JUVENILE COURT

America's juvenile courts play a central role in protecting children from maltreatment and providing guidance and reform for children who break the law. This chapter discusses the day-to-day work of juvenile court, or as it is called in some states, family court.

Juvenile court has authority over three groups of children: abused and neglected children, juvenile delinquents, and status offenders. A status offense is misbehavior that is not delinquency but that nevertheless brings a child under the authority of the juvenile court. The traditional status offenses are truancy, smoking and drinking under age, running away, curfew violations, and so-called ungovernable behavior.

§ 15–1 BIRTH OF JUVENILE COURT

America's first juvenile court was established in 1899 in Chicago. The Progressive Era reformers who created the juvenile court were concerned primarily with the criminal justice system's harsh treatment of delinquent children. Prior to the juvenile court, children who broke the law were arrested, jailed, brought to trial, and punished similarly to adults. Children as young as six languished in jail with adult criminals.

What stood the Chicago juvenile court apart from earlier reforms was that it removed youthful offenders *altogether* from the criminal justice system.

Rather than subject children to trial, conviction, and punishment as criminals, proceedings in juvenile court were civil. The juvenile court adjudicated the youngster a delinquent rather than a criminal, and provided individualized treatment rather than punishment. The goal in juvenile court was to save the child from a downward spiral leading to a life of crime. The reformers who created the juvenile court believed rehabilitation was superior to the retribution meted out by criminal law. Julian Mack, an early judge of the Chicago juvenile court put it this way in 1909, "Why is it not just and proper to treat these juvenile offenders . . . as a wise and merciful father handles his own child whose errors are not discovered by the authorities? Why is it not the duty of the state, instead of asking merely whether a boy or girl has committed a specific offense, to find out what he is, physically, mentally, morally, and then if it learns that he is treading the path that leads to criminality, to take him in charge, not so much to punish as to reform, not to degrade but to uplift, not to crush but to develop, not to make him a criminal but a worthy citizen." (Julian W. Mack, The Juvenile Court, 23 *Harvard Law Review* 104, 107 (1909)).

In addition to delinquency, the Chicago juvenile court had authority over neglected and dependent children, which the 1899 law defined as any child under sixteen "who for any reason is destitute or homeless or abandoned; or dependent upon the public for support; or has no proper parental care or guardianship; or who habitually begs or receives alms; or who is found living in any house of ill fame or with any vicious or disreputable person; or whose home, by reason of neglect, cruelty or depravity on the part of its parents, guardian or other person in whose care it may be, is an unfit place for such child." (Illinois Juvenile Court Law, Section 1). This definition became the model for juvenile court laws across the United States.

Juvenile courts spread across the country. The early juvenile court was as much social agency as law court. For that reason, the formal procedures of the courtroom were relaxed. In many juvenile courts the judge sat at a desk rather than on an elevated bench. The child and interested adults sat at the desk with the judge. Usually, the child had no attorney. Everyone provided input and the judge decided what was needed to turn the young offender away from crime. Most delinquents were placed on probation. Some were sent to reform schools or other institutions. In cases of abuse or neglect, the judge could remove children from home or leave them at home under the supervision of the court's probation officers. (For in-depth history of juvenile court, *see* John E.B. Myers, A Short History of Child Protection in America, 42 *Family Law Quarterly* 449 (2008); John E.B. Myers, *Child Protection in America: Past, Present and Future* (2006); John E.B. Myers, *A History of Child Protection in America* (2004)).

In the 1960s, the U.S. Supreme Court decided two cases dealing with the juvenile court—*Kent v. United States*, 383 U.S. 541, 86 S. Ct. 1045 (1966) and *In re Gault,* 387 U.S. 1, 87 S. Ct. 1428 (1967). Both decisions shaped America's juvenile courts for the twentieth century and the twenty-first. In *Gault,* the

Supreme Court ruled that minors accused of delinquency have the right to notice of the charges, the right to remain silent, the right to counsel, and the right to confront and cross-examine witnesses.

§ 15–2 JUVENILE DELINQUENCY

Juvenile delinquency is illegal conduct by a minor that would be a crime if committed by an adult. When a minor is suspected of delinquency, police investigate. The minor may be questioned and searched. If the investigation points to the minor, an arrest may follow. Once arrested on a serious matter, the minor is typically taken to the juvenile detention center. At the detention center, an intake worker—often a probation officer—interviews the minor, considers the police report, and decides whether the minor should be released or detained. The intake worker and/or a prosecutor decides whether to file formal delinquency charges against the minor. If charges are filed, and the minor is detained, the minor must be taken before a juvenile court judge as soon as possible so the judge can rule on the legality of further detention.

Once a minor is charged with delinquency, the minor has the right to an attorney. Because most minors (and their parents) cannot afford private defense attorneys, the judge assigns the public defender's office to represent the minor. The public defender meets with the minor, explains the charges, listens to the minor's side of the story, and helps the minor decide whether to admit or deny guilt. The state is represented by a prosecutor.

Plea bargaining occurs in juvenile court delinquency proceedings, and most minors plead guilty. Only a small percentage of minors deny guilt and insist on a trial, or, as it is called in many states, an adjudicatory hearing. A juvenile court adjudicatory hearing regarding delinquency looks much like the trial of an adult. The minor is represented by counsel. A prosecutor represents the government. Formal rules of evidence and procedure apply. Witnesses are called and cross-examined. The minor has the right to testify but cannot be compelled to do so.

Adults charged with serious crimes have a right under the U.S. Constitution to trial by jury. In juvenile court, however, the U.S. Supreme Court ruled in *McKeiver v. Pennsylvania,* 403 U.S. 528, 91 S. Ct. 1976 (1971), that minors accused of delinquency do not have a constitutional right to jury trial. The Supreme Court reasoned that the constitutional right to a jury trial in criminal cases does not apply in juvenile court because delinquency proceedings are civil not criminal.

Since the Supreme Court's 1971 decision in *McKeiver* that the Constitution does not require juries in delinquency cases, there has been a movement to "get tough" on juvenile delinquents. As a result, defense attorneys have renewed the argument that minors accused of delinquency should have the right to trial by jury in juvenile court. In 2008, the Kansas Supreme Court agreed, ruling in *In re L.M.,* 286 Kan. 460, 186 P.3d 164 (2008), that Kansas minors accused of delinquency have a constitutional right to a jury. In 2009 the Louisiana Supreme Court rejected the argument that minors accused of delinquency have a constitutional right to a jury trial in juvenile court. (*In re A.J.*, 27 So. 3d 247 (La. 2009)).

If a minor pleads guilty or is found guilty following an adjudicatory hearing, the judge decides the appropriate disposition. Unlike criminal prosecutions against adults, where the sentencing judge imposes punishment in the form of incarceration, a fine, or, if the defendant is deserving, probation, the juvenile court judge is concerned more about rehabilitation than punishment. The judge, aided by a report from the juvenile probation officer, and input from counsel, fashions a disposition that is intended to turn the young offender away from crime. Most youth are placed on probation and may be ordered to go to school, obey their parents, perform community service, and stay away from bad influences. If the youth has mental health or substance abuse issues, the disposition may include therapy. To the extent it will teach a lesson, punishment is part of disposition in juvenile court. The goal of disposition is individualized intervention to put the youth on the right track.

Some teenagers commit serious, calculated, callous crimes. Some of these teens deserve to be punished like adult criminals. Moreover, some teens are already committed to a life of crime and are unlikely to benefit from the therapeutic approach of the juvenile court. The law allows such "hardened" youth to be transferred from juvenile court to criminal court where they are prosecuted as adults. In making the transfer decision, the juvenile court judge considers the minor's age and IQ, the nature and seriousness of the crime, whether the youth is naive or sophisticated in the ways of crime, whether the minor has been in trouble before, and the likelihood the minor can be rehabilitated in juvenile court.

The overarching theory of juvenile court is that youth are malleable. With the right package of individualized services, most youth can be saved from the downward spiral that leads to crime as a career. Sadly, there are times when the theory of the juvenile court gets lost in crowded court dockets, overworked professionals, and underfunded programs. Today's juvenile court is stretched thin. Yet, few argue that juvenile court should be abandoned as a failure. Every day, dedicated judges, probation officers, social workers, and attorneys pour their energies into turning kids away from crime. Failure is common, but success stories abound. Thousands of minors benefit from interaction with the juvenile court.

§ 15-3 STATUS OFFENSES

As conceived at the beginning of the 20th century, the juvenile court was intended as a refuge for a broad range of children in difficulty. Thus, the court had jurisdiction over delinquent children, abused and neglected children, and children who were simply poor. In addition, the juvenile court had jurisdiction over so-called status offenders. A status offense is conduct by a minor that is not a crime but that nevertheless justifies intervention by the juvenile court. As mentioned earlier, the traditional status offenses include running away from home, truancy, and smoking and drinking under age. In addition, the juvenile court had authority over so-called "ungovernable children"—that is, older children who refused to obey the "reasonable" demands of their parents. A parent at wits' end with their teenager's disobedience could ask a juvenile court judge to assume control of the child and order the child to behave or face the possibility of commitment to a reform school or other institution.

The extent to which juvenile courts dealt with status offenses varied from place to place. In the closing decades of the 20th century, experts recommended narrowing or eliminating juvenile court authority over status offenses. In particular, experts called for an end to the practice of placing status offenders in the same institutions with delinquents. Congress responded in 1974 with passage of the Juvenile Justice and Delinquency Prevention Act. This law required states receiving federal funds to stop institutionalizing status offenders in facilities for juvenile delinquents.

Today, juvenile courts in many states retain authority over status offenses. As before, however, the degree of juvenile court involvement with these children varies. In many communities, juvenile courts are so overwhelmed with delinquency and maltreatment cases that little time and few resources are available to help status-offending youth.

§ 15-4 PROTECTING CHILDREN FROM ABUSE AND NEGLECT: DEPENDENCY PROCEEDINGS IN JUVENILE COURT

In the United States, protecting children from abuse and neglect is the responsibility of parents, and, when parents fail, professionals and government. All states require professionals who work with children to report suspicions of abuse and neglect to police or child protective services (CPS). CPS agencies, staffed by social workers have broad responsibility for child protection. CPS social workers work closely with law enforcement, attorneys, and juvenile court.

§ 15-5 FEDERAL LEADERSHIP IN CHILD PROTECTION

The day-to-day work of child protection is carried out at the local level. However, Congress plays an important role in setting national child protection policy. Prior to the 1970s, the federal government played a minor role in child protection. The federal Children's Bureau was created in 1912, although the Bureau devoted little attention to maltreatment until the 1960s. The Social Security Act of 1935 created Aid to Families with Dependent Children, and authorized the Children's Bureau "to cooperate with State public-welfare agencies in establishing, extending, and strengthening, especially in predominantly rural areas, [child welfare services] for the protection and care of homeless, dependent, and neglected children, and children in danger of becoming delinquent." (Social Security Act, U.S.

Statutes at Large, Volume 49, Part 1, Title V, Part 3, Section 521, 74th Congress, 1st Session, Chapter 531, August 14, 1935). Yet, as late as 1973, Senator Walter Mondale wrote, "Nowhere in the Federal Government could we find one official assigned full time to the prevention, identification and treatment of child abuse and neglect." (Letter of Transmittal from Walter F. Mondale to Harrison A. Williams dated March 15, 1974. Located at Child Abuse Prevention and Treatment Act, 1974. Public Law 93–247 (S. 1191), Questions and Answers, Analysis, and Text of the Act, Prepared for the Subcommittee on Children and Youth of the Committee on Labor and Public Welfare, United States Senate. 93rd Congress, 2nd Session. Page VII. April, 1974). It was not until 1974 that the federal government assumed a leadership role in responding to child abuse and neglect.

1974—Child Abuse Prevention and Treatment Act

In 1973, hearings were conducted in the U.S. Senate and House of Representatives on bills to create the Child Abuse Prevention and Treatment Act (CAPTA). In January, 1974, President Nixon signed CAPTA into law. CAPTA authorized federal funds to improve the response to physical abuse, neglect, and sexual abuse. CAPTA provided funds to train professionals, funds for multidisciplinary centers on child abuse and neglect, and money for demonstration projects.

1980—Adoption Assistance and Child Welfare Act

Child abuse reporting laws and enhanced awareness of abuse produced an increase in intervention. By the mid-1970s, a rising number of children in foster care set off alarm bells in Congress, resulting in the Adoption Assistance and Child Welfare Act of 1980. The Act required states seeking federal foster care funds—all states—to make "reasonable efforts" to avoid removing children from maltreating parents. When removal was necessary, reasonable efforts were required to reunite families. Every child in foster care had to have a "permanency plan" to return the child home or move toward termination of parental rights. For children who could not go home, Congress provided financial incentives for adoption. Finally, the Act provided financial support for adoptive parents who adopted children with special needs.

1997—Adoption and Safe Families Act

The effort to preserve families was the key component of the 1980 Adoption Assistance and Child Welfare Act. "Family preservation" was the dominant paradigm of child protection in the 1980s. In the 1990s, however, critics argued that over-reliance on family preservation sometimes led to tragedy. One forceful critic of over-reliance on family preservation was Richard Gelles, who challenged the effectiveness of family preservation in his 1996 book, *The Book of David: How Preserving Families Can Cost Children's Lives.* Gelles criticized research supporting family preservation programs, and argued for a shift in policy toward what he called "A New Child-Centered Policy." Gelles wrote, "The essential first step in creating a safe world for children is to abandon the fantasy that child welfare agencies can balance the goals of protecting children and preserving families, adopting instead a child-centered policy of family services. This is not a new policy, but rather a return to the policy of the early 1960s that established child safety as the overriding goal of the child welfare system. . . . It is time to abandon the myth that 'the best foster family is not as good as a marginal biological family.' The ability to make a baby does not ensure that a couple have, or ever will have, the ability to be adequate parents. The policy of family reunification and family preservation fails because it assumes that *all* biological parents can become fit and acceptable parents if only appropriate and sufficient support is provided" (pp. 148–149). An equally forceful critique came from Elizabeth Bartholet, who wrote in her 1999 book, *Nobody's Children: Abuse and Neglect, Foster Drift, and the Adoption Alternative*, "There is no evidence that the treatment and other parent-support services which may be offered in the most serious abuse and neglect cases are helpful in reforming parents and protecting children." (p. 109).

The 1980 Adoption Assistance and Child Welfare Act helped many children and parents. Yet, the number of children in foster care did not decline. Many children languished in out-of-home care. Moreover, Richard Gelles, Elizabeth Bartholet, and others charged that the reasonable efforts and family preservation requirements caused social workers to leave children in dangerous homes. Congress responded with the Adoption and Safe Families Act of 1997 (ASFA). Although ASFA did not abandon family preservation, it made child safety the top priority. When children were placed in foster care, ASFA established strict time lines to return them to their parents or terminate parental rights so children could be adopted. In cases of sexual abuse and chronic physical abuse, ASFA authorized states to dispense at the beginning of the case with *any* effort to reunify the family, and to move directly to termination of parental rights.

Across the history of child protection, we see pendulum swings in the debate over family privacy versus intervention to keep children safe. These swings are reflected in the federal legislation described above. The Child Abuse Prevention and Treatment Act of 1974 contained broad definitions of maltreatment, encouraging greater intervention. By contrast, the Adoption Assistance and Child Welfare Act of 1980, with its emphasis on family preservation, pushed the pendulum away from intervention. Finally, the Adoption and Safe Families Act of 1997 placed top priority on child safety, once again shifting the emphasis toward intervention. The intervention pendulum swings back and forth, never reaching the extremes, and never standing still.

§ 15–6 DIFFERENTIAL RESPONSE

In the early twenty-first century, the most noteworthy development in child protection has been the spread of what is commonly called differential response (DR), also known as alternative response, or dual track. The Children's Bureau describes this approach:

> Differential response . . . is a way of structuring child protective services (CPS) that allows for more than one method of initial response to reports of child abuse and neglect. . . . DR responses typically fall into two major categories:
>
> > [1] Investigative response (IR) (also called the traditional response or high-risk assessment). These responses involve gathering forensic evidence and making a formal determination of whether child maltreatment has occurred or the child is at risk of abuse or neglect.
> >
> > [2] Alternative response (AR) [is] usually applied in low-and moderate-risk cases (p. 2), [and involves offers of help, which parents are free to accept or reject].

(U.S. Children's Bureau, Child Welfare Information Gateway. *Differential Response to Reports of Child Abuse and Neglect. Issue Brief* (2014)).

A primary goal of DR is to adopt a positive, cooperative, voluntary, "family friendly" approach to parents, and to avoid the involuntary, and sometimes adversarial, investigative approach of traditional CPS. In 2010, Congress gave a boost to DR by requiring states to adopt policies to triage low risk cases away from traditional CPS investigation, and into DR.

DR is not a new idea. Since the earliest days of formal child protection in the 1800s, professionals sorted between high and low risk cases, reserving formal investigation and court involvement for the former. DR is little more than a refinement and expansion of existing practice.

Critics of DR worry that the expansion of voluntary services is draining already scarce resources away from traditional CPS. As well, critics of DR believe that funneling large numbers of children into voluntary services, where there is no meaningful investigation, places children at risk. It is true that several evaluation studies suggest DR does not compromise child safety (Children's Bureau, 2014, p. 10). Hughes and his colleagues, however, published a critique of DR research. Hughes and colleagues write, "In our review, we identified significant problems in research methodology and implementation that presented threats to internal, external, and construct validity, thereby calling into question the reliability and accuracy of many of the claims and conclusions made in these studies." Hughes and colleagues opine that research does not support the conclusion that DR keeps children safe. "We conclude that the many claims found in DR research studies and program literature related to children's safety are overreaching." (Ronald C. Hughes et al., Issues in Differential Response, 23 *Research on Social Work Practice* 493 (2013)). Bartholet reviewed the research supporting DR, and concluded, "DR represents a dangerous direction for children." (Elizabeth Bartholet, Differential Response: A Dangerous Experiment in Child

Welfare, 42 *Florida State University Law Review* 573–644 (2015)).

Differential response may prove to be a flash in the pan; the latest in a long line of fads in child welfare. In all likelihood, traditional, investigation-based CPS will remain society's primary tool for keeping kids safe. Ideally, CPS will "steal" the best features of DR.

§ 15-7 DEFINING ABUSE AND NEGLECT

The juvenile court has authority to intervene in the family to protect children from abuse and neglect. Definitions of abuse and neglect vary slightly from state to state. The following definitions are typical:

Physical abuse is nonaccidental physical injury inflicted on a child by an adult. Physical abuse takes many forms: hitting with hands, fists, or weapons; kicking; burning; poisoning; twisting arms or legs; squeezing; drowning; stabbing; and strangling. Devastating and often fatal brain injuries are inflicted when babies are shaken by frustrated caretakers, resulting in Shaken Baby Syndrome (SBS). The term SBS is being replaced with Abusive Head Trauma. Much physical abuse results from "corporal punishment" that goes too far.

Sexual abuse is sexual activity between a child and an adult. Sexual abuse also includes sexual activity between a child and an adolescent. Sexual activity includes inappropriate sexual touching, penetration, and use of children in pornography.

Psychological abuse is a pattern of adult behavior that conveys to a child the idea that the child is worthless, unloved, unwanted, or all three. Sexual abuse is essentially psychological abuse. Many physically abused or neglected children are also psychologically abused.

Every year, millions of children witness domestic violence. Witnessing domestic violence is sometimes a form of neglect.

Neglect occurs when a caretaker deliberately or inadvertently fails to provide a child with essential food, clothing, shelter, medical care, or love. At its core, neglect occurs when the "care" is missing from "caretaker."

§ 15-8 DECISION TO INVOLVE THE JUVENILE COURT

Cases of possible child abuse and neglect come to official attention when reports of suspected maltreatment are received by child protective services (CPS). Approximately one third of initial reports are screened out because they do not involve maltreatment. For cases that are screened in, CPS workers conduct an investigation or place the case in the differential response track.

Following investigation, if no maltreatment is detected, the case is closed. On the other hand, if abuse or neglect is substantiated, CPS workers make a series of decisions. How serious is the maltreatment? What is the risk the child will be hurt again? Is it safe to leave the child at home, or must the child be removed and placed with relatives or in a foster home? Can the case be handled safely and effectively without involving juvenile court? In quite a few cases—particularly neglect cases—CPS workers decide juvenile court is not needed, and CPS offers services to alleviate neglect.

The juvenile court is invoked when maltreatment is serious, when the child is at risk, when it is unsafe to leave the child at home, or when maltreating parents increase the risk to the child by refusing to cooperate.

Formal proceedings in juvenile court are commended by filing a petition. The petition contains a description of the facts of the case and an allegation that the child is abused or neglected and in need of the court's protection. A copy of the petition is given to the parents.

§ 15-9 EMERGENCY REMOVAL OF CHILD FROM HOME

One difficult decision CPS workers make is whether to remove a child on an emergency basis from an unsafe home. Often, this decision is made in the middle of the night, in chaotic circumstances, and with less than complete information.

CPS agencies have procedures for assessing risk and determining when a child needs to be removed in an emergency. In addition to mastering the principles of risk assessment, safety evaluation, and casework, CPS workers need to understand that the Constitution places limits on emergency removal.

The Fourteenth Amendment to the Constitution guarantees due process of law, and the U.S. Supreme Court has interpreted the Fourteenth Amendment to protect parental rights. As the Ninth Circuit Court of Appeals put it in *Wallis v. Spencer,* 202 F.3d 1126, 1136 (9th Cir. 2000), "Parents and children have a well-established constitutional right to live together without governmental interference."

In addition to the Fourteenth Amendment, the Fourth Amendment protects citizens from unreasonable searches and seizures by police *and* government social workers. Removing a child from parents is a "seizure" for Fourth Amendment purposes. Under the Constitution, CPS may not remove a child from parents unless (1) parents consent to removal or (2) before removal, CPS obtains a court order or warrant authorizing removal or (3) absent a court order or warrant, an emergency exists that necessitates immediate removal to protect the child from serious harm or death. The emergency exception to the requirement of a pre-removal warrant is known as the exigent circumstances exception.

When it comes to emergency removal, CPS workers balance the need for child protection against the right of parents to custody of their children free from unwarranted government intrusion. The Fifth Circuit Court of Appeals discussed the delicate balancing of interests in *Gates v. Texas Department of Protective and Regulatory Services,* 537 F.3d 404 (5th Cir. 2008):

There is no doubt that child abuse is a heinous crime, and the government's interest in stopping abuse and removing children from abusive situations is paramount. . . . Deciding what is reasonable under the Fourth Amendment will require an assessment of the fact that the courts are dealing with a child who likely resides in the same house, and is under the control of, the alleged abuser. The analysis cannot be divorced from that fact, but that fact does not override all other Fourth Amendment considerations.

Therefore, we hold that the government may not seize a child from his or her parents absent a court order, parental consent, or exigent circumstances. Exigent circumstances in this context means that, based on the totality of the circumstances, there is reasonable cause to believe that the child is in imminent danger of physical or sexual abuse if he remains in his home. This is a flexible inquiry that considers all of the facts and circumstances with no one factor being dispositive. . . . Whether there was time to obtain a court order is . . . one factor that informs the reasonableness analysis. . . . Other non-exclusive factors . . . are the nature of the abuse (its severity, duration, and frequency), the strength of the evidence supporting the allegations of abuse, the risk that the parent will flee with the child, the possibility of less extreme solutions to the problem, and any harm to the child that might result from the removal. (p. 429).

On rare occasions, parents whose child was removed sue CPS. (*Gates v. Texas Department of Protective and Regulatory Services*, 537 F.3d 404 (5th Cir. 2008); *Rogers v. County of San Joaquin*, 487 F.3d 1288 (9th Cir. 2007); *Doe v. Kearney*, 329 F3d 1286 (11th Cir. 2003); *Tenenbaum v. Williams*, 193 F3d 581 (2d Cir. 1999)). In such lawsuits, parents claim the removal violated their constitutional rights under the Fourteenth and Fourth Amendments.

When a child is removed in an emergency, the law requires CPS to immediately file a petition in juvenile court. Within a short time—often the next day—a hearing is held before a juvenile court judge (or referee or commissioner). The purpose of the hearing is to determine whether the child should remain in out-of-home care or be returned to the parents. At the hearing—which goes by various names, including detention hearing and initial hearing—the judge informs the parents of the nature of the proceedings, including the specific allegations in the petition.

At the detention hearing, CPS is represented by a government attorney. The judge assigns attorneys for the parents and, in many states, for the child. After listening to the attorneys, the CPS worker, and the parents, the judge decides whether CPS made a reasonable effort to avoid removing the child from the home. Assuming reasonable efforts were made, the judge decides whether to "detain" the child in out-of-home care or return the child to the parents. The detention hearing is often quick—on the order of a few minutes to an hour.

With the detention hearing out of the way, the attorneys get down to the task of resolving the case or preparing for trial, often called an adjudicatory hearing. As is true with all types of litigation, few juvenile court cases go all the way to a contested adjudicatory hearing. Most cases settle. The attorney for CPS negotiates with the attorneys for the parents and the child in an effort to reach a solution that is acceptable to all parties. In cases that settle, the parents acknowledge they need help. The parents, CPS, and the child's attorney agree that the child meets one or more of the definitions of maltreatment. The agreement is presented to the judge, who typically approves the agreement and makes a ruling that the child is subject to the juvenile court's authority. The child is then called a "dependent of the court" or a "child in need of protection."

Once the judge rules that a child is a dependent of the court, the next step is disposition—what is the goal for this child and family? CPS prepares a report for the judge outlining the agencies' goals for the family and the services that will be provided to help the parents achieve the goals. In most cases, the goal is reunification of the family.

§ 15-10 ADJUDICATION

Cases that do not settle go to contested adjudicatory hearing before a juvenile court judge, referee, or commissioner. In most states, there is no jury in juvenile court. At the adjudicatory hearing, CPS is represented by its attorney. The parents have the right to hire an attorney of their choosing. Most parents cannot afford to hire an attorney, and the judge appoints an attorney to represent the parents.

Does the child need an attorney? The practice in many states until recently was not to appoint attorneys for children in juvenile court dependency proceedings. Rather, the judge appointed a guardian ad litem to look after the child's interests. A guardian ad litem is an individual—not necessarily an attorney—assigned to safeguard a child's interests in litigation. Today, the trend is to appoint an attorney for the child. Although there is some disagreement about the proper role for a child's attorney, in most states the attorney conducts an investigation, communicates with the child, and advocates in court for the position the attorney believes is best for the child.

In addition to an attorney for the child, juvenile courts in many states appoint a court-appointed special advocate (CASA) for children in dependency proceedings. CASAs are volunteers—college students, retirees, parents, etc.—who are interested in helping abused and neglected children. CASAs receive training about child maltreatment, the child protection system, and juvenile court. Typically, each CASA volunteer is assigned only one or two children. The CASA gets to know the child and, in most communities, the CASA goes to court when their child's case in on. Juvenile court judges often place great stock in the opinions of CASA volunteers because it is common for the CASA to know the child better than any of the professionals assigned to the case.

§ 15–11 DISPOSITION

If the judge sustains the petition and rules the child was maltreated, the next step is disposition. The judge receives recommendations from CPS, considers the parents' wishes, consults the child if the child is old enough to have a useful opinion, and listens to the attorneys.

If the child can live safely at home, then home placement is the preferred disposition. The judge's dispositional order outlines the services the parents will receive to keep the child safe and reduce the likelihood of further maltreatment. The order may provide that the child receive therapy or other intervention.

If the child cannot live safely at home, the dispositional order provides for the child's placement and approves a plan to work toward family reunification. In some cases of severe maltreatment, there is no realistic hope of reunification, and the disposition is to move expeditiously toward termination of parental rights.

§ 15–12 POST-ADJUDICATION PLACEMENT AND REVIEW

Every year, some half a million children enter America's foster care system. A rural county may have a dozen children in out-of-home care, while a large urban county has thousands. Keeping track of these children and providing services to the children and their families is one of the greatest challenges facing child welfare.

There are myriad rules and regulations to keep kids from falling through cracks in the foster care system. In tandem with efforts by social workers, the juvenile court retains authority over the children it adjudicates, and the court holds periodic post-adjudication hearings to review progress. The timing of review hearings varies from state to state, but a common approach is to review progress every 6 months.

To prevent children from languishing in out-of-home care, the federal Adoption and Safe Families Act (ASFA) requires states to consider termination of parental rights for children who have been in foster care 15 of the previous 22 months. ASFA's push toward termination is not required for children in the care of relatives or in cases where termination is not in the child's best interest. ASFA's time limits keep pressure on social workers and judges to reunite families or move toward adoption.

§ 15-13 TERMINATION OF PARENTAL RIGHTS

There is no relationship more revered than the relationship between parent and child. The parent-child relationship is protected by the Constitution from unwarranted government interference. (Chapter 2). Yet, some parents are so thoroughly incompetent, incapable, or abusive that in order to save the child, society must sever the parent-child relationship. The solemn responsibility for determining when such severance is necessary is entrusted to judges of the juvenile and family court.

The law of every state has detailed provisions governing termination of parental rights. The party seeking termination—CPS in juvenile court—has the burden of proof and must establish grounds for termination by clear and convincing evidence. To terminate the parent-child relationship, CPS must establish serious parental fault such as abandonment of the child, mental illness or intellectual disability that is incompatible with minimally adequate parenting, or serious maltreatment that is likely to persist. If fault is established, the judge determines whether termination of parental rights is in the child's best interest.

A judgment terminating parental rights permanently severs the legal parent-child relationship. The "parent" no longer has rights to custody, visitation, or even contact with the child. Severance of the parent-child relationship frees the child for adoption.

See the Pennsylvania Supreme Court's decision in *Adoption of C.M.*, 255 A.3d 343 (Pa. 2021). The Supreme Court explains differences in termination of parental rights in the child welfare system and in private adoption cases.

§ 15–14 FOSTER CARE

The federal government defines foster care broadly to include "24-hour substitute care for children outside their own homes." (45 C.F.R. § 57). Under the federal definition, foster care includes children living with relatives, nonrelative foster family homes, group homes, institutions, and preadoptive homes. State definitions of foster care vary.

Foster care is intended to be a temporary stop—a short layover on the journey to permanence for children removed from home. Most foster children eventually are reunified with their parents. When reunification is impossible, the journey takes a different turn, often in the direction of adoption.

§ 15–14[A] NUMBER AND CHARACTERISTICS OF CHILDREN IN FOSTER CARE

The number of children in foster care fluctuates over time. Until recently, there were few national statistics on foster care, making it difficult to tell how many children were in care at any given point in time. Across the 20th century, approximately 1% of American children were in foster care at any given time. The percentage of poor children in foster care always exceeded 1%.

Today, the foster care population hovers around 500,000. Although a half million children is unacceptably high, it is well to remember that foster children make up a tiny fraction of the total child population. Most children are not abused or neglected, and most who are are not in foster care.

Children of color are overrepresented in the child welfare system. African Americans make up 15% of the U.S. population but 32% of the foster care population. Native American and Alaskan Natives represent 1% of the U.S. population but 2% of children in foster care. Whites are 60% of the population but 40% of the foster care population.

§ 15–14[B] AGING OUT OF FOSTER CARE

Every year, approximately 20,000 foster children reach age 18 and "age out" of the child welfare system. Unfortunately, many of these young people do not fare well. Children who age out of foster care have increased rates of homelessness, incarceration, and mental illness. Some sell drugs to earn money. Others sell their body. Courtney and his colleagues described a longitudinal study of former foster youth in Illinois, Iowa, and Wisconsin:

> In summary, youth making the transition from foster care are faring worse than their same-age peers, in many cases much worse, across a number of domains of functioning. They approach the age of majority with significant educational deficits and relatively few of them appear to be on a path that will provide them with the skills necessary to thrive in today's economy. They are less likely to be employed than their peers, and earnings from employment provide few of them with the means to make ends meet. This is reflected in the economic hardships many of them face and the need that many of them have for government assistance. A large number continue to struggle with health and mental health problems. Too many of them have children for whom they cannot provide a home. They are much more likely than their

peers to find themselves involved with the criminal justice system.

(M.E. Courtney, A. Dworsky, G. Ruth, T. Keller, J. Havicek, & N. Bost, Midwest Evaluation of the Adult Functioning of Former Foster Youth: Outcomes at Age 19. *Chapin Hall Working Paper,* University of Chicago. p. 71 (2005)).

To help foster youth prepare for adulthood, Congress in 1986 created the Independent Living Program. The program provides federal funds to states to help foster youth achieve independence. In 1999, Congress strengthened the program with the Foster Care Independence Act, including the John H. Chafee Foster Care Independence Program. Under the Chafee program, federal funds allow states to pay educational expenses for foster youth aging out. Additional funds are available to extend Medicaid eligibility to age 21. Money is available to assist former foster youth with housing.

It is important to keep in mind that foster care itself is not responsible for the difficulties children experience. Berzin compared outcomes for foster youth and similarly situated youth who were not in care. Berzin's findings "suggest that youth with foster care experience and matched youth do not differ to a statistically significant degree on any of the outcomes measured. This finding differs from the results of previous research, which suggests that many educational and employment outcomes are worse for youth with foster care experience than for other youth. This study does not find such differences. . . . The results challenge the notion that foster care placement is uniquely responsible for negative outcomes. . . . [V]ulnerabilities for foster youth seem to stem from characteristics that existed well before youth's placement in care." (S.C. Berzin, Difficulties in the Transition to Adulthood: Using Propensity Scoring to Understand What Makes Foster Youth Vulnerable, 82 *Social Service Review* 171–196, 19–191 (2008)).

§ 15-15 INDIAN CHILD WELFARE ACT (ICWA)

Prior to 1978, 25% to 35% of Native American children were removed from their parents for alleged abuse or neglect. The majority of these children were placed in non-Indian foster homes, adoptive homes, and institutions. (25 U.S.C. § 1901(4). Lisa L. Atkinson, Best Interest of the Child, 58 *Judges' Journal* 6 (2019)). In 1974, Congress held hearings on the issue. Calvin Isaac, Chief of the Mississippi Band of Choctaw Indians, testified before Congress:

> One of the most serious failings of the present system is that Indian children are removed from the custody of their natural parents by non-tribal government authorities who have no basis for intelligently evaluating the cultural and social premises underlying Indian home life and childrearing. Many of the individuals who decide the fate of our children are at best ignorant of our cultural values, and at worst contemptuous of the Indian way and convinced that removal usually to a non-Indian household or institution; can only benefit an Indian child.

Congress enacted ICWA in 1978. (25 U.S.C. §§ 1901, et seq.). The law is intended to reduce the number of Native American children inappropriately removed from their homes. Congress reported, "The wholesale separation of Indian children from their families is perhaps the most tragic and destructive aspect of Indian life today."

In state juvenile court proceedings, ICWA requires social workers and judges to inquire whether a child is Native American. (*See In re Josiah T. v. E.M.*, 71 Cal.App.5th 388, 286 Cal.Rptr.3d 267 (Cal. Ct. App. 2021)). Under ICWA, a child is an Indian if the child is a member of an Indian tribe or is eligible for membership in a tribe. (25 U.S.C. § 1903(4)). If there is reason to believe a child is Native American, notice is given to the child's tribe and the tribe has the right to participate in the proceeding. For Indian children living on or domiciled within a reservation, the tribe may have exclusive jurisdiction. (25 U.S.C. § 1911(a)). In some cases, the case is transferred from state court to a tribal court.

ICWA applies to foster care placement, termination of parental rights, and adoption. (25 U.S.C. § 1903(1)). When an Indian child is removed from parents due to maltreatment, social workers must make "active efforts" to reunite the child with the family. "Active efforts" are greater than the "reasonable efforts" required for non-Indian parents. In making active efforts, social workers must take into account the child's tribe's social and cultural conditions and way of living. To terminate parental rights to an Indian child, evidence of unfitness must be established by proof beyond a reasonable doubt. (*See In re V.L.R.*, 507 S.W.3d 788 (Tex. Ct. App. 2015)).

A number of courts created an exception to application of ICWA known as the "existing Indian family doctrine." The California Court of Appeal explained in *In re Alexandria P.*, 228 Cal. App. 4th 1322, 176 Cal. Rptr. 3d 468, 484 (2014), "The existing Indian family doctrine is a judicially created exception to the ICWA for factual situations when the minor has never been a member of an Indian home or exposed to Indian culture. It was first applied by the Kansas Supreme Court in *Matter of Adoption of Baby Boy L.* (1982) 231 Kan. 199, 643 P.2d 168. That court has since repudiated the doctrine, as have courts in many other states." A federal regulation provides: "There is no exception to application of ICWA based on the so-called 'existing Indian family doctrine. . . .' " (25 C.F.R. § 23.103(b)). When this regulation becomes law, it will put an end to the doctrine.

§ 15-16 INTERSTATE COMPACT ON THE PLACEMENT OF CHILDREN

Juvenile courts sometimes place children across state lines. When they do, it is necessary to comply with the Interstate Compact on the Placement of Children (ICPC), which is in force in every state. The purpose of the ICPC is to enhance cooperation between states to the end that children are placed in appropriate foster homes, institutions, or adoptive homes.

Social workers seeking to place a child in another state send a detailed form to social workers in the receiving state. The placement does not occur until social workers in the receiving state notify social workers in the sending state "that the proposed placement does not appear to be contrary to the interests of the child." (ICPC Article III(d)). Once a child is placed across state lines, the sending state retains authority over the child as well as financial responsibility for the child.

The ICPC does not apply to cross-border placements with parents and other close relatives. (ICPC Article VIII(a)). As the California Court of Appeal put it in *In re Z.K.*, 201 Cal. App. 4th 51, 133 Cal. Rptr. 3d 591 (2011), "The ICPC governs conditions for out-of-state placement in foster care or as a preliminary to a possible adoption. . . . The ICPC is applicable only to foster care and possible adoption—neither of which would involve natural parents. Accordingly, compliance with the ICPC is not required for placement with an out-of-state parent." The ICPC does not play a role in child custody litigation in family court.

§ 15–17 SPECIAL IMMIGRANT JUVENILE STATUS

Federal immigration law allows certain children who are in the United States without documentation to become permanent residents. The program is called Special Immigrant Juvenile Status (SIJ). The child must be a victim of abuse, neglect, abandonment, or similar maltreatment. A court—

typically a juvenile court—makes a finding that reunification with one or both parents is not a viable option, and that returning the child to the child's home country is not in the child's best interest. The court's findings are submitted to federal immigration authorities, and federal authorities decide whether to grant SIJ status. (*See* Shannon Aimee Daugherty (Note) Special Immigrant Juvenile Status: The Need to Expand Relief, 80 *Brooklyn Law Review* 1087 (2015); *Bianka M. v. Superior Court*, 245 Cal. App. 4th 406, 199 Cal. Rptr. 3d 849 (2016)).

CHAPTER 16

ETHICAL ISSUES AND MALPRACTICE IN FAMILY LAW

Ethical issues pervade law practice. This Chapter touches on ethical issues of special relevance to family law. The chapter also examines legal malpractice in family law.

§ 16–1 DUAL REPRESENTATION

Married couples seeking a divorce may ask a lawyer to represent both of them. The couple typically says, "Our divorce is amicable, and we can't afford two lawyers. Will you represent both of us?" Dual representation is a bad idea even in uncontested cases. The potential for conflicts of interest is too high. Regarding claims of legal malpractice arising out of conflict of interest *see Ex parte Lindsey*, 298 So. 3d 1061 (Ala. 2021).

§ 16–2 DILIGENCE AND COMMUNICATION

Clients are deeply personally concerned about their case. It is vital to keep clients informed of developments. Regular communication—even when nothing new is happening—is respectful to the client and helps the client understand you are not ignoring them. When clients contact the office, make sure you or someone on your staff gets back to the client promptly.

§ 16–3 YOU DON'T HAVE TO BE A PIT BULL TO BE A GOOD ADVOCATE

The adversary system of justice is, well, adversarial. Yet, even in highly contested cases, attorneys are expected to act professionally toward witnesses, the judge, and each other. The California Court of Appeal, in *Marriage of Davenport,* 194 Cal. App. 4th 1507, 125, Cal. Rptr. 3d 292 (2011), ended its opinion with good advice for all attorneys: "Zealous advocacy does not equate with 'attack dog' or 'scorched earth'; nor does it mean lack of civility. Zeal and vigor in the representation of clients are commendable. So are civility, courtesy, and cooperation. They are not mutually exclusive."

§ 16–4 CLIENT TRUST ACCOUNT

All client funds must be deposited in a client trust account. Client funds cannot be deposited in the attorney's personal account.

§ 16–5 CAN YOU PROVIDE A SECOND OPINION?

An attorney cannot provide legal advice to a person who is represented by counsel. Sometimes, family law clients who are represented seek a second opinion from another attorney. It is ethical to offer a second opinion without contacting the client's attorney. (*Oklahoma Bar Association v. Butner*, 976 P.2d 542 (Okla. 1998)).

§ 16-6 SEXUAL RELATIONSHIP WITH CLIENT

It is unethical to have a sexual relationship with a client. (*Iowa Supreme Court Attorney Disciplinary Board v. Moothart,* 860 N.W.2d 598 (Iowa 2015); *Iowa Supreme Court Attorney Disciplinary Board v. Blessum,* 861 N.W.2d 575 (Iowa 2015); *Cleveland Metropolitan Bar Association v. Sleibi*, 42 N.E.3d 699 (Ohio 2015); *In re Phillips*, 413 S.C. 472, 776 S.E.2d 565 (2015); *In re Vogel*, 482 S.W.3d 520 (Tenn. 2016)).

§ 16-7 LEGAL MALPRACTICE

Lawyers practicing family law can be sued for malpractice. The elements of a malpractice cause of action are: (1) an attorney-client relationship; (2) the attorney failed to exercise the degree of skill and diligence required by the circumstances; (3) damage; and (4) causation. (*O'Shea v. Lindenberg,* 64 Cal. App. 5th 228, 278 Cal. Rptr. 3d 654 (2021); *Saussy v. Bonin,* 125 So. 3d 1 (La. Ct. App. 2013); *Collins v. Missouri Bar Plan,* 157 S.W.3d 726 (Mo. Ct. App. 2005)). The New York Court of Appeals wrote in *Arvan Industries Inc. Retirement Trust v. Brown Raysman, Millstein, Felder & Steiner*, 96 N.Y.2d 300, 303–304, 751 N.E.2d 936, 727 N.Y.S.2d 688 (2001), "To sustain a cause of action for legal malpractice . . . a party must show that an attorney failed to exercise the reasonable skill and knowledge commonly possessed by a member of the legal profession."

Some malpractice claims are brought by non-clients, including children and the former spouse of the client.

The most common malpractice claims against family law attorneys relate to property division. (*Faber v. Herman,* 731 N.W.2d 1 (Iowa 2007)). Mallen and Smith write, "The most commonly alleged error against a family lawyer concerns the property settlement agreement or how the marital property is divided in the divorce proceedings." (Ronald E. Mallen & Jeffrey M. Smith, *Legal Malpractice* § 28:8, p. 1277 (2011)).

The Nebraska Supreme Court's decision in *Rice v. Poppe*, 302 Neb. 643, 924 N.W.2d 344 (2019) reminds us of the importance of taking and keeping notes of interactions with clients. The fact that the lawyer in this case kept notes of his interview with the client who sued him helped the lawyer prevail against a claim of malpractice.

CHAPTER 17

FAMILY LAW ATTORNEY AS TRIAL ATTORNEY

Most family law attorneys are in court on a regular basis arguing motions and trying cases. Thus, family law is typically a litigation practice. This chapter introduces issues of evidence law that arise in family law cases. The chapter begins with expert testimony. Attention then shifts to hearsay in family law proceedings. Next, the chapter addresses technical rules governing admission of documents in evidence. The chapter ends with discussion of privileges.

§ 17–1 OPINION TESTIMONY FROM LAY AND EXPERT WITNESSES

Expert testimony is frequently offered in family law trials. The expert may be a mental health professional, accountant, vocational expert, appraiser, or actuary. Experts provide opinions and recommendations on a broad range of subjects, from the best interests of children to the value of businesses.

Experts do not testify in all family law trials. Lay witnesses, by contrast, including the parties, testify in virtually every trial. The primary office of the lay witness is to provide factual information to the trier of fact. Often, however, lay witnesses offer opinion. Occasionally, one hears of a supposed rule called the rule against opinion testimony from lay witnesses. In truth, there is no such rule. Lay witnesses offer opinions all the time. The point with lay witnesses is that they should as much as possible limit their testimony to factual information that is within their personal knowledge. The more specific, factual, and detailed a lay witness's testimony, the better. If some aspects of a lay witness's testimony stray into opinion, that usually does not make the testimony objectionable.

Federal Rule of Evidence (FRE) 701 authorizes opinion testimony from lay witnesses, and provides:

> If a witness is not testifying as an expert, testimony in the form of an opinion is limited to one that is: (a) rationally based on the witness's perception; (b) helpful to clearly understanding the witness's testimony or to determining a fact in issue.

Judges allow opinions from lay witnesses on a broad range of subjects. For example, a lay witness could testify that a person appeared ill, in pain, injured, drunk, or sober. The Florida Court of Appeal's decision in *Bush v. State,* 809 So. 2d 107 (Fla. Ct. App. 2002) involved Munchausen Syndrome by Proxy inflicted by a mother. When the child was finally rescued, the child's health improved dramatically. The court ruled that it was proper for a lay witness to describe the child's improved health following rescue. The court noted, "A lay witness may describe a person's physical appearance using opinions that do not require special skill, so long as the opinions are based upon observations of the witness. . . . Here, the lay witness did not testify that Jennifer seemed 'healthier,' which would have been improper because [the lay witness] did not know

Jennifer during her care with [the mother]." (pp. 119–120). If the lay witness *had* known Jennifer before *and* after her rescue, the witness could have testified that Jennifer appeared healthier.

In *Hicks v. State,* 6 So. 3d 1099 (Miss. Ct. App. 2009), the defendant had an argument with his seventy-two-year-old mother so he took an ironing board and hit her with it multiple times. The defendant claimed he acted in self-defense when his mother came at him with a knife. An experienced police officer investigated the case and testified as a lay witness regarding the insignificant nature of wounds on the defendant. The defense objected that expert testimony was needed to describe injuries. Disagreeing, the Mississippi Court of Appeal ruled that it was proper for the officer to describe the defendant's injuries.

A lay witness may describe a person's state of mind: happy, sad, depressed, frightened, etc. In *People v. Acosta,* 338 P.3d 472 (Colo. Ct. App. 2014), the defendant was caught in the act of inappropriate conduct with a child. The child's father angrily confronted the defendant. It was proper for the father to testify that the defendant was "very guilty-looking."

May a lay witness offer an opinion that someone seemed insane or out of touch with reality? Clearly, a lay witness could describe a person's behavior, and testify to things the person said. In *People v. Clark,* 432 N.W.2d 173 (Mich. Ct. App. 1988), the defendant walked into a church, drew a gun, and robbed parishioners. At Clark's robbery trial it was proper for parishioners to describe the defendant's behavior during the robbery. The Michigan Court of Appeals wrote, "The testimony of lay witnesses may be competent evidence of a defendant's mental illness." (p. 178).

In *Ex parte Milteer*, 571 So. 2d 998 (Ala. 1990), the Alabama Supreme Court wrote, "Generally, the testimony of a lay witness on the issue of sanity is competent and admissible where the lay witness has known the defendant for a long period of time." (p. 1000).

When it comes to testimony about mental illness, many aspects of the subject require expert testimony. Basic observations about a person's conduct, however, often fall within the competence of lay witnesses.

There are limits on opinion testimony from lay witnesses. Thus, a lay witness cannot diagnose mental illness, and a lay witness should not opine, "The best interest of the child will be served by placing the child with the father." These opinions require an expert.

§ 17–2 WHO MAY PROVIDE EXPERT TESTIMONY

FRE 702 describes who qualifies to provide expert testimony. The Rule states:

> A witness who is qualified as an expert by knowledge, skill, experience, training, or education may testify in the form of an opinion or otherwise if: (a) the expert's scientific,

> technical, or other specialized knowledge will help the trier of fact to understand the evidence or to determine a fact in issue; (b) the testimony is based on sufficient facts or data; (c) the testimony is the product of reliable principles and methods; and (d) the expert has reliably applied the principles and methods to the facts of the case.

To qualify as an expert, a professional must possess sufficient "knowledge, skill, experience, training, or education." A professional need not be the foremost authority on a subject to provide expert testimony. Nor must a professional understand every nuance of a subject. Publication is not necessary. Indeed, most expert witnesses do not publish.

Before a professional may testify as an expert, the judge must be satisfied that the professional is qualified. The normal procedure is for the attorney offering the professional's testimony to put the professional on the witness stand and ask questions about the person's education, training, and experience. The opposing attorney has the right to voir dire the witness in an effort to persuade the judge that the person is not an expert. In most cases, there is no challenge to the expert's qualifications.

Expert testimony is allowed when an expert can help the trier of fact comprehend technical, clinical, or scientific issues. The subject of an expert's testimony does not have to be completely beyond the ken of the trier of fact. Often, an expert adds depth and clarity to subjects that are somewhat familiar to the trier. On the other hand, if the trier is adequately equipped to decide an issue without assistance, expert testimony is inadmissible.

§ 17-3 BASES FOR EXPERT TESTIMONY

Expert witnesses base their testimony on a broad range of facts and data. In the medical and mental health fields, experts rely on many sources of information, including interviews of the individual, discussions with others, consultation with other experts, psychological and medical tests, research in the literature, and written documentation, including hospital records and police reports. Accountants, appraisers, and actuaries rely on a similarly broad basis of information.

The rules of evidence permit experts to formulate court testimony based on the types of facts and data experts rely on in their normal, day-to-day professional work outside the courtroom. FRE 703 provides:

> An expert may base an opinion on facts or data in the case that the expert has been made aware of or personally observed. If experts in the particular field would reasonably rely on those kinds of facts or data in forming an opinion on the subject, they need not be admissible for the opinion to be admitted. But if the facts or data would otherwise be inadmissible, the proponent of the opinion may disclose them to the jury only if their probative value in helping the jury evaluate the opinion substantially outweighs their prejudicial effect.

Rule 703 specifies that experts may base opinions on information that is *not* admissible in evidence, so long as other professionals in the expert's field rely on such information.

Although an expert's opinion may be based on inadmissible evidence, including inadmissible hearsay, FRE 703 provides, "But if the facts or data would otherwise be inadmissible, the proponent of the opinion may disclose them to the jury only if their probative value in helping the jury evaluate the opinion substantially outweighs their prejudicial effect." If an attorney objects to an expert disclosing inadmissible evidence that the expert considered in preparing to testify, the judge balances the importance of the inadmissible evidence to a proper understanding of the expert's testimony, against the possibility that the jury will place too much emphasis on the inadmissible evidence. Depending on how the judge views this balance, the judge may prohibit the expert from disclosing to the jury some or all of the inadmissible evidence that supports the expert's testimony. The expert testimony is still admissible; only the inadmissible evidence that supports the testimony is kept from the jury. On the other hand, the judge may conclude that the trier of fact needs to hear the inadmissible evidence in order to gain a full understanding of the expert's opinion.

§ 17-4 OPINIONS ON ULTIMATE ISSUES

In every case, there are ultimate facts and ultimate legal issues. Rule FRE 704(a) allows expert witnesses to testify regarding ultimate facts, but not ultimate legal issues. The ultimate facts are the facts that one side must prove to win its case. Suppose, for example, that Sue broke into a house in order to steal. Sue is charged with burglary, which is the breaking and entering of the dwelling house of another at night with the intent to commit a felony therein. The ultimate facts are: (1) breaking, (2) entering, (3) the dwelling house of another, (4) at night, and (5) with the intent to commit a felony inside the dwelling.

In a rape prosecution, the crime is defined as sexual intercourse accomplished by force and against the will of the victim. Penetration is an element of the crime, and is an ultimate fact.

In the burglary case, lay witnesses could testify to the ultimate facts required for conviction. In the rape case, the victim and/or an expert witness could testify regarding penetration.

The ultimate *legal* issue in the burglary and rape cases is whether the defendant is guilty or innocent. As mentioned above, expert witnesses may testify to ultimate facts, but *not* ultimate legal issues such as guilt or innocence. Thus, an expert should not venture an opinion on whether the defendant in a criminal case is guilty or innocent. Nor should an expert express an opinion on *who* committed a crime. Guilt, innocence, and identity are for the jury to decide, not experts. In child custody litigation, there is controversy over whether experts should offer opinions on the ultimate issues of a child's best interest, or which parent should have custody. This issue is discussed in Chapter 7.

§ 17-5 THE REASONABLE CERTAINTY STANDARD FOR EXPERT TESTIMONY

When eliciting an expert's opinion, it is common for an attorney to ask, "Doctor, do you have an opinion, based on a reasonable degree of certainty, whether Ms. Jones was mentally ill?" In *People v. Gilmore,* 653 N.E.2d 58, 60 (Ill. Ct. App. 1995), for example, an expert testified, "to a reasonable degree of medical and psychiatric certainty that defendant was mentally ill and legally insane at the time of the alleged offense." The expert testimony in *Gilmore* illustrates the so-called "reasonable certainty" standard: An expert must be reasonable certain the opinion is correct. (*See Cooper v. Takeda Pharmaceutical America, Inc.,* 191 Cal. Rptr. 3d 67 (Ct. App. 2015)).

The rules of evidence do not *require* experts to testify in terms of reasonable certainty. Yet, attorneys so often ask questions in the language of reasonable certainty that it is helpful to understand the meaning of the term. It may surprise you to learn that no one knows the meaning of reasonable certainty. Lewin concluded: "Although judges expect, and sometimes insist, that expert opinions be expressed with 'reasonable medical certainty,' and although attorneys ritualistically intone the phrase, no one knows what it means!" (Jeff L. Lewin, The Genesis and Evolution of Legal Uncertainty About "Reasonable Medical Certainty," 57 *Maryland Law Review* 380 (1998)).

Expert witnesses do not have to be completely certain their opinion is correct. The Iowa Supreme

Court observed in *State v. Tyler,* 867 N.W.2d 136, 153 (Iowa 2015), "There is no requirement that the expert be able to express an opinion with absolute certainty." At the same time, experts may not speculate or guess. The California Court of Appeal wrote in *Pedeferri v. Seidner Enterprises,* 216 Cal. App. 4th 359, 375 (2013), "Where an expert bases his conclusion upon assumptions which are not supported by the record, . . . his conclusion has no evidentiary value and should be excluded." *See also Pratt v. Ferguson,* 3 Cal. App. 5th 102 (2016). In a similar vein, the California Court of Appeal wrote in *Cooper v. Takeda Pharmaceuticals America, Inc.*, 191 Cal. Rptr. 3d 67, 83 (Ct. App. 2015), "Courts are to ensure that opinions are not speculative, based on unconventional matters or grounded in unsupported reasoning." Thus, experts may not guess, but, at the same time, they do not have to be 100% certain they are right. Reasonable certainty lies between guesswork and certainty—closer to the latter.

Not only does reasonable certainty have no clear meaning, the phrase can cause confusion because it is a legal term, not a term employed in medicine or mental health. Bradford (2001) comments, "Many lawyers and judges believe the phrase is a medical term of art. Physician commentators, however, have described the phrase as a legal term of art." (Glenn Bradford, Dissecting Missouri's Requirement of "Reasonable Medical Certainty," 57 *Missouri Bar Journal* 136, 137 (2001)). Poythress wrote, "I've always had a pretty healthy skepticism about phrases like 'reasonable medical certainty.' . . . Left undefined, there is a risk that lay jurors will think that the opinions are somehow an outgrowth of quasi-objective, scientific investigation." (Norman Poythress, Concerning Reform in Expert Testimony: An Open Letter from a Practicing Psychologist, 6 *Law and Human Behavior* 39, 41 (1982)). Melton and his colleagues observe, "There is a danger that, because of the law's preference for certainty, experts will over-reify their observations and reach beyond legitimate interpretations of the data." (Gary B. Melton, John Petrila, Norman G. Poythress & Christopher Slobogin, *Psychological Evaluations for the Courts: A Handbook for Mental Health Professionals and Lawyers* p. 11 (3d ed. 2007)).

Because reasonable certainty has no clear meaning, a more useful way to think about the value of expert testimony is to ask: In formulating an opinion, did the expert consider all relevant facts? Does the expert have adequate understanding of pertinent clinical, scientific, accounting, etc., principles? Did the expert use methods of assessment that are appropriate, reliable, and valid? Are the expert's inferences, assumptions, and conclusions reasonable and defensible?

The concept of reasonable certainty should not be confused with the burden of proof. The burden of proof is the level of certainty by which a trier of fact must be persuaded by the evidence that is presented by the party with the burden of proof. The law that applies to a case determines which party has the burden of proof. Three burdens of proof are used: (a) Beyond a reasonable doubt; (b) Preponderance of the evidence; and (c) Clear and convincing evidence.

As discussed above, in many courts, experts must be reasonably certain their opinions are right. It is important to understand that the certainty needed for expert testimony does *not* vary with the type of litigation or the burden of proof. Experts do not have to be more certain in criminal cases, where the burden of proof is highest, than in civil cases. Regardless of the type of litigation—criminal or civil—experts should ensure the correctness of opinions.

Occasionally, attorneys ask experts whether they are certain of their opinion beyond a reasonable doubt or by a preponderance of the evidence. An accurate response to such a question is, "Counsel, when I reach an opinion, I do not employ the legal concept of burden of proof. Burdens of proof are legal constructs, and are not used in psychology. Instead, I use clinical and scientific principles to reach my opinion. In reaching my opinion, I took all the steps I could to ensure that my opinion is correct. I am reasonably certain of my opinion, and, by reasonably certain, I mean I am confident my opinion is correct."

§ 17-6 DIRECT EXAMINATION OF EXPERT WITNESSES

Once the judge approves a professional as an expert witness, testimony begins with direct examination. An expert's direct testimony typically takes one or more of the following forms: an opinion, an answer to a hypothetical question, or a lecture providing technical or clinical information to the trier of fact.

Opinion is the most common form of expert testimony. For example, an expert might opine that a child experienced abusive head trauma. An expert might testify that a child or a parent is depressed. An expert might opine of the value of a marital/community property business, a pension, the value of goodwill, or the value of a minority interest in a closely held corporation.

Less often than an opinion, an expert is asked a hypothetical question. The attorney describes a hypothetical set of facts that parallel the facts of the case on trial. Then, the expert is asked for an opinion about the hypothetical facts. The trier of fact applies the expert's opinion about the *hypothetical* facts to the *actual* facts of the case.

Many attorneys avoid hypothetical questions on direct examination. The hypothetical can seem stilted and artificial.

Experts are more likely to encounter hypothetical questions during cross-examination. The cross-examiner may try to weaken the expert's opinion by asking about a hypothetical set of facts that differs from the facts described by the expert. The cross-examiner then asks, "If the hypothetical facts I have suggested turn out to be true, would that change your opinion?" When a cross-examiner asks a far-fetched hypothetical question, the expert might answer, "If the facts were as you suggest, my opinion could change, yes. Of course, the facts you suggest were not the facts I observed."

In some cases, the expert limits testimony to a lecture intended to give the trier of fact technical, clinical, or scientific information that it needs to evaluate the evidence. With this form of expert testimony, the expert does not render an opinion. The expert's testimony is limited to educating the trier of fact.

§ 17–7 CROSS-EXAMINATION OF EXPERT WITNESSES

One of the most effective cross-examination techniques with experts is to get the expert to agree to the facts, inferences, and conclusions that support the expert's opinion, and then dispute one or more of those facts, inferences, or conclusions.

The cross-examiner might ask whether the expert's opinion would change if certain facts were different (hypothetical question). The attorney might ask the expert whether other experts could come to different conclusions based on the same facts.

Rather than attack the expert's facts, inferences, and conclusions during cross-examination, the attorney may limit cross-examination to pinning the expert down to a limited set of facts, inferences, and conclusions, and then, when the expert has left the witness stand, offer another expert to critique the expert's testimony.

An expert witness can, with important limits, be cross-examined with quotes from books and articles. The rule of evidence on point is FRE 803(18). The rule sates:

Statements contained in a treatise, periodical, or pamphlet [can be admitted in evidence] if:

(A) the statement is called to the attention of an expert witness on cross-examination or relied on by the expert on direct examination; and

(B) the publication is established as a reliable authority by the expert's admission or testimony, by another expert's testimony, or by judicial notice.

If admitted [in evidence], the statement may be read into evidence but not received as an exhibit.

§ 17–8 HEARSAY

Hearsay evidence plays an important role in family law trials. Hearsay is an out-of-court statement (an assertion of fact) that is repeated in court to prove the truth of the statement (the truth of the matter asserted). It is useful to divide the definition into its three components. A person's words are hearsay when: (1) The person's words were intended by the person to describe something that happened; and (2) The person spoke prior to the court hearing where the person's words are repeated (The person's assertion was "out-of-court"); and (3) The person's out-of-court statement (assertion) is repeated in court to prove that what the person said actually happened (the *out*-of-court assertion is repeated *in* court to prove the truth of the matter asserted).

§ 17-9 EXCEPTIONS TO THE HEARSAY RULE

There are more than thirty exceptions to the rule against hearsay, but only a handful play a day-to-day role in family law litigation.

§ 17–9[A] EXCITED UTTERANCE EXCEPTION

An excited utterance is a hearsay statement that describes a startling event (FRE 803(2)). The statement must be made while the declarant is under the emotional stress caused by the startling event. The theory behind the excited utterance exception is that statements made under significant stress are likely to be true. The following factors are considered by judges in deciding whether a hearsay statement is an excited utterance: (1) *Nature of the event.* Some events are more startling than others, and the judge considers the likely impact a particular event would have on a person of similar age and experience. (2) *Amount of time between startling event and statement relating to the event.* The more time that passes between a startling event and a declarant's statement describing the event, the less likely a judge is to conclude the statement is an excited utterance. Although passage of time is important, elapsed time is not the only factor judges consider. Judges have approved delays ranging from a few minutes to many hours. (3) *Was the declarant upset?* Indications that the declarant was distraught when the declarant spoke are important. Was the declarant crying, frightened, or otherwise upset when the statement was made? (4) *Declarant's speech pattern.* In some cases, the way a person speaks—*e.g.*, pressured or hurried speech—indicates excitement. (5) *Was the statement spontaneous?* Spontaneity is a key factor in the excited utterance exception. The more spontaneous a statement, the more likely it meets the requirements of the exception. (6) *Did questions elicit the statement?* The fact that a declarant was asked questions does not necessarily destroy the spontaneity required for the excited utterance exception. However, as questions become suggestive, spontaneity may dissipate, undermining the exception. (7) *First safe opportunity.* In many abuse cases, victims remain under the control of an abuser for hours after an abusive incident. When the victim is finally released to a safe person, the victim has the first safe opportunity to disclose what happened. A victim's statement at the first safe opportunity may qualify as an excited utterance even though considerable time elapsed since abuse occurred. (8) *Rekindled excitement.* A startling event such as abuse may be followed by a period of calm, during which excitement abates. If victim is later exposed to a stimulus that reminds the victim of the startling event, the victim's excitement may be rekindled. Rekindled excitement sometimes satisfies the excited utterance exception.

§ 17–9[B] MEDICAL DIAGNOSIS OR TREATMENT EXCEPTION

All states have a diagnosis or treatment exception for certain hearsay statements made to professionals providing diagnostic or treatment services (FRE 803(4)). The rationale for the diagnosis or treatment exception is that hearsay statements to professionals providing diagnostic or treatment services are reliable because the patient has an incentive to be truthful with the professional.

The person to whom a patient speaks may be a physician, psychiatrist, psychologist, nurse, social worker, paramedic, EMT, or medical technician. The diagnosis or treatment exception includes the patient's statements describing medical history, as well as statements describing present symptoms, pain, and other sensations. The exception includes the patient's description of the cause of illness or injury.

Unlike the excited utterance exception, the patient does not have to be upset for the medical diagnosis or treatment exception to apply.

§ 17–9[C] STATE OF MIND EXCEPTION

The state of mind exception allows hearsay statements describing the declarant's physical or mental condition *at the time* the declarant speaks (FRE 803(3)). The following statements are admissible under the state of mind exception, "I want to live with my mom." "I'm afraid of my mother." "I love grandma and grandpa." "If the judge makes me live with my dad, I'll run away."

§ 17–9[D] RESIDUAL EXCEPTION

Most states have a hearsay exception known as a residual or catchall exception, which allows use in court of reliable hearsay that does not meet the requirements of one of the traditional exceptions (*e.g.*, excited utterance, medical diagnosis or treatment) (FRE 807). In addition to a generic residual exception, which applies in all kinds of cases, most states have a residual hearsay exception for reliable statements by children in child abuse cases. Some states have a residual exception for domestic violence cases.

When a declarant's hearsay statement is offered under a residual exception, the most important question is whether the statement is reliable. The judge considers the totality of the circumstances to evaluate reliability, including: The more spontaneous a statement, the more likely a judge is to find it reliable. Reliability may be influenced by the type of questions asked. When questions are suggestive, the possibility increases that the questioner influenced the statement. It should be noted, however, that suggestive questions are sometimes necessary to elicit information, particularly when the information is embarrassing. The smaller the number of suggestive questions, the more likely a judge is to conclude that a person's statement is reliable. Reliability may be enhanced if a declarant's statements are consistent over time. When a declarant's emotions are congruent with the hearsay statement, the reliability of the statement may be enhanced. Evidence that the declarant had or lacked a motive to fabricate affects reliability. When a declarant's behavior alters in a way that corroborates the declarant's statement, it may be appropriate to place increased confidence in the statement. None of these factors is a litmus test for reliability. Judges consider the totality of circumstances to evaluate reliability.

§ 17–9[E] PRIOR INCONSISTENT STATEMENTS

A witness may be impeached with a prior inconsistent statement. When a prior inconsistent statement is offered both to impeach, *and* for the truth of the matter asserted, the statement is hearsay. The FRE allow some, but not most prior inconsistent statement to be admitted for the truth. State evidence codes vary on when prior inconsistent statements are admissible for the truth, as well as to impeach.

§ 17–9[F] PARTY ADMISSIONS

A party's own words—written or oral—are admissible against the party. FRE 801(d)(2) contains five types of party admissions: (A) Personal admissions; (B) Adoptive admissions; (C) Admissions by an authorized agent; (D) Statements by an employee of a party, within the scope of the employee's duties; (E) Statements by co-conspirators during the course of, and in furtherance, of the conspiracy.

1. Personal Admissions: Personal admissions abound in family law litigation. The statement, "I forgot to make last month's child support payment," is admissible against the speaker for the truth of the matter asserted, as is, "I won't get a job if it means paying child support," as is, "I get paid under the table," as is, "My monthly income is $10,000." A person's postings to their Facebook page are party admissions. (*State v. Inkton*, 60 N.E.3d 616 (Ohio Ct. App. 2016)). A party's tax return is admissible against the party as an admission. (*In re Sillins*, 264 B.R. 894, 898 (N.D. Ill. 2001); *Greenspan v. LADT*, 191 Cal. App. 4th 486, 121 Cal. Rptr. 3d 118 (2011)). The old shibboleth, "Anything you say can be used against you" is generally true.

2. **Adoptive Admissions:** A party can adopt the truth of a statement uttered or written by a non-party. For example, Husband asks his employer to write a letter describing husband's job responsibilities and salary. Husband uses the letter to secure an auto loan. In family court litigation, Wife could offer the letter as evidence of husband's income, arguing that husband adopted the contents of the letter. A person's tax return can be an adoptive admission or a personal admission. (*Greenspan v. LADT*, 191 Cal. App. 4th 486, 121 Cal. Rptr. 3d 118 (2011)).

3. **Authorized Admissions:** When a party authorizes another to make statements on the party's behalf, the statements are admissible against the party. *Melamed v. Melamed*, 50 N.E.3d 669 (Ill. Ct. App. 2016), was an action to increase child support. Husband acknowledged that bank records and tax documents were prepared for Husband's company. The Illinois Appellate Court ruled that "the documents can be viewed as statements by a person authorized by the party to make a statement concerning the subject."

§ 17–9[G] BUSINESS RECORDS EXCEPTION

The business records exception is contained in FRE 803(6). The exception allows admission of:

> A record of an act, event, condition, opinion, or diagnosis if: (A) the record was made at or near the time by—or from information transmitted by—someone with knowledge; (B) the record was kept in the course of a regularly conducted activity of a business, organization, occupation, or calling, whether or not for profit; (C) making the record was a regular practice of that activity; (D) all these conditions are shown by the testimony of the custodian or another qualified witness, or by a certification that complies with Rule 902(11) or (12) or with a statute permitting certification; and (E) neither the source of information nor the method or circumstances of preparation indicate a lack of trustworthiness.

Routine records of a business of any size, including sole proprietorships, close corporations, and professional practices, are generally admissible as business records. Documents regarding compensation, including pay stubs, are business records. Documents describing deferred compensation for employees are business records. A business's tax documents and tax returns are business records. An employee's business calendar containing appointments and business travel is a business record. Bank documents are business records. (*Greenspan v. LADT*, 191 Cal. App. 4th 486, 524, 121 Cal. Rptr. 3d 118 (2011)). On the other hand, purely personal documents are not business records, even when the document is written while at work.

The foundation to qualify a document as a business record includes testimony from the custodian of records, or a certification from the custodian that satisfies the requirements of FRE 902(11) or an applicable statute. If the foundation is laid in court, with the custodian of records, the elements of the foundation are: (1) The document was written by an employee of the company or agency; (2) The source of the information in the document works for the company, and has personal knowledge of what is discussed in the document. The person who wrote the report does not have to have personal knowledge of the events; (3) The document was made at or near the time of the events discussed in the document. The time limit is flexible, and can be considerably longer than what would satisfy the excited utterance exception. The point of the time limit is to ensure that the document was prepared while events were fresh in memory; (4) It is a routine practice of the business to prepare documents of the sort offered; and (5) The document was prepared in the regular course of business.

The witness who lays the foundation does not have to be the author of the document. Nor does the witness have to have personal knowledge of the events described in the document. Instead, the witness must be familiar with how the company or agency prepares and maintains documents.

The witness who lays the foundation for the business records exception also authenticates the document and satisfied the best evidence rule.

§ 17–9[H] PUBLIC RECORDS EXCEPTION

The public records exception—FRE 803(8)—covers documents prepared by government agencies. The exception provides:

> A record or statement of a public office if: (A) it sets out; (i) the office's activities; (ii) a matter observed while under a legal duty to report, but not including, in a criminal case, a matter observed by law-enforcement personnel; or (iii) in a civil case or against the government in a criminal case, factual findings from a legally authorized investigation; and (B) neither the source of information nor other circumstances indicate a lack of trustworthiness.

The public records exception embraces public records prepared by federal, state, and local government employees. The exception includes records of child support services, tax authorities, and public pension plans. Public records become self-authenticating by obtaining the seals, signatures, and certifications specified by FRE 902. Many courts, especially in civil cases, rule that government documents can be admitted under the public records exception or the business records exception.

§ 17-10 AUTHENTICATION OF DOCUMENTS

Before a document is admissible to prove the contents of the document, five matters must be resolved: (1) Relevance (FRE 402), (2) Authentication (FRE 901–902), (3) Best evidence rule (FRE 1002), (4) Hearsay, (FRE 802) and (5) Probative value versus danger of unfair prejudice (FRE 403). The following subsections assume the document is relevant, and that probative value is not substantially outweighed by the danger of unfair prejudice. Analysis focuses on authentication and best evidence. Hearsay is discussed above.

FRE 901 and 902 govern authentication. Rule 902 provides that certain documents are self-authenticating. Documents that are not self-authenticating fall under Rule 901, and require the proponent of the document to "produce evidence sufficient to support a finding that the item is what the proponent claims it is." In other words, is this document the real McCoy? The Maryland Court of Appeal wrote, "Authentication has been defined as 'the act of proving that something (as a document) is true or genuine, esp[ecially] so that it may be admitted as evidence'. Black's Law Dictionary 157 (10th ed. 2014). Authentication of a matter prior to its admission 'is not an artificial principal of evidence, but an inherent necessity', (7 J. Wigmore, Evidence § 2129 (Chadbourn Rev. 1978)), and is integral to establishing relevancy. *See* 2 McCormick on Evidence § 221 (7th ed. 2013)." (*Sublet v. State*, 442 Md. 632, 113 A.3d 695 (2015)).

§ 17–10[A] PRELIMINARY MATTERS

The law regarding authentication is intertwined with the law governing determination of preliminary facts, that is, facts that must be determined as a condition precedent to the admission of evidence (FRE 104). Rule 104 allocates the determination of preliminary facts between the judge and the jury. Some preliminary facts are decided by the judge alone (Rule 104(a)). Other preliminary facts are for the jury to decide, after the judge finds that sufficient evidence of the preliminary fact has been introduced "to support a finding that the fact does exist." (Rule 104(b)).

By way of example, Rule 104(a) provides that the following preliminary facts are for the judge alone: competence of a person to testify, whether a witness qualifies as an expert; existence and application of privileges, whether an out-of-court statement is hearsay, and, if it is, whether it meets the requirements of a hearsay exception.

Among the preliminary facts that are for the jury to decide—Rule 104(b)—the most pertinent is authorship of documents, that is, did a particular person create a document? The process begins with the judge listening to evidence pro and con of authorship, and deciding whether a reasonable juror could find the document is authentic. If the answer is yes, then the document is admissible, provided other rules of evidence are fulfilled (*e.g.*, hearsay). Once a document is admitted, the jury decides how much, if any, weight to give the document.

In most states, there is no jury in family law litigation. In bench trials, questions about preliminary issues are decided by the court.

§ 17-10[B] DISCOVERY AND STIPULATIONS REGARDING AUTHENTICATION

In many family law trials, authentication is not disputed because the matter is resolved before trial via discovery or stipulation. Some courts have rules requiring parties to resolve such matters in advance.

Documents produced in response to discovery requests generally are implicitly authenticated. In *Stumpff v. Harris*, 31 N.E.3d 164 (Ohio Ct. App. 2015), the Ohio Court of Appeal wrote, "Numerous courts, both state and federal, have held that items produced in discovery are implicitly authenticated by the act of production by the opposing party." The Ohio court noted that implicit authentication is appropriate when the person responding to discovery has the capacity to authenticate the document, but may be inappropriate when person lacks that capacity.

§ 17-10[C] RULE 902—SELF-AUTHENTICATION

A document that is self-authenticating requires no extrinsic evidence to establish authorship. The court examines the document, and, if all is order, authentication springs from the document itself.

1. Rules 902(1) and (2): Public Document Signed by Public Employee and Under Seal.

Government documents generated by federal, state, and local agencies are self-authenticating when the document bears an official seal *and* the signature of a public employee "purporting to be an execution or attestation." (Rule 902(1)(B)). If a public employee has no official seal, Rule 902(2) makes the employee's signature self-authenticating if the signature is accompanied by the signature of another public employee, who certifies under seal "that the signer has the official capacity and that the signature is genuine."

2. Rule 902(4): Certified Copies of Public Records. An official record is self-authenticating when it is certified as correct by the custodian of the record or another qualified person. Many government documents can be self-authenticating under Rule 902(4).

3. Rule 902(5): Official Publications. Rule 902(5) authenticates publications of public authorities. This rule embraces government manuals, and would include, for example, officially published child support guidelines. The official nature of the document is garnered from the appearance of the document.

4. Rule 902(8): Notarized Documents. A notarized signature is self-authenticating.

5. Rule 902(10): Federal Statute Declares Signature or Document Authentic. Rule 902(10) provides that a signature or document is self-authenticating when a federal statute so provides. For example, 26 U.S.C. § 6064 provides, "The fact that an individual's name is signed to a [tax] return . . . shall be prima facie evidence for all purposes that the return . . . was actually signed by him."

6. Rules 902(11): Certification of Business Records. The business records exception to the hearsay rule contemplates testimony from the custodian of records to lay the foundation for the exception, and to authenticate the documents. (Rule 803(6)(D)). Rule 902(11) eliminates the need for actual testimony from the custodian. The custodian certifies that the records comply with Rule 803(6). States have similar rules, eliminating the need for *viva voce* testimony from the custodian.

§ 17-10[D] RULE 901—DOCUMENTS THAT ARE NOT SELF-AUTHENTICATING

For non-self-authenticating documents, the law does not presume that the document is genuine. The proponent of the document must produce evidence to satisfy Rule 901, which provides, "The proponent must produce evidence sufficient to support a finding that the item is what the proponent claims it is." Evidence that is sufficient to authenticate can be direct or circumstantial. (*Smith v. Smith*, 196 So.3d 1191 (Ala. Civ. App. 2015); *Sublet v. State*, 442 Md. 632, 113 A.3d 695, 711 (2015); *Donati v. State*, 84 A.3d 156 (Md. Special App. 2014)). The proponent does not have to rule out possibilities that are inconsistent with authentication. (*United States v. Gagliardi*, 506 F.3d 140 (2d Cir. 2007)).

Rule 901(b) contains a list techniques that are commonly used to authenticate documents, identify voices, and lay the foundation for real evidence—things. The subsections that follow describe the techniques used most frequently in family court.

1. Witness with Personal Knowledge. Rule 901(b)(1) describes the most straight forward way to lay the foundation for many items of evidence: Offer testimony from a witness with personal knowledge. Thus, to authenticate a signature, offer testimony from a witness who knows the signature. To authenticate an email, offer testimony from the person who wrote the email. To identify a voice, offer testimony from someone who knows the voice, and the speaker. To authenticate that a document is a "copy" printed from a computer, put the person on the stand who printed the document. A pay stub can be authenticated by the bookkeeper who generated the pay stub, or the employee who received it.

2. Opinion on Handwriting. In the digital age, handwritten documents and signatures are less common than they were in ancient times, before 2000. Yet, it is sometimes necessary to prove who penned a handwritten document, or signed a word processed document, a check, or a credit card receipt. Needless to say, the author can authenticate her own handwriting. Rule 901(b)(2) allows a person who is familiar handwriting to opine on authorship. In cases where no one is familiar with handwriting, a handwriting expert can compare the disputed document/signature with authenticated exemplars, and offer an opinion on authorship (Rule 901(b)(3)). As an alternative to a handwriting expert, Rule 901(b)(3) allows the party seeking to prove authorship to ask the jury to compare the disputed document to the exemplars, and decide.

3. Content and Distinctive Characteristics. It is sometimes possible to establish authorship of a document by pointing to content that could only be known to one person, or to peculiarities of spelling, word choice, word order, or phrasing. Rule 901(b)(4) speaks to this approach by providing that authentication can be established by, "The appearance, contents, substance, internal patterns, or other distinctive characteristics of the items, taken together with all the circumstances." This method of authentication is used to authenticate emails, text messages, Facebook postings, and other electronic communications.

4. Reply Letter Doctrine. A disputed communication—letter, text, email, etc.—can be authenticated with evidence that it was written in response to another, authenticated, missive. This is the reply letter doctrine, and it is regularly deployed to authenticate electronic communications.

§ 17-10[E] AUTHENTICATION OF ELECTRONIC COMMUNICATIONS

Electronic communications—texts, emails, Facebook, etc.—often provide powerful evidence in family court. (Jay M. Zitter, Authentication of Electronically Stored Evidence, Including Text Messages and E-Mail, 34 A.L.R.6th 253 (2008, with annual updates)). People routinely say things in electronic communications that make authors blush.

1. Authentication Is a Two Step Process. First, the party seeking to prove the contents of an email, text message, Facebook post, or other electronic communication typically takes a photograph of the electronic medium displaying the message, and prints out a hard copy, or prints a screenshot. The person who took the photo, and printed out the hardy copy, or the screen shot, can authenticate these documents as having come from a particular phone or computer. The person has personal knowledge for purposes of Rule 901(b)(1), and can testify that the phone or computer was working properly to satisfy Rule 901(b)(9).

Not infrequently, a party shows up in court with cellphone, tablet, or computer in hand, and asks the judge to look at the offending message on the spot, or to listen to a voice message. Many family court judges will oblige.

Once the document is authenticated as an accurate copy of the electronic communication, the proponent moves to step two: Prove authorship of the document. (*In re L.P.*, 749 S.E.2d 389 (Ga. Ct. App. 2013); *State v. Henry*, 292 Neb. 834, 875 N.W.2d 374 (2016); *State v. Davis*, 61 N.E.3d 650 (Ohio Ct. App. 2016)).

2. Email. An email typically begins with "From" and "To." Because it is possible to fake emails, the fact that an email states that it is From "John Brown" is *not* sufficient, by itself, to authenticate John as the author. (*State v. Eleck*, 130 Conn. App. 632, 23 A.3d 818, 822 (2011); *Sublet v. State*, 442 Md. 632, 113 A.3d 695, 711 (2015); *Tienda v. State*, 358 S.W.3d 633, 641–642 (Tex. Ct. App. 2012)). The "From" portion of the email is relevant, but it must be fortified with other evidence. The reply letter doctrine, in conjunction with the "From" line, is often sufficient. (*People v. Downin*, 357 Ill. App. 3d 193, 828 N.E.2d 341, 293 Ill. Dec. 371 (2005)). In many cases, the necessary evidence is gleaned from the contents of the email—for example, "I dropped the kids off at soccer practice, as usual. Sally still has a band aid on her arm, but I put antibiotic on it, and it is better." In *State v. Manuel*, 357 S.W.3d 66, 75 (Tex. Ct. App. 2011), the Texas Court of Appeal explained: "Characteristics to consider in determining whether e-mail evidence has been properly authenticated include (1) consistency with the e-mail address in another e-mail sent by the alleged author; (2) the author's awareness, shown through the e-mail, of the details of the alleged author's conduct; (3) the e-mail's inclusion of similar requests that the alleged author had made by phone during the time period; and (4) the e-mails reference to the author by the alleged author's nickname." A witness could describe a history of email communications to and from a particular email address. (*State v. Bohlman*, 2006 WL 915765 (Minn. Ct. App. 2006)). An email sometimes contains a picture of the author, or a unique screen name. (*Culp v. State*, 178 So. 3d 378 (Ala. Crim. App. 2014)). A party's admission that he sent an email will suffice. (*Kearley v. State*, 843 So. 2d 66 (Miss. Ct. App. 2002)). In most cases, authentication is achieved without resort to expert testimony tracing the electronic communication to a particular device.

3. Text Messages. Text messages typically contain the name of the sender, and often a phone number. Like emails, texts can be faked, and judges typically want evidence in addition to a screen shot or photo of the text. (*State v. Eleck*, 130 Conn. App. 632, 23 A.3d 818, 822 (2011)). In many cases, the necessary evidence is found in the string of back and forth text messages. Often, a text makes no sense unless it is from a particular person. (*People v. Green*, 107 A.D.3d 915, 967 N.Y.S.2d 753 (2013)). The authentication factors described above for emails work as well for texts. (*State v. Koch*, 334 P.3d 280 (Idaho 2014); *State v. Davis*, 61 N.E.3d 650 (Ohio Ct. App. 2016)).

4. Facebook. Authorship of a message posted to Facebook can be authenticated with circumstantial evidence similar to that employed with emails and texts. (*United States v. Hassan*, 742 F.3d 104 (4th Cir. 2014); *State v. Palermo*, 168 N.H. 387, 129 A.3d 1020 (2015); *State v. Ford*, 782 S.E.2d 98 (N.C. Ct. App. 2016); *Manuel v. State*, 357 S.W.3d 66 (Tex. Ct. App. 2011)). In *United States v. Barnes*, 803 F.3d 209 (5th Cir. 2015), the prosecution offered enough evidence to authenticate defendant as the author of Facebook posts. A witness testified she had observed defendant using Facebook, she recognized his Facebook account, and the Facebook messages matched the defendant's manner of communicating.

§ 17–10[F] DOCUMENTS COMMONLY OFFERED IN FAMILY LAW CASES

This subsection discusses authentication of documents commonly offered in family court cases.

1. **Pay Stubs.** A pay stub can be authenticated by testimony from a witness with knowledge. (Rule 901(b)(1)). A pay stub should qualify as a business record under Rule 803(6), and a certificate by the custodian of records will authenticate the stub pursuant to Rule 902(11).

2. **Tax Returns.** A tax return can be authenticated with testimony from a witness with knowledge. (Rule 901(b)(1)). A business tax return should qualify as a business record, and a certificate by the custodian of records will authenticate the stub. (Rule 902(11)).

3. **Documents Prepared by Child Support Services.** Documents prepared by child support services can be authenticated by a witness with knowledge. (Rule 901(b)(1)). Rule 901(b)(7) provides that public records can be authenticated with evidence that the record is from the office where such records are kept. Child support services documents are self-authenticating when they bear a seal and signature (Rule 902(1) and (2)) and when they are certified (Rule 902(4)).

4. **Loan Applications.** This may come as a surprise to you, but some child support litigants underestimate their income. In *Marriage of Calcaterra*, 132 Cal. App. 4th 28, 33 Cal. Rptr. 3d 246 (2005), husband estimated his net monthly income to

be $1,715. Yet, he signed a loan application placing his monthly income at $28,000! The trial judge found husband committed perjury, and ruled that his income for purposes of child support was the higher amount. The Court of Appeal approved.

A party's signature on a loan application can be authenticated by someone with knowledge that the party signed the document (Rule 901(b)(1)), and this includes an admission from the party herself. A person who is familiar with the party's signature can authenticate the signature (Rule 901(b)(2)).

§ 17–11 BEST EVIDENCE RULE

When a party seeks to prove the contents of a document or recording, the party must produce the original. This is the best evidence rule. (Rule 1002). A duplicate of an original is typically a photocopy of a document, and, pursuant to Rule 1003, a duplicate is admissible to the same extent as an original. Any trial lawyer will tell you, however, if you have the original, use it.

When a hard copy of a document is offered, best evidence issues seldom arise because the hard copy is either the original or a duplicate. Best evidence issues arise when a witness attempts to describe what a document says. At that point, opposing counsel may object, "This violates the best evidence rule. The witness is describing the contents of the document. The best evidence rule requires the production of the original."

§ 17–12 PRIVILEGE

States have detailed laws establishing privileges for confidential communications between certain professionals and clients. Among the privileges are the attorney-client privilege, the physician-patient privilege, and the psychotherapist-client privilege.

Privileges protect confidential communications from disclosure in litigation. A subpoena does not override privilege. When a professional is on the witness stand in court, and a question calls for disclosure of privileged material, an attorney or the professional objects. The judge rules on whether a privilege applies.

§ 17–12[A] PHYSICIAN-PATIENT PRIVILEGE

The patient is the holder of the physician-patient privilege, although the doctor is required to assert the privilege for the patient. The privilege covers private communications between doctor and patient, as well as information the doctor observes by examining the patient. The physician-patient privilege applies in civil cases, but not criminal prosecutions.

§ 17–12[B] PSYCHOTHERAPIST-CLIENT PRIVILEGE

The psychotherapist-client privilege covers confidential communications between clients and psychotherapists. The client is the holder of the privilege. The mental health professional is required to assert the privilege on the client's behalf. The privilege applies to individual therapy and group therapy. The privilege extends to civil and criminal cases.

§ 17–12[C] PATIENT-LITIGANT EXCEPTION TO PRIVILEGE

In the world of personal injury (tort) litigation, when an injured person sues someone for personal injuries, and seeks damages for physical or psychological damage, the injured plaintiff often places her physical or mental condition in issue, waiving privilege. This waiver is known as the patient-litigant exception to privilege.

In child custody litigation, one parent may seek access to the other parent's privileged communications with medical or mental health professionals. Does contesting custody trigger the patient-litigant exception, waiving claims of privilege? In other words, by seeking custody of children, does a parent place her medical or mental health condition in issue? There are times when a court needs to know a parent's psychological functioning, and the best evidence of the parent's condition may be privileged records or testimony from a treating professional. On the other hand, it is good public policy to encourage parents to seek professional guidance and therapy. If a parent believes private information shared with a professional could be used in court to deprive the parent of their child, the parent may not get the therapy they need to be a better parent.

Although courts are not always consistent on this question, most decisions hold that contesting custody does not, by itself, invoke the patient-litigant exception to privilege. (*See Darab N. v. Olivera*, 242 Cal. Rptr. 3d 891, 897 (2019); *Manela v. Superior Court*, 177 Cal. App. 4th 1139, 99 Cal. Rptr. 3d 736 (2009); *Brooks v. Brooks*, 239 So. 3d 758 (Fla. Ct. App. 2018); *Zarzaur v. Zarzaur*, 213 So. 3d 1115 (Fla. Ct. App. 2017)). The Alabama Evidence Code provides, "There is no [psychotherapist-client] privilege under this rule for relevant communications offered in a child custody case in which the mental state of a party is clearly an issue and a proper resolution of the custody question requires disclosure." (Ala. R. Evid. 503(d)(5)).

Should a parent contesting custody be able to subpoena the child's privileged records? The outcome varies from case to case. (*See Ex Parte Johnson*, 219 So. 3d 655 (Ala. Civ. App. 2016) (child's records were privileged); *Rinehart v. Svensson*, 204 Vt. 390, 169 A.3d 198 (2017) (release of children's mental health records to father not in children's best interest)).

§ 17–12[D] CHILD CUSTODY EVALUATIONS AND PRIVILEGE

When a judge orders a child custody evaluation performed by a forensic mental health professional, the expectation is that the professional will testify, and the professional's custody evaluation will be submitted to the court. In this context, privileges do not apply. Mental health professionals who perform custody evaluations have parents sign documents acknowledging that communications during the evaluation are not confidential, and that privileges do not apply.

§ 17–12[E] ROUTINE MENTAL HEALTH COUNSELING

Before, during, or after divorce or separation, parents and children may benefit from mental health counseling. Regarding confidentiality and privilege, there is an important difference between a forensic child custody evaluation, on one hand, and routine mental health counseling, on the other. As mentioned in § 17–12[D], communications during formal custody evaluations are not confidential or privileged. By contrast, confidential communications during routine mental health counseling are.

Mental health professionals who provide counseling to parents and children have different approaches to participating in court. Some professionals want nothing to do with court or lawyers, will not write letters to the judge, or communicate with counsel. These professionals will testify only if subpoenaed. Other professionals are willing—with proper consent, of course—to talk to lawyers, and to inform the court of a client's progress in counseling. Testimony from a child or parent's counselor is often very powerful evidence.

§ 17–12[F] CHILD'S PSYCHOTHERAPY RECORDS

Occasionally, a parent embroiled in custody litigation subpoenas the child's psychotherapy records. The therapist may file a motion to quash the subpoena, based on the psychotherapist-client privilege. In *Ex Parte Johnson*, 219 So.3d 655 (Ala. Civ. App. 2016), the Court of Civil Appeals quashed a father's subpoena for his child's privileged records.

INDEX

References are to Pages
